For Lenny, Zvi, and Gadi
The three men who make my life complete

And for Shira, Jana and Chavi
The three women who have brought a new level of love to us all

Table Of Contents

Acknowledgments

In keeping with the nature of the Internet, it is fitting to acknowledge two groups of people instrumental in the creation of this book. One set of people I know only through cyberspace. The other set of people is physically present in my daily life.

My appreciation goes to all those who voluntarily maintain Jewish Internet sites. Many of those people are mentioned by name throughout this book. Others are anonymous. Without their efforts, the valuable cyberspace resources in Judaica would remain diffused throughout the Internet and their cumulative impact sorely diminished. The Jewish community is indeed richer for the efforts of these individuals.

On a more personal note, my deepest thanks go to Elinor Haber of Nassau BOCES and Dr. David Klein of Hofstra University. These two people served as my initial trainers on the Internet and introduced me to a world far broader than any I could ever have envisioned. I am indebted, too, to the Academic Computing Center of Hofstra University headed by Dr. Lanny Udey, which has generously provided the public schools of my area with access to the Internet. And finally, I am grateful to my friend and colleague Adele Bildersee, whose companionship in learning I treasure.

To both these sets of people I say thank you.

Mikol melamdei hiskaltee. From all those who have taught me have I gained wisdom.

Introduction

When Moses Maimonides attempted in his work *A Guide to the Perplexed* to define God, he did so by explaining what God was not. Taking a cue from Maimonides, let us consider what this book is not.

This book does not pretend to be a comprehensive work. The ever-changing world of the Internet precludes any printed text from encompassing the entire range of material available on the Internet, even in a small, well-defined area. Resources are added constantly, sites are moved, and indexing tools remain rudimentary. The scope and depth of electronic resources may indeed be unplumbable. What we are offering here are some of the most useful sources of information in the area of Judaica that were current as of the date of this book's publication. By pointing the reader toward the major sites that house Judaica information, we hope to direct the reader to areas that he may monitor as they continue to grow and develop.

Second, this book is not a "how to" guide but rather a "where is" guide. It assumes that the reader is fairly comfortable traveling the highways and byways of the Internet and adept at navigating through its waters. Here we are concentrating on how to use these tools to locate interesting Judaica resources. In addition, the reader should be aware that redundancy is commonplace on the Internet. A resource may appear at one site and be mirrored or pointed to in many others. One should not be surprised if one comes across the same material in a number of locations.

Finally, for the purposes of this book, Judaica resources have been defined as information pertaining to some area of interest or study in a Jewish field. Materials created by Jews that do not fit this definition have been excluded. With the advent of hypertext markup language (HTML) authoring tools, almost anyone can construct a simple Web page. Indeed, in the past years we have seen an explosion of Jewish Web sites. This has led to an increased winnowing of material for inclusion in this book. We have "upped the ante" for selection criteria, looking, as Andrew Tannebaum once commented, to point to libraries rather than books. Entire host names have been favored over even portions of sites, and many personal pages have been disregarded, as have sites deemed too local in nature to interest a wide audience. Informational sites have been favored over those seeking to sell a product or service, except where that item is noteworthy or unique. In some areas resources have been included that touch on the developments in a given field of study in Israel. Unless otherwise indicated, all sites are in English. Where the material in the second edition covered the period up to June 1996, the citations in this edition were accurate at the time of publication. Changes and updates to the material in this book will be noted on the author's home page at **www.jewishinternetguide.com**.

Our ultimate goal is to entice the reader into exploring the rich treasures of Jewish study that lie scattered throughout the electronic universe. Sometimes the reader may use this book as a guide to locating a specific resource. At other times his exploration may be more like one who is paddling around in the ocean, occasionally glimpsing a familiar landmark ashore. Whatever the purpose, we hope the reader will find material here that is stimulating, informative, and entertaining. As the *Haggadah* commands, *tze ulemad,* go and learn!

NEWSGROUPS AND LISTSERVS

NEWSGROUPS AND READING LISTS

Interactive discussion is at the heart and soul of the Internet. Several thousand discussion groups, sometimes called Usenet groups, exist, each devoted to a particular topic of interest. These discussions are free and open to the public. Messages posted to the discussion group for the previous few weeks are available for all to see and comment upon. Older messages are often archived and may be searched.

Newsgroups of particular interest to those searching for Judaica resources include:

Alt.music.jews
Alt.personals.jewish
Clari.world.mideast.israel
Clari.news.jews
Soc.culture.jewish
Soc.culture.israel
Soc.culture.jewish.holocaust
Talk.politics.mideast

In addition to offering discussions and informational tidbits, many of the newsgroups provide informative FAQs (Frequently Asked Questions). For example, soc.culture.jewish has an extensive FAQ with Jewish reading lists on a variety of topics, including:

General reading list
Traditional liturgy, practice, lifestyle, and holidays reading list
Kabbalah, mysticism, and messianism reading list
Reform Judaism reading list
Conservative Judaism reading list
Reconstructionist Judaism reading list
Humanistic Judaism reading list
Hasidism reading list
Zionism reading list
Anti-Semitism reading list
Intermarriage and conversion reading list
Periodicals list
List of books for Jewish children

While the newsgroups you can read are dependent upon what is offered by your Internet service provider, you can access the previously mentioned reading lists and FAQS at **http://shamash.org/lists/scj-faq/html/rl**. If you are interested in reading a newsgroup not made available by your provider, send a message to the administrator of the system asking if he would consider adding it to the newsgroup offerings.

LISTSERVS

If your newsreader does not provide you with access to a discussion group you want to follow on a regular basis, you can subscribe to the discussion through a service called a listserv. When you send in a subscription request, you will receive every message in your mailbox that is posted to the discussion group. In the case of active discussion groups, you may find yourself overwhelmed with mail. The difference between reading a discussion through a listserv and through a newsreader is the difference between having the newspaper delivered to your home daily and going to the library to read the newspaper. When you read material through a listserv, you have to actively manage your account, just like taking the newspapers out for recycling. When you go to the library to read the newspaper, you just dip into the areas you are interested in and can forget about the management aspects.

Listservs are also used as a means of participating in online courses. For those interested in Judaica, a number of different courses are offered regularly through listservs. In addition, many discussion groups with Judaic content are often not available through newsreaders. There are several hundred discussion groups of Jewish interest on the Internet. For these reasons, one might consider subscribing to a listserv and actively managing one's mail account.

Generally speaking, to subscribe to a listserv you send a message to listproc@the server. In some cases the term *listserv* or *majordomo* is used. For example, to subscribe to Tachlis, a nuts and bolts discussion group about *aliyah*, one would send a message that looks like this:

listproc@shamash.org

because the discussion group is housed on the Shamash server. Leave the subject blank. As the body of the message, you would write:

subscribe tachlis your name

Typically, you include your name for listserv or listproc groups but not for majordomo lists. It is important to understand that you are addressing a computer that understands only these specific terms. Extra phrases or politeness will only confuse it. As with newsgroups, old messages from listservs are often archived and may be searched.

Discussion groups have exploded in popularity since the last edition of this book. The technology has evolved to the point where anyone with even minimal technical skills can own and operate a discussion group. Therefore, this edition of the book excludes listservs and discussion groups as entries. In addition to the listservs noted on the major search engines such as Shamash, Virtual Jerusalem, Jewishnet, Maven, and Hareshima, you can locate discussions on Jewish topics through the following major collections of general listservs:

Name	Address	Description
Liszt	**http://www.liszt.com**	90,095 mailing lists searchable by keyword or browsable by subject
Tile.net	**http://tile.net/lists/**	Search by name, description,domain, or topic
CataList	**http://www.lsoft.com/lists/listref.html**	Search 32,364 public lists by topic, domain, or size
Egroups	**http://www.egroups.com/**	Groups are searchable by keyword or browsable by subject. Information on creating your own discussion group is also available.

Many of the resources listed in the main body of the book host their own discussion groups that you can sign up for as well.

DISPLAYING HEBREW CHARACTERS

Many sites offer information in Hebrew format. These include libraries with bibliographic citations, Israeli discussion groups, clippings from Israeli newspapers, and interactive lessons in the Hebrew language. There are several solutions to the problem of how to display information in Hebrew characters.

READING HEBREW ON THE WEB WITH WINDOWS 95/98 AND NETSCAPE

Nadav Caine at Stanford University in his home page, **http://www.stanford.edu/~nadav/hebrew.html**, has an excellent, step-by-step explanation of how to configure Netscape to display Hebrew. It presupposes that you are using Netscape 1.1 or greater. His Web page offers pointers to the appropriate Hebrew fonts, and his explanation of how to install them follows:

In order to enable Netscape to display Hebrew, follow these steps:

1. Shift-click to download the self-extracting archive "webfont.exe" of two Hebrew fonts that work well with Netscape. When your browser prompts you for the directory in which to put this file, choose the Windows System directory, which is normally c:\windows\system\.
2. Now, minimize this webrowser window, and from the main Windows screen (the Program Manager), select "Run" from under "File." Click on "Browse," and then open the Windows System folder (again, it's usually c:\windows\system\) Click on "webfont.exe" and then "OK" and then "OK" again. This will turn the one file into the necessary font files automatically. (There will be a "read me" file, too, added into your Windows system directory, if you want to read it.)
3. Click on "Control Panel" (usually in the "Accessories" group) and then on the "Fonts" icon. Click on "Add" and then scroll all the way down and add both Web Hebrew AD and Web Hebrew Monospace. Your PC is now Hebrew-ready. (Note that different Hebrew fonts work

with different applications, depending on how they are "mapped" onto the keyboard. In addition, other factors are involved in Netscape's use of fonts.) Thus, if you already have some Hebrew fonts, they may or may not work with the Web sites listed in the following section. Conversely, these Hebrew fonts may not work with other Hebrew programs such as Dagesh that you may already have installed on your PC. The important thing is that the fonts offered here will not interfere with any other fonts or applications you are using, so don't worry!

4. Go back to Netscape (i.e., maximize this window). Now select "Preferences" under "Options" above. Choose "Fonts and Colors." Click on "Browse" for the Proportional font, find "Web Hebrew AD" from the list, and choose it. Then click on "Browse" for the Fixed font, find "Web Hebrew Monospace," and choose that. Close the windows and you're all set to go. Now you will have both Hebrew and English on Netscape.

READING HEBREW ON THE WEB WITH WINDOWS 95/98 AND INTERNET EXPLORER

1. Follow the previous steps one through three.
2. Having installed the Hebrew fonts on your computer, you now have to tell Internet Explorer how to use them. Go to the "Tools" menu and choose "Internet Options" from the list. At the bottom of the general page there is a section on fonts. When you click on the fonts section, you will see "Language Script." Keep that as Latin-based. For the "Web page font" choose "Web Hebrew AD." For the "plain text font" choose "Web Hebrew monospace." Click OK when finished, and you should be ready to search the Web.
3. With Internet Explorer 5 you are often asked to download "Hebrew Text Display Support" and "Uniscribe," both of which are provided by Microsoft on a CD-ROM that is often shipped with the Windows operating system. If you do not have the necessary files, just choose Cancel when asked to perform the download, and the page should appear anyway. Uniscribe is Microsoft's proposed way of displaying non-Latin characters and should be the future solution for the difficulties in reading Hebrew

online. If problems persist, go to View->Encoding and choose one of the Hebrew options. Then refresh the page.

READING HEBREW ON A MACINTOSH

1. Download a file containing the Ariela font from **http://www.israweb.co.il/hebrew/mac.html**
2. The font is compressed so you must expand it using Stuffit Expander. Drop Ariela.hqx on Stuffit Expander to create a font suitcase.
3. Drop the Ariela suitcase on your system folder.
4. Quit your browser and open it up again so that it will recognize the newly added font.
5. Tell your browser to use these fonts. In Netscape go to Options->Preferences->Fonts and Colors and choose Ariela as both your fixed and your proportional fonts. In Internet Explorer choose it for both the Web page font and the plain text font.

READING HEBREW ON AMERICA ONLINE

As of this writing, America Online's browser does not display Hebrew fonts. Even if you have downloaded Hebrew fonts onto your machine, America Online does not offer you the opportunity to install them on its browser. Perhaps this situation will change once AOL fully integrates Netscape into its system. For now, however, the only solution is to install Hebrew fonts into Netscape or Internet Explorer, following the previous directions. Then log onto the Internet using America Online, minimize the AOL display, and view the Hebrew site through Netscape or Internet Explorer.

PROBLEMS WITH HEBREW DISPLAYS

Sometimes Hebrew displays rather strangely on your screen. A number of explanations exist for these problems. There are two main problems with HTML documents containing Hebrew text: encoding the Hebrew letters, and displaying them from right to left. Sometimes Hebrew text appears on the page looking like English vowels with strange diacritical marks. This problem often results when the author of the Web page has used the incorrect ASCII code. If the author assumes that his readership is usually looking only at Hebrew text, he may not include the necessary HTML tag on his site to instruct the browser to use the Hebrew ISO 8859-8 display. If the user's browser is set to use ISO 8859, which displays Latin text as the default, he will see gibberish on Hebrew pages. Unfortunately, there is nothing the end user can do to solve this problem.

The other problem that plagues Hebrew text is directionality. Computers store text as it is typed sequentially, and text can be stored either logically or visually. Gabi Dabon describes how these approaches vary:

> Consider, for example, the following mixed line of text:
>
> **one שתם three**
>
> The order in which we type, and read, this text is:
>
> **O, n, e, ם, י, י, ת, ש, t, h, r, e, e**
>
> If the text is stored in this order, it is called logical order. Text that is stored in its logical order is easy to edit, since the correct (logical) order of letters and words is always maintained. However, this requires software that is smart enough to know how to display BiDi text; all modern operating systems that support Hebrew use this method for handling text, and reversing the display is done at the level of the OS.
>
> The other method of storing BiDi text is called visual order and is based on reversing Hebrew text while it is typed and storing it already reversed. In the last example, the visual order would be:
>
> **O, n, e, ם, י, י, ת, ש, t, h, r, e, e**
>
> This method requires very little sophistication from the program that *displays* the text, because the text is already stored in the order it should be displayed; but editing such text can be difficult, because the stored order does not reflect the way the text is written.
>
> It would seem that logical order is always the natural choice for storing any kind of text, including text that is mainly Hebrew. But things are complicated when we consider some types of mixed text, such as text whose main direction is right to left (RTL), like Hebrew text, which contains some English words. In this case, logical order alone becomes ambiguous. Consider for instance the following text, in logical order:
>
> **ד, ו, ג, מ, א, s, i, l, l, y**

If the main language of the paragraph containing this text is English, the main direction is LTR (—>) and the text should be displayed as:

דוגמא silly

But if the main language is Hebrew, then the direction is RTL (<—) and we should get:

Silly דוגמא

That is, BiDi text stored in logical order should also have a directionality in addition to the letters themselves; this is why all word processors that handle Hebrew (and store it in logical order; this includes all modern word processors and excludes older QText for DOS) must have a way of choosing the direction of a paragraph.

Web page authors should include an HTML tag, indicating the direction in which the text should be read. Unfortunately, this sometimes does not occur, resulting in Hebrew characters that are written backward. Consult Gabi Dabon's article at **http://www.tau.ac.il/~danon/Hebrew/HTML_and_Hebrew.html** for an excellent discussion of these issues and some suggested solutions.

One final problem arises on sites written with the assumption that the viewer is using Hebrew-enabled Windows. In many of these cases, you cannot do a search on these sites because, even with Hebrew fonts on your machine, you cannot display the Hebrew in the search box. The answer to this problem is a shareware utility called Hebrew Keys **(http://www.hebrewkeys.com)**, which can be downloaded and installed, allowing you to perform your searches. Also, several Israeli sites, including the Israeli libraries' union catalog and Dapey Reshet, offer a virtual keyboard that allows you to cut and paste the appropriate Hebrew letters into a seach box.

ISRAELI LIBRARIES AND UNIVERSITIES

Many libraries in Israel are networked together using a common automation system called ALEPH. This commonalty of approach makes searching Israeli libraries a fairly easy matter. Commands are the same, regardless of the library being searched. Searching capabilities in ALEPH are trilingual, with displays possible in English, Hebrew, and Arabic. So successful has it been that ALEPH has been adopted in the United States by the library of the Jewish Theological Seminary as its software of choice.

Until recently, the only way to access Israeli library catalogs was through telnet. You would telnet to one of the libraries and from there move seamlessly to another. To begin a search, you would telnet to **aleph.biu.ac.il** and log in as **aleph**. This would take you to Bar Ilan University Library. From there you could search all the other Israeli university libraries.

Recently, however, this process has been enormously simplified through the efforts of the Israel Academic Inter-Library Network. Its home page at **http://libnet1.ac.il/~libnet/malmad-israel.htm** provides the means to search almost all of the university libraries through the Web rather than through telnet and should be the first place to go to locate holdings of most Israeli university libraries.

Another exciting development has been the creation of MALMAD, the Israel Center for Digital Information Services (**http://libnet.ac.il/~libnet/malmad.htm**), headed by Elhanan Adler. Using this URL as a portal, it is possible to access the electronic journal subscriptions of the libraries arranged by title and subject, the Israeli union list of serials, and the Israeli union catalog. When you enter the last two sites as a non-Hebrew Windows user, click on "browse" and you will be presented with an ingenious virtual Hebrew keyboard, enabling you to search in Hebrew by pasting the letters from the keyboard into the search box. Clicking on the "databases and full text" section of MALMAD will also lead you to RAMBI, an index of journal articles on Jewish studies, where you can make use of the same Hebrew keyboard.

Increasingly, Israeli libraries are developing their own Web sites, which seek to simplify access to their holdings and offer pointers to other resources. An excellent example is the Web site of the University of Haifa

Library at **http://www-lib.haifa.ac.il.** This Web site offers information about the library, access to electronic journals and texts in English and Hebrew, and links to other Israeli, Judaic, and worldwide resources. The libraries of the other Israeli universities may be accessed through their home pages as follows:

Bar Ilan University	**http://www.biu.ac.il**
Ben Gurion University	**http://www.bgu.ac.il**
Hebrew University	**http://www.huji.ac.il**
Technion,	**http://www.technion.ac.il**
University of Haifa	**http://www.haifa.ac.il**
Tel Aviv University	**http://www.tau.ac.il**
The Open University	**http://www.openu.ac.il**
Weizmann Institute	**http://www.weizmann.ac.il**

KEEPING CURRENT

In the world of flux that characterizes the Internet, the only constant is change. New resources and sites appear daily. To stay current, the interested reader can monitor several locations that concentrate specifically on Judaica material.

One of the best ways to learn about new sites is to sign up for current awareness newsletters. **Jewish-announce** from Shamash (**http://jewish-announce@shamash.org**) sends out daily listings of both new Web sites and events in the Jewish world. **Maven-announce (www.maven.co.il)** compiles a weekly newsletter specifically devoted to new Web sites. In addition, most of the major Jewish search engines and home pages listed in this book under "major Jewish sites" have a "what's new" section that are worth periodic visits.

A number of software programs will also alert you as to changes on a given Web site. If there is a site you follow regularly, you may wish to use one of these alert services. In addition, many of the major Jewish sites have e-mail subscriptions you can join for free that will apprise you of new additions to their pages. And finally, traditional print media should not be overlooked as a source of information on new Web sites. As the Internet has become more pervasive throughout our lives, many groups and organizations now routinely publicize their Web sites along with other standard press releases and advertisements.

WHAT'S NEW IN THIS EDITION

The major change that has taken place in cyberspace since the original edition of this book, which included material up to May 1995, has been the development of the World Wide Web. Materials in the older gopher format have almost entirely migrated to the Web, whose ease of navigation has also superseded protocols such as ftp and telnet. The following observations are made on the basis of the material contained in this edition, which was current as of June 2000.

HISTORY OF THE JEWISH INTERNET

The Jewish Internet is now old enough to have a history. The rise of both Shamash and Jerusalem One (now called Virtual Jerusalem) in 1993 heralded the birth of the Jewish Internet for large-scale audiences. For a look at what the Jewish Internet looked like in those days, check Andrew Tannenbaum's site at **http://www.shamash.org/trb/judaism.html**. He has wisely archived his one-page index of sites as of November 29, 1993, which had grown to fifty links by October 1994. Another page frozen in time (**http://web.macam98.ac.il/~dovw/jw/jewish96.html**), written by Lucia Wright of Ben Gurion University, provides insight into the early contents of the Jewish Internet. Zvi Lando, the originator of Jerusalem One, has chronicled the development of the Jewish Internet through four stages of *aliyah*. You can read his insightful treatment of the topic, told from an insider's point of view, and sample some of his well-designed Jewish Web sites at **http://www.connect.co.il/history/**.

In the ensuing years we have gone through a tremendous amount of change, both in the number of informational resources and the formats in which they have written. Strange as it may seem, this edition of *The Jewish Guide to the Internet* probably presents the most stable set of resources yet. The first edition of the book was written when gophers were still dominant. The second edition came out just as material housed on gophers was migrating to the Web. Many individuals and organizations were using host sites as guests. By this edition, most organizations have filed for their own host names, so even if the content on their pages changes, their locations most probably will not. This change reflects the maturation of the Jewish Internet.

GROWTH OF DISCUSSION GROUPS

Discussion groups have exploded in popularity since the last edition of this book. The technology has evolved to the point where anyone with even minimal technical skills can own and operate a discussion group. It has become almost impossible to track the thousands of listservs that now address Jewish topics. Many of the larger and older groups are housed on the established Jewish sites such as Shamash and Virtual Jerusalem. However, the sheer number of discussion groups precludes their inclusion in this edition. If you are interested in locating listservs, check the section covering them earlier in this book.

Online conversations on many topics of Jewish interest take place constantly on the Internet. Unlike listservs and newsgroups, these discussions happen in real time. Some Internet service providers such as America Online offer chat rooms on specific topics to their customers. In other cases, you may need to download and install a special piece of software to allow you to participate in chat rooms. One of the best-known examples of this type of software is ICQ, originally developed in Israel by the Mirabelis Company. Other discussions take place through forums such as the two hosted by MSN, The MSN Jewish Community at and the MSN Israel Community at **http://communities.msn.com**.

NEW FORMATS

Another area of growth has been in the formats in which information is presented online. It is now routine to see sites that incorporate streaming audio and video programs that can be viewed through Real Player, MP3, and Microsoft's Media Player. These formats are used for music, radio programs, and instructional material. Java applets also appear in abundance and are used effectively in online games and tutorials such as Zigzag World's Hebrew Keyboard Tutor. Increasing numbers of pages are making use of Shockwave for both design and instructional purposes.

Documents are often presented in .pdf format, which can be read through Adobe Acrobat's free reader. A Pdf document is essentially a photographic reproduction of a page that thereby preserves graphical and tabular forms often lost when the document is transformed into ASCII text. With the rise of personal data appliances such as the Palm

Pilot, many sites are looking to transform Web pages into formats compatible with the Palm. You can now download the current issues of *The Jerusalem Post* and *Haaretz* to read on your Palm Pilot.

WEB RINGS

The proliferation of Web sites has often made it difficult to locate information on a given topic. Search engines and directories solve some of these problems. Recently, a new solution has evolved in the form of Web rings. As the webring.org page defines them, "this completely free service offers easy access to hundreds of thousands of member websites organized by related interests into easy-to-travel rings. Anytime you find yourself at a webring member page, just click on the navigation buttons or hypertext links to travel to other sites in the ring."

Andrew Rajcher of Australia was one of the earliest designers of Jewish Web rings. His home page at **http://home.vicnet.net.au/~argorn/jew-ring.htm** describes what the rings do and the criteria and mechanism for joining them. HaReshima (**http://www.hareshima.com**) lists the following Web rings:

Name	Address
Holocaust Web Ring	**http://www.netbistro.com/electriczen/holoring.html**
Jewish Youth Web Ring	**http://www.jewishyouth.com/jewring.htm**
Klezmer Web Ring	**http://www.geocities.com/Broadway/Stage/2452/Klezmerring.htm**
Chabad Web Ring	**http://www.geocities.com/Colosseum/Loge/7744/**
Counter-Missionary Web Ring	**http://members.xoom.com/3DTorah/**
Jewish Roots Web Ring	**http://pw1.netcom.com/~barrison/jewgenwebring.html**
General Jewish Web Ring	**http://members.aol.com/JermyMP/jewish.html**
Jewish Women's Web Ring	**http://www.geocities.com/Heartand/Hills/1330/women.html**

MAJOR JEWISH SEARCH ENGINES

HaReshima

ADDRESS: http://www.HaReshima.com

DESCRIPTION: Meaning "the list," this site's major categories include business, congregations, culture, entertainment, holidays, kids, Israel, kosher, media, medical, organizations, regional, resources, study, and women, with a total of 181 subcategories. Special areas for trivia contest, Hebrew calendar, best of the list, friends contest, and new sites are available. You can add a URL for consideration and sign up for a free newsletter. The site is searchable.

IGuide

ADDRESS: http://www.iguide.co.il

DESCRIPTION: Sponsored by Netvision since 1994 and searchable in English and Hebrew, this Yahoo-style directory was created by John Neystadt and Nadav Har'El. It allows advanced searching and offers a guide to the Israeli Internet, along with a classified guide and technical guide. Categories in the classified guide include Commercial Companies, the Arts, Computers, Education, Entertainment, Government and Politics, Online, News, Recreation, Reference, Regional, Professional, and Society and Culture. The technical guide is of particular note for its information on the Israeli Internet, including statistics, a comparison chart of service providers, and a list of all Israeli sites by host. New sites can be viewed by category and alphabetically, and you can sign up to receive an online newsletter.

Maven

ADDRESS: http://www.maven.co.il

DESCRIPTION: Begun as Matthew Album's A–Z collection on ANJY, this is one of the oldest and most comprehensive Jewish directories online and supports Boolean searching with AND and OR operators. Short annotations of over 6,000 sites in the categories of Business and Economics, Communities and Synagogues, Computers and Internet, Education, Entertainment, Food and Drink, Government and Politics, Holocaust and Antisemitism, Hospitals and Medicine, Israel, Judaism, Law, News and Information, Regional Resources, Science and Technology, Shopping and Gifts, Social and Personal, Sports and Hobbies, The Arts,

Travel and Tourism, Women and Feminism, and Youth and Students are provided. You can view all subjects alphabetically as well. Sign up for an online newsletter highlighting new additions to the directory, suggest a link for inclusion, and view the list of new additions to the directory. This is an excellent starting point for all Jewish sources.

NU?—The JAFI Portal

ADDRESS: http://www.jewishsites.org

DESCRIPTION: Created by the Jewish Agency, this searchable, Yahoo-style directory has categories for Israel, Our Communities and Life, Judaism, Education, Youth and Students, Jewish Gastronomy, Government and Politics, Holocaust and Antisemitism, News and Information, Health, Business and Finance, Shopping, Travel and Tourism, Culture, and Social and Personal. Short descriptions are provided for each entry. You can add a URL, check out the top 10 sites of the month, and access the Jewish Resource Center with material from the online courses offered through the Jewish University in Cyberspace (J.U.I.C.E.).

SABRAnet

ADDRESS: http://www.sabranet.com

DESCRIPTION: Dating back to 1995, this English and Hebrew directory provides access to Israeli sites in the areas of Agencies and Institutions, Culture, Entertainment, News and Information, Science and Technology, and Trade and Commerce. Sidebars provide quick access to headline news, sports, discussion forums, classifieds, chat rooms, radio, and shopping. This is an excellent starting point for English speakers searching for Israeli sites.

Yehud Links

ADDRESS: http://www.yehud.com/

DESCRIPTION: A portal to sites of interest to the Jewish community and arranged into the categories of Anti-Semitism, Arts and Culture, Business and Economy, Education, Entertainment, Family, Food, Health and Medicine, Holidays, Holocaust, Israel, News and Media, Organizations, Religion, Reference, Regions, Science, Shopping, Sports and Recreation, Synagogues, and Youth. You can suggest a site; rate existing sites; check sections on new listings, top rated, and "cool" sites; and receive updates to the directory by e-mail. Quick links to news, free e-mail, chats, and a variety of other topics are available, along with links to 14 Jewish online directories and 14 general ones. Advanced searching capabilities are also available. If you are looking for sites of interest to traditional Jews, this is a good starting point.

Zipple

ADDRESS: http://www.zipple.com

DESCRIPTION: Zipple was created in 1998 by Jenesis Communications of Illinois and is committed to creating a Jewish portal that organizes both commercial and not-for-profit Jewish Web sites, as well as quality Web sites created by individuals from around the world "to present an outstanding resource for anything relating to Judaism, Israel, and the Holocaust." Major categories include Arts and Humanities, Directories, Food, Education, History, the Holocaust, Israel, Life Cycle, Jewish Holidays, Organizations, People, Politics, Religion, Jewish Portals, Jewish Communities, and Women. In addition to serving as a portal, Zipple also hosts two Jewish chats and offers Judaica shopping. Along with its index, Zipple offers free e-mail, free greeting cards through Blue Mountain, free singles listings, and you can sign up for a free newsletter.

Hot Max

ADDRESS: http://www.jcn18.com/jhot00.htm

DESCRIPTION: JCN18.com, a pioneering Jewish Web zine produced by the Jewish Communication Network, has been discontinued, but its directory, Hot Max, is still online with 1,815 links. The searchable Yahoo-style directory has categories for Arts and Entertainment, Business and Economy, Community, Education, Middle East, News, Reference, Shopping, Tradition, Travel, Gophers, and Usenet and Listserv.

Israel.com

ADDRESS: http://www.israel.com

DESCRIPTION: Major categories in this Israeli-based searchable directory include Arts and Culture, Business and Economy, Government and Politics, History and People, Education and Reference, News and Media, People of the Book, and Travel and Tourism. The site also hosts discussions and categorizes threads by topic. You can get free e-mail, check the guest book and the classifieds, suggest an URL for inclusion in the directory, and find additional sites through Maven and Iguide.

Jewish Community Online

ADDRESS: http://www.Jewish.com/search

DESCRIPTION: Jewish Community Online (JCOL) was established in 1995 as an outgrowth of the America Online site by that name and has a directory of 4,700 sites. The philosophy of the site "is to serve all Jews from the most observant to the most secular. We are proud to be inclusive." Major categories include Arts and Culture, Education, Family, Food, Holidays, Holocaust and Anti-Semitism, Indices, Introduction to Judaism, Israel, Jewish City Guides, Most Useful Websites, News, Organizations, Other Communities, Social Action, Special Interests, Spirituality and Torah, Synagogues, Websites of the Week, and Youth. You can add a URL for consideration and sign up for a free newsletter. In addition to serving as a portal, JCOL also hosts its own content in the areas of personals, an online store, job hunting, "ask a rabbi," daily news and columnists, radio broadcasts, basic Judaism, recipes and *kashrut*, Jewish life cycle, a Jewish summer camp guide, and a schedule of chat groups and bulletin boards of Jewish interest on America Online. The site is also searchable.

Neto Hi-Tech

ADDRESS: http://www.neto.co.il/

DESCRIPTION: Specialized English and Hebrew search engine focusing on the high-tech industry in Israel. You can search by word or company or by categories, including Communications, Education, Electronics, Electro-Optics, Finance, Government, Health Care, Human Resources, International, Internet, Media, Microelectronics, Military, Multimedia, Software, Research and Development, and International. There are quick links to stock quotations and information for Israeli high-tech companies on Wall Street, local high-tech news, and job listings. You can sign up for a free newsletter as well. This is an excellent starting point for information on Israeli high-tech companies.

HEBREW LANGUAGE SEARCH ENGINES

Israel Online

ADDRESS: http://www.iol.co.il

DESCRIPTION: One of the most popular Hebrew portals, this site associated with *Haaretz* has sections on Software Utilities, News, shopping, Communities and Life Style, and Recreation, in addition to the main index, that has areas for Business, Recreation, Computers, Shopping, Sports, Art, News, Education, Family and Society, Science and Health, Travel, and Politics. Sites are annotated and rated and language is noted. The entire site is searchable.

Nana Nana

ADDRESS: http://www.nana.co.il

DESCRIPTION: A search engine from Netvision, Israel's largest ISP. Searching is possible in English, Russian, Hebrew, and Arabic. Advanced searching possible. Sites are rated by viewers, annotated, and with country of origin indicated. Major categories include Art and Entertainment, News and Media, Computers and Internet, Private Sites, Society and Family, Business and Economy, Education and Science, Law and Order, Tourism and Leisure, Sports and Health, Shopping and Services, and Download Software Archive. Quick links to listings of new sites, shopping, forums, chats, and free e-mail. You can suggest a URL for inclusion in the directory as well.

Tapuz

ADDRESS: http://www.tapuz.co.il

DESCRIPTION: This searchable Yahoo-style site whose name suggests Tel Aviv, the big "orange," is one of Israel's leading Hebrew-language directories. It includes sections on Business, Recreation, Computers, Shopping, Sports, Education, Family and Society, Science and Health, Travel, and Politics. Sites are annotated and rated. There is a news section, access to chats, forums, maps, phone directories, and a "clementine" section for kids.

Walla

ADDRESS: http://www.walla.co.il

DESCRIPTION: The earliest and still one of the leading Hebrew-language directories, *Walla* means "yahoo" in Israeli slang and looks much like its namesake. It includes sections on Business, Recreation, Computers, Shopping, Sports, Art, News, Education, Family and Society, Science and Health, Travel, and Politics. Sites are annotated and rated, and region of origin is noted. You can create a "my Walla" page with your own preferences for viewing. The entire site is searchable.

A

ADDRESS: http://www.a.co.il

DESCRIPTION: Describing itself as "a start page for search engines in Israel," this site provides access to11English-language search engines, 4 Hebrew-language ones, and the Israeli white pages of Bezeq. You can conduct a search across them or input words into a particular engine in order to take advantage of its unique capabilities. There is also a directory in Hebrew of sites relating to Education, Telephones, Software, Organizations, Sports, Support, People, Sites, Health, Arts, News, Economics, Stocks, and New Sites.

Achla

ADDRESS: http://www.achla.co.il

DESCRIPTION: Annotated listings of general sites arranged in a directory, with major categories of Health, Computers and the Internet, the Community, Law, Education, Business and Economics, Leisure and Sports, Tourism, and Culture and the Arts. Annotation indicates the language of the site and where it comes from. Some Hebrew displays do not work well in non-Hebrew Windows browsers. There are quick links to weather, news, telephone white pages, sports, and radio sites. Site is searchable.

Dapey Reshet

ADDRESS: http://www.reshet.co.il

DESCRIPTION: Portal with a unique virtual typewriter, allowing even those without typing capabilities in Hebrew to enter search terms. Quick links to listings of News, Shopping, Airport Travel, This Week in the Knesset, Classifieds, and Chats. Hosts a large number of forums, has archives of the Israeli Internet watch dog dating back to 1996, and has listings for many popular topics.

Gizmoo

ADDRESS: http://www.gizmoo.co.il

DESCRIPTION: Allows you to input words in English and get the search results in Hebrew.

Hebsearch

ADDRESS: http://www.info.co.il

DESCRIPTION: Allows you to search Israeli and Jewish servers in Hebrew or English.

Isralink

ADDRESS: http://www.isralink.co.il/

DESCRIPTION: English and Hebrew portal built around current news stories. Searching is done through other engines in English and Hebrew. The directory of resources covers standard topics.

Kinneret

ADDRESS: http://www.kinneret.co.il

DESCRIPTION: English and Hebrew site that lists English, Hebrew, and children's Internet portals. Also provides listings of English and Hebrew sites for News, Banks, Stores, Magazines, Fun, Sports, Chat, Games, and Travel. Sections for site of the week and tip of the week are also available.

Netex

ADDRESS: http://www.netex.co.il/

DESCRIPTION: By downloading and installing this free utility, you can enter the name of a site in English or Hebrew, such as "New York Times," and you will be taken to the site immediately.

Netking

ADDRESS: http://www.netking.com/

DESCRIPTION: From this Israeli Internet service provider comes an annotated listing of general sites arranged in a directory, with major categories of Health, Computers and the Internet, the Community, Law, Education, Business and Economics, Leisure and Sports, Tourism, and Culture and the Arts. Annotation indicates the language of the site and where it comes from. Some Hebrew displays do not work well in non-Hebrew Windows browsers. There are quick links to weather, news, telephone white pages, sports, and radio sites. Site is searchable.

Other Hebrew Search Engines

ADDRESS:

DESCRIPTION: For a variety of searches, try some of the smaller Hebrew search engines, including:

Atraf—http://www.atraf.co.il
Sababa—http://sababa.co.il
Portaljob—http://www.portaljob.co.il

Madlik—http://www.madlik.co.il
Indexnet—http://www.indexnet.co.il
Gogo—http://www.gogo.co.il
Falafel—http://www.falafel.co.il
Clicknet—http://www.clicknet.co.il
Sharks—http://www.sharks.co.il

Sivuv

ADDRESS: http://www.sivuv.co.il

DESCRIPTION: Allows non-native speakers of English to use tools such as Yahoo, Lycos, and Infoseek without the need to translate their terms into English. Instructions are given in English, and searchers may enter terms in Hebrew and receive results in English.

Start.Co.il

ADDRESS: http://www.start.co.il

DESCRIPTION: Conduct your search in any or all of 8 English-language search engines and 8 Hebrew ones. Do a search for e-mail through 3 services, and check Israeli telephone listings through 2 services. There are quick links to 5 major Israeli sites in the areas of News, Computers, Business, Leisure, Travel, Food, Weather, Lotteries, Sales, and Classifieds.

Zooloo

ADDRESS: http://www.zooloo.co.il

DESCRIPTION: Yahoo-style directory, with major categories of Health, Culture, Community and Family, Computers and the Internet, the Law, Education, Business and Economics, Leisure, Judaism, Malls, Sports, Tourism, and Databases and News. Listed sites can be viewed in order of ranking by Internet surfers, by Zooloo, by date, and by name. It has quick links to Israeli news sites and radio stations, worldwide weather and stock market quotations, along with listings of headlines from Galei Zahal, Channel Two, Walla, Hadashot, Nana, and Maariv. A Zooloo Magazine section is also provided, with a variety of articles produced by Zooloo. There are quick links to listings of new sites, maps, tax calculators, forums, courses, and chats. You can personalize the page, suggest a URL for inclusion in the directory, and build your own page.

MAJOR JEWISH SITES

INSTITUTIONAL PAGES

Israel Information Service

ADDRESS: http://www.israel.org

DESCRIPTION: Begun in 1994 by the Ministry of Foreign Affairs as a gopher, this site, with more than 14,000 pages, offers one of the most extensive sets of resources about Israel on the Internet. In addition to current news and updates, you can find basic facts about the country; a historical timeline; and details about Zionism, foreign affairs, the government, law, culture, economy, and religions of Israel. There are biographies of Israeli leaders and an extensive section on the peace process as well. You can personalize the page, join a variety of mailing lists, check older material stored in the original gopher archive, and search the entire site. This is a major starting point for any information about the State of Israel.

Shema Yisrael Torah Network

ADDRESS: http://www.shemayisrael.co.il/

DESCRIPTION: This portal to traditional Judaism provides a large number of resources and also hosts many traditionally minded sites worldwide. There are numerous articles on the weekly *parsha*, written by various rabbis; sections on the *daf yomi*; the teachings of the Chofetz Chaim; online reading rooms for adults and children; a password-protected women's corner; and forums for all age groups. Educational materials include resources for special education and access to Pirchei Shoshanim, as well as archives for *Mishnah Yomi* and *Halachah Yomi*. The network also hosts traditionally minded sites in Great Britain, South Africa, and France and has sections for shopping and music. Finally, there are a number of searchable directories available including one for synagogues, *mikvaot*, Jewish schools, and cemeteries. This is a rich resource for materials from the strongly traditional Jewish community.

Torah.net

ADDRESS: http://www.torah.net

DESCRIPTION: Funded by HaMa'ayan Institutions of Be'er Sheva, under the leadership of Rabbi Natan Spector, this site in English, Hebrew, and French is looking to increase the amount of Torah-related mate-

net. You will find *divrei Torah* in three languages on the a, holidays, on education and prayer, a calendar with all ally important times, a discussion forum, and a Bet *Hora'ah,* can ask halachic questions. Its links are divided into sections for Je Supersites, Online Study, History and Education, Shopping, Kids, Family, Communities and Institutions, Services, Reference, and Forums. The site also provides a glossary of Jewish terms and hosts a number of traditionally minded sites. This is an excellent portal for material from the strongly traditional point of view.

Virtual Jerusalem

ADDRESS: http://www.virtualjerusalem.com

DESCRIPTION: Virtual Jerusalem began life as Jerusalem One. As one of the major Jewish sites on the Internet, Virtual Jerusalem hosts many organizations, services, and discussion groups on its server and also provides a great deal of original content. Topics covered include News, Business, Travel, Jewish Living, Torah, History, Food, Teens, Shopping, and Holidays. You can join chat groups, check bulletin boards, send a prayer to the Kotel and watch the Kotel Kam, send a greeting card, and listen to VJ Radio. You can also sign up for free e-mail and subscribe to a wide variety of listservs hosted by Virtual Jerusalem.

Ahavat Israel

ADDRESS: http://www.ahavat-israel.com

DESCRIPTION: Founded on the principles of Ahavat Am Israel, Ahavat Torat Israel, and Ahavat Eretz Israel, this very traditional site features original material related to Jewish ideals, laws, customs, and holidays, and Israel. It also houses musical clips, humorous stories, games, classifieds, and software resources. Its Jewish links section houses a directory of sites in the areas of Jewish Studies, Eretz Israel, News, Business, and the Holocaust. You can participate in a forum group, join a chat room, and send postcards from the site as well.

Jewish Communication Network

ADDRESS: http://www.jcn18.com

DESCRIPTION: "A pioneering Jewish web zine produced by the Jewish Communication Network," JCN has ceased publication. However, it still sponsors JewishPersonals.com, JewishMatch.com, and JewishMall.com. Its search engine, Hot Max, is still online but has not been updated. It serves as a frozen moment in time in the history of the Jewish Internet.

JewishNet

ADDRESS: http://jewishnet.net

DESCRIPTION: Created by Dov Winer, this site is subtitled "The Global Jewish Information Network" and was one of the first directories online, with much of the material on it dating back to 1995. The searchable directory indexes links in the areas of Israel Zionism and Aliyah, Talmud Torah and Observance, Holocaust and Antisemitism, Jewish Scholarship and Universities, Jewish Education, Culture, Organizations, Denominations, Communities, Newspapers, Radio and TV, Youth and Students, Women and Feminism, Personal Concerns, Social Activism and Politics, Jewish Genealogy, Professional Groups, Hebrew, Hebrew Support and Yiddish, Networks, Software and Computers, Tourism, and Jewish Food. The site is notable for the access it provides to older, but often still useful, resources in the form of lists of Web servers, IRC, chat and MOO groups, and Jewish libraries. Of particular note is the old, but still informative, list of discussion groups and usenet news groups arranged alphabetically and by subject. Access to files from ftp and gopher servers is also available. While some of the material in these resources is dated, other files still have value. At the very least, the collection serves as a primary source document in the history of the Jewish Internet.

Kosher Delight

ADDRESS: http://www.kosherdelight.com

DESCRIPTION: Although this site describes itself as an online magazine, it houses a directory of Jewish resources, specializing in links to kosher restaurants worldwide and Jewish education. There are categories for Holidays, Travel, Business, Art, and Politics as well. The section on Peace features many links to the Arab world. You can suggest a site for inclusion and check out listings in new categories.

Shamash

ADDRESS: http://shamash.org

DESCRIPTION: Founded by Avrum Goodblatt in 1993, "Shamash is the oldest and best-known Jewishly oriented service accessible through the Internet. Shamash serves the full spectrum of Jewish religious, educational, cultural, communal, and social service organizations interested in utilizing new electronic technologies to share information and deliver services to the Jewish community worldwide." The site hosts numerous mailing lists and archives, a large searchable database of *divrei Torah*, and an extensive kosher restaurant database. There are links to online resources about the Holocaust and computers as well. You can sign up for a newsletter announcing new events in the Jewish online and offline world. The section on Judaica leads to many of the organizations that use Shamash as their server. While the age of this service is showing, it still houses many important and useful resources.

Top 10% of Israeli Sites

ADDRESS: http://www.top.co.il

DESCRIPTION: This site, covering Israeli-based home pages, was created in anticipation of Israel's 50th anniversary and does not appear to have been updated since 1998. It does have a good collection of links in 21 categories that are annotated briefly. The site is searchable, and you can nominate pages for consideration.

PERSONAL PAGES

A Wagner

ADDRESS: http://www.geocities.com/TimesSquare/7833/my-isra.htm

DESCRIPTION: This huge collection of links focuses on Israel and provides material in the areas of Israeli Internet Service Providers, Israeli Government and Politics, News and Weather, the Holocaust, Jewish (Religious and Athiest), Culture and Entertainment, the Internet, and Science and Education. The site features many links not included in other starting pages, such as the Arab view of the peace process.

(Almost) Complete Guide to Www in Israel

ADDRESS: http://math.technion.ac.il/~nyh/israel/

DESCRIPTION: "After almost four years of faithful service to the Israeli public, and to other people interested in Israel, the two sites Nadav Har'El's 'The (almost) Complete Guide to the Israeli Internet' and John Neystadt's 'Israeli Internet Guide' have merged to create iGuide—Your Guide to the Israel Internet." IGuide is covered in the Search Engines section of this book. Nadav Har'El's original page, created in 1994 when he was a student at the Technion, is still available, at least temporarily. It has 1,600 resources in the categories of Commercial Companies, News, Arts, Recreation, Computers, Reference, Education, Regional Resources, Entertainment, Professional Resources, Society and Culture, and Online Resources.

Digital Genizah

ADDRESS: http://www.uscj.org/metny/middletown/GENIZAH.HTM

DESCRIPTION: Created by Mark C. Bassell for the Temple Sinai's home page (of Middletown, New York), this extensive collection of sites is arranged alphabetically, with special sections on Children, Food, Histories, Holidays, Israel, Learning, and World religions. There is also a link to the author's *Cyber Guide for the Perplexed,* with information on using search engines and submitting sites to them and technical resources for web site creation. This is a huge and inclusive collection that should be considered an excellent starting point.

Eliezer Segal

ADDRESS: http://www.acs.ucalgary.ca/~elsegal/

DESCRIPTION: Eleizer Segal is a Canadian scholar whose home page includes newspaper articles he has written for Canadian Jewish publications and the full text of Uncle Eli's Passover *Haggadah,* which has been described as the *Haggadah* written by Dr. Seuss. You can also find image maps for a page of Talmud, the 10 *sefirot* of Kabbalah, varieties of Orthodox Judaism, the ascent to the *Merkavah,* and an interactive site for learning to chant from the Torah and the *Haftorah.*

For Every Jew

ADDRESS: http://www.foreveryjew.com/

DESCRIPTION: This Mexican-based Chabad site provides online courses in subjects such as Torah, Talmud, *Mussar, Tanya, Shulchan Aruch,* and *Mishneh Torah.* In many cases, a large amount of primary source material is provided online as well.

Frum Side of the Web

ADDRESS: http://www.cs.brandeis.edu/~walrus

DESCRIPTION: Originally designed by Oizer Alport and now maintained by Nachum Shanske, this site houses a collection of links to the Orthodox world. Categories include *Divrei Torah* on the *Parshios;* Jewish Learning (not *Parsha*-based); Yeshivos and Schools; Online Classical Texts; Kiruv (Outreach) Organizations; Collections of Links to Jewish Resources; Miscellaneous; Holidays, Calendars and *Zmanim;* National Organizations; Jewish Boston, Sights, Sounds, and Tastes; Sight and Sound Guide to Shabbos Koidesh; Books and Magazines; Israeli News; Hebrew and

Yiddish; and Fun Stuff. Despite the fact that this page has not been updated since the end of 1997, it still contains useful information.

Harry Leichter's All Things Jewish

ADDRESS: http://www.haruth.com/JewishIndex.html

DESCRIPTION: Haruth is a publishing and Web design company. Its owner, Harry Leichter, has compiled an extensive collection of Jewish links, with a particular emphasis on Jewish communities worldwide, Jewish Music, Publications worldwide, Travel, Women, Marranos, Kabbalah, *Kashrut*, Museums, *Sephardim*, Torah Study, the Weekly *Parsha*, and Yiddish. In all, there are 92 categories of material. This is a rich and comprehensive collection.

Jacob Richman

ADDRESS: http://www.jr.co.il

DESCRIPTION: Jacob Richman is an American *oleh* who works in the Israeli computer industry. His personal page has been online since April 24, 1996, and offers a rich variety of resources. His section on *Aliyah* provides links to information about *aliyah* centers, appliances, housing, jobs, learning Hebrew, *olim* organizations, useful addresses, Web links, and why one would make *aliyah*. The Charity section not only lists a large number of Israeli and Jewish groups, but also has an extensive section of Torah resources online. The Computer Jobs in Israel section includes a valuable salary survey, and the Dictionary defines several hundred Hebrew words, with an emphasis on computer terms. Check the Hotsites section for links in 32 different subject areas. If you have interests in any of the topics covered by Mr. Richman, this is an excellent starting point.

Jewish 1000

ADDRESS: http://Jewish1000.com/

DESCRIPTION: Chosen from English-language pages, this site includes home pages that meet the following criteria; interesting content for the Jewish community, appealing appearance, significant number of links, and updated frequently. Pages are divided into 18 categories, and the number of sites in each section is listed. The best of the best are cited in the Top 50 section. You can also recommend a site for consideration. This is an excellent starting point for beginning an exploration of the English-language Judaica Web world.

Jewish Express

ADDRESS: http://www.jewishexpress.com

DESCRIPTION: This new entrant into the Jewish directory field has a limited number of listings in the categories of Dining, Holidays, Real Estate, Shidduchim, Shopping, Synagogues, Torah, and Travel. You can sign up for free singles listings and free e-mail.

Jewish Ring Home Page

ADDRESS: http://home.vicnet.net.au/~aragorn/jew-ring.htm

DESCRIPTION: Andrew Rajcher of Australia was the first to introduce the concept of the Web ring to the Jewish community. His home page describes what a Web ring is and how to join it. You can use this home page as a starting point for exploring the Jewish Web ring.

Jewish Web Ring Exchange

ADDRESS: http://members.aol.com/JeremyMP/jewish.html

DESCRIPTION: Jeremy Padawer has posted another Jewish Web ring exchange that you can explore from this site.

Leonard Grossman's Lengthy List of Jewish Links

ADDRESS: http://www.mcs.net/~grossman/jewish.html

DESCRIPTION: Created for West Suburban Temple Har Zion's home page, this collection includes sections for Israel, United Synagogue and JTS, Holidays, Family, Genealogy, Jewish Publications, Directories, Resources and Museums, Food, Humor, Calendars, Art and Gifts, Literature, Psychology and Philosophy, Study, Synagogues and Temples, Singles, Judaism in Its Variety, and Holocaust Studies.

Mish Mash

ADDRESS: http://mishmash.virtualave.net

DESCRIPTION: Created by Lori Sheiman, this site boasts over 10,000 sites in categories, including the branches of Judaism, Business, Computer, Cooking, Culture, Education, Entertainment, Family, Health, History, Holidays, the Holocaust, Jewish Communities, Judaica, Judaism, Link Launchers, Media, Parenting, Politics, Social, Sports, Tourism, and Women. Links are arranged alphabetically within categories and subcategories and have brief annotations. This sheer size of this site makes it an excellent starting point.

Over 300 Jewish Links

ADDRESS: http://www.chebucto.ns.ca/~ab522/jewish.html

DESCRIPTION: This site presents a list of over 300 links divided into 48 categories, with a strong emphasis on Canadian sites.

Ultimate Jewish/Israel Launcher

ADDRESS: http://ucsu.colorado.edu/~jsu/launcher.html

DESCRIPTION: Created by Steve Ruttenberg, this site from the Jewish Student Union of the University of Colorado is one of the veterans of the personal home pages on the Internet. This version, dating back to 1998, houses more than 4,600 links in the categories of Politics, Judaism, Culture, Local Resources, People, History, Antisemitism, Information, Travel, Business, Academic Groups, and Organizations. The interactive features of the site allow you to check the biographies of famous Jews, add a link to the database and vote on its contents, and sign the guest book. You can also search the site. The Biography section of the site became so popular that the students created a new site called Yahoodi, which is described in a separate entry.

Yahoodi

ADDRESS: http://www.yahoodi.com

DESCRIPTION: An outgrowth of the Ultimate Jewish/Israel Link Launcher, this searchable database profiles famous Jews in 54 categories. The site includes a section defining who is a Jew for the sake of inclusion in the database. You can also suggest additional people. The biographies consist of references to Internet sites rather than original material. This is an excellent starting point for Jewish biographical material.

ACADEMIC JEWISH STUDIES

Jewish Studies from St. Johns University

ADDRESS: http://www.stjohns.edu/library/staugustine/JewishStudiesTOC.html

DESCRIPTION: This large, browsable collection of links to resources on anti-semitism, archaeology, culture, the Diaspora, history, the Holocaust, Israel and Zionism, journals, Judaism, *kashrut*, mailing lists, mysticism, organizations, social issues, and links to academic institutions and libraries was last updated in 1998 but is still a useful resource.

Jewish Studies Guide

ADDRESS: http://www.columbia.edu/cu/libraries/indiv/area/Jewish/

DESCRIPTION: This large, searchable collections of links in Jewish studies was created by Middle East and Jewish librarian Frank Unlandherm. Subjects include *aliyah*, anti-semitism, bibliographies in Jewish Studies, a directory of scholars in Jewish Studies, electronic journals, the Holocaust, Israel, Jewish holidays, Judaism, Hebrew language and literature, libraries with major Jewish Studies collections, Major Jewish Organizations, Palestine and the Palestinians, publishers, Sephardic Jewish communities, women, and Yiddish language and literature. The site was last updated in 1998 but is still a very useful resource.

Jewish Studies Network

ADDRESS: http://h-net2.msu.edu/~judaic

DESCRIPTION: Discussions, reviews, pre-print articles, and syllabi related to all aspects of Judaic studies. Of particular note are H-Judaic, a moderated, scholarly discussion group; *The Jewish Studies Newsletter*, and *JSN Book Reviews* provided here. This is an excellent starting point for information about academic Jewish studies.

Jstudies.org

ADDRESS: http://www.JStudies.org/

DESCRIPTION: This site provides bibliographies, suggested books, and links to sites in the field, as well as a list of graduate students and scholars in various areas of study. In addition, it supports a mailing list and discussion groups and provides a large selection of links arranged by subject area. This is an excellent starting point for information relating to the area of academic Jewish studies.

American Jewish Literature

ADDRESS: http://www.ngc.peachnet.edu/Academic/Arts_Let/LangLit/dproyal/jewish.htm

DESCRIPTION: Information on literary criticism about Stanley Elkin, Cynthia Ozick, Philip Roth, Woody Allen, E. M. Broner, Art Spiegelman, Joseph Heller, Grace Paley, and E. L. Doctorow. Of particular note is the selected bibliography of texts on Jewish-American literature.

Association for Jewish Studies

ADDRESS: http://www.brandeis.edu/ajs

DESCRIPTION: Information about the membership, conferences, publications, and constituent Jewish studies societies of this organization devoted to the promotion of academic Jewish studies. Of particular note is the rentable mailing list of members and listing of job openings.

China Judaic Studies Association

ADDRESS: http://servercc.oakton.edu/~friend/chinajews.html

DESCRIPTION: Tours, publications, links, and activities of this group that seeks to promote Judaic studies in China.

Hebrew College

ADDRESS: http://www.hebrewcollege.edu

DESCRIPTION: Information about the courses, admissions policy, Hebrew programs, adult education, youth programs, online courses, alumni, library, affiliates, and faculty of this Boston-based school.

Institute for Islamic-Judaic Studies

ADDRESS: http://www.du.edu/~sward/institut.html

DESCRIPTION: Information about the work and publications of this group, headed by Dr. Seth Ward and based at the University of Denver. Includes table of contents for past publications, conference and course information, and calls for papers.

Jewish University in Cyberspace (JUICE)

ADDRESS: http://www.jajz-ed.org.il/juice/index.html

DESCRIPTION: Sign up for free, online courses in a variety of Jewish subject areas.

Orion Center for the Study of the Dead Sea Scrolls

ADDRESS: http://orion.mscc.huji.ac.il/

DESCRIPTION: This searchable site offers access to the activities, publications, annual symposiums, and e-mail discussion group on the Dead Sea Scrolls. Also available are the regularly updated bibliography on the Scrolls, news articles, links, and a bulletin board for conferences, paper calls, and job openings. Photographs of manuscripts from Qumran, the site of the Scrolls' discovery, are provided as well.

Semantics of Ancient Hebrew Database

ADDRESS: http://www.ed.ac.uk/~dreimer/SAHD

DESCRIPTION: A cooperative research project based at Leiden University, which is attempting to create a Greek and Hebrew database in English transliteration.

Sino-Judaic Institute

ADDRESS: http://www.sino-judaic.org/

DESCRIPTION: Dedicated to "promoting friendship and understanding between Chinese and Jewish peoples," this organization also works with the remnant of the Jewish community in Kaifeng. Its home page provides selections from its journal, *Points East*, and describes the projects, activities, and publications of the group. Of particular note is the material the site provides on the history of the Jews of Kaifeng.

Virtual Jewish University

ADDRESS: http://www.bar-ilan.edu

DESCRIPTION: Bar Ilan's virtual Jewish university, complete with course catalog, bookstore, faculty listings, academic adviser, FAQ, and course demonstration. Courses receive academic credit and may be transferred to other institutions.

ALIYAH

Jewish Agency for Israel

ADDRESS: http://www.jafi.org.il/comehome/index.htm

DESCRIPTION: This searchable site in Russian, French, Spanish, and English has special sections on *Aliyah*, Preparation, *Oleh* Rights, Jobs, Housing, the Army, General Information for the *oleh*, *Ulpanim* and Useful Tips for the *Oleh* and the Veteran. It includes a link to the archives of Tachlis, the nuts and bolts *aliyah* discussion group, with discussions on appliances, where to live, jobs, banking, and *ulpanim*. This is the first site to check for *aliyah* information.

Aliyah Resources

ADDRESS: http://www.weizmann.ac.il/home/comartin/aliyah.html

DESCRIPTION: A narrative discussion with embedded links about the process of *aliyah*.

Association of Americans and Canadians in Israel

ADDRESS: http://www.aaci.org.il

DESCRIPTION: Information about the organization, as well as pre-*aliyah* information, regional and branch programming, and the AACI Israel Jobnet.

Discover Aliyah Online

ADDRESS: http://www.ujia.org.il/discover/discover.htm

DESCRIPTION: Free, downloadable database of information for prospective *olim* created by the British UJIA.

English Speaking Residents Association in Israel

ADDRESS: http://www.esra.org.il

DESCRIPTION: This home page details the activities and services of this group that represents English speakers in Israel. Links created by the ESRA's computer club to Jewish and Israeli sites, as well as online buying sites, are also available. The group sponsors a gardening club as well.

Flathunting

ADDRESS: http://members.tripod.com/~flathunting

DESCRIPTION: Archives of two listservs where individuals can offer or search for apartments to rent in either Jerusalem or Tel Aviv. An interactive map of Jerusalem is planned.

Immigration.co.il

ADDRESS: http://www.immigration.co.il

DESCRIPTION: A Russian-language site with discussion groups and information about aliyah.

Israel Aliyah Center of North America

ADDRESS: http://www.aliyah.org/

DESCRIPTION: As of this writing, this site was under construction.

Kef International

ADDRESS: http://www.feldcom.com/kef/

DESCRIPTION: This shipping company specializes in service to Israel and offers a detailed description of the process of international shipping. It also has information on customs and storage. Of particular note is the information, prices and KEF recommendations on 220-volt appliances, sample shipping contract, and tax chart for *olim*.

Kesher Online

ADDRESS: http://www.kesheronline.com

DESCRIPTION: *Kesher* means "connection," and this site allows you to connect with friends and family abroad.

Ministry of Immigration and Absorption

ADDRESS: http://www.moia.gov.il

DESCRIPTION: English, Hebrew, and Russian site with contact information, publications, types of assistance, and statistics and research of interest to *olim*. Of particular note are the numerous charts detailing the monetary amounts offered by various assistance programs.

National Employment Database from AACI

ADDRESS: http://www.jobnet.co.il

DESCRIPTION: Searchable site with listings in English and Hebrew of jobs in Israel, particularly in the high-tech field. Information is offered on salaries, job fairs, Israeli computer news, Israeli news sources, professional organizations, *olim* organizations, selected government links, and *aliyah* offices, along with an employment terms dictionary and salary survey.

Parents of North American Israelis (PNAI)

ADDRESS: http://www.pnai.org

DESCRIPTION: Information about the membership and services of the organization, as well as access to its publication, *The Bridge*.

Real Aliyah Information Pages

ADDRESS: http://members.tripod.com/realaliyah/

DESCRIPTION: Akiva Marks provides a personal and practical perspective on taxes, housing, banking, making a living, benefits and subsidies, schooling, medical issues, transportation, and appliances in Israel.

Rentals in Beit Shemesh

ADDRESS: http://members.tripod.com/ShemeshRentals

DESCRIPTION: General information about Ramat Beit Shemesh, as well as apartment rental listings.

Revivim

ADDRESS: http://www.revivim-insurance.com

DESCRIPTION: Information in English and Hebrew on insuring shipments to Israel sent by sea is provided at this site. Also available are an *aliyah* timeline, links to *aliyah* information, and pages about Israel and movers.

Settling in Modi'in

ADDRESS: http://www.lerner.co.il/modiin/

DESCRIPTION: From this site you can sign up for a listserv about Modi'in, moderated by Reuven Lerner, and check some of its archives. There is also a list of useful telephone numbers, a .gif map of Modi'in, the Margalit bus schedule in Hebrew and English, and a list of Jewish studies in Modi'in in Hebrew. Additional information about the "city of the future" is available in Hebrew from http://www.webscape.co.il/modiin/main/modiin2.htm.

Settling in Ramat Beit Shemesh

ADDRESS: http://www.cs.huji.ac.il/~momo/rbs/

DESCRIPTION: News, community information, and list archives of this discussion group on living in Ramat Beit Shemesh are available here, along with a map of the community.

Strand Freight

ADDRESS: http://www.strandfreight.com

DESCRIPTION: The home page of this company, which specializes in shipping to Israel, features information about the services it offers, along with a useful FAQ about the details of transporting goods to Israel.

Teen to Teen

ADDRESS: http://www.ttt.org.il

DESCRIPTION: A magazine for teens whose families have made *aliyah*. Includes articles written by the youngsters, jokes, an advice column, creative writing, and profiles of the authors.

Tehilla

ADDRESS: http://www.tehilla.com/index.shtml

DESCRIPTION: The Union for Religious Aliyah provides information about opportunities in Israel, employment, housing, education, and rights. Of particular note are Tehilla's publications, available in full text—*Bayit Ne'eman*, with useful housing information, and Tehilla's house organ, *Derech Tehilla.*

Telfed—South African Zionist Federation

ADDRESS: http://www.telfed.org.il/

DESCRIPTION: Information on *aliyah* as well as a job bank, a "find a friend" service, and an online magazine are provided at this site for South Africans making *aliyah*. Information about a joint counseling service, being run by Telfed and the British Olim Society, and a forum for former South Africans living in Israel, called a Network for Professionals, are also available.

ISRAELI WANT ADS

Classified Israeli Ads

ADDRESS: http://www.classads.co.il

DESCRIPTION: If you are looking for employment, a new person in your life, home rentals, real estate, a car, computers, or other merchandise or services in Israel, check this searchable English-language site. You can also place an ad and send an Internet postcard here.

IsraelAds

ADDRESS: http://IsraelAds.listbot.com

DESCRIPTION: Archives and subscription form to read or join this listserv that offers items from Israel for sale.

ANTI-SEMITISM

Anti Defamation League

ADDRESS: http://www.adl.org/

DESCRIPTION: This searchable site has information about the organization, categorized press releases, background briefings, and focus articles on a variety of hate groups and their leaders, the work of the legislative center, and material about terrorism. Of particular note is ADL's Hate Filter, which can be used on the Internet. This is an excellent starting site for information about anti-Semitism.

Antisemitism in the World Today

ADDRESS: http://www.jpr.org.uk/antisem/index.shtml

DESCRIPTION: This searchable site, from the Institute for Jewish Policy Research, details antisemitic trends worldwide by country. Archived material dating back to 1996 is also available. This is another excellent starting point for anti-Semitic issues worldwide.

SICSA—Vidal Sassoon International Center for the Study of Antisemitism

ADDRESS: http://sicsa.huji.ac.il/

DESCRIPTION: This site offers a searchable bibliography of over 30,000 items housed in this library at the Hebrew University. Publications and research undertaken by the institute are also available, along with a selected bibliography on Holocaust denial. This is an excellent starting site.

Stephen Roth Institute for the Study of Contemporary Antisemitism and Racism

ADDRESS: http://www.tau.ac.il/Anti-Semitism/institute.html

DESCRIPTION: Housed in the Wiener Library at Tel Aviv University, this institute contains one of the largest collections of anti-Semitic, Nazi, and extremist literature in the world. The Web site provides access to its database, list of publications, annual reports, news, and updates. It is also an excellent starting point for research in this area.

Antisemitism Reading List

ADDRESS: http://shamash.org/lists/scj-faq/HTML/rl/ant-index.html

DESCRIPTION: Part of the soc.culture.jewish newsgroup, this list of books covers Topics in antisemitism, what led to the Holocaust, medieval oppression; anti-Semitism today, including hate groups; Judaism and Christianity; and Judaism, freemasonry, and other rumors.

Jewish Defense League

ADDRESS: http://www.jdl.org/

DESCRIPTION: News, organizational information, profiles of anti-Semitic individuals and those who fight against them, and reports of actions taken by the group to combat anti-Semitism are available here.

ART

Israel Art Guide

ADDRESS: http://www.israelartguide.co.il

DESCRIPTION: Searchable database of thousands of Israeli artists, with many of their works on display. Of particular note is the listing of current exhibitions at galleries and museums throughout Israel. This is an excellent starting point for information about Israeli art.

American Guild of Judaic Art

ADDRESS: http://www.jewishart.org

DESCRIPTION: This organization serves as a referral service devoted to promoting professional Jewish artists. Its home page offers a hypertext directory of members, bulletin board discussions, and a list of upcoming events, as well as an Education section with book reviews written by members. Also of note is the Speakers' Bureau listings.

Fenster Museum of Jewish Art

ADDRESS: http://www.jewishmuseum.net/

DESCRIPTION: Information about and online exhibits in archaeology, ritual objects, life cycle items, ethnology, and Jewish history from this Tulsa, Oklahoma, Jewish art museum. The site also features Oklahoma Jewish history materials.

Israel Images

ADDRESS: http://www.israelimages.com

DESCRIPTION: A searchable site of photographs and images of Israel and the Holy Land arranged by subject. The company will search for pictures for a fee and is also available for special assignments.

Israeli Association of Painters and Sculptors

ADDRESS: http://www.gallery.co.il

DESCRIPTION: English and Hebrew site with information about the organization, its constituent artists, and their exhibitions.

Jewish Artists Network

ADDRESS: http://www.jewishartists.com

DESCRIPTION: This site describes itself as "a meeting place for professional Jewish artists and a place to hire and purchase from professional Jewish artists."

Jews in Comics

ADDRESS: http://www.geocities.com/Athens/Acropolis/5756/JWISHC.HTM

DESCRIPTION: A hypertext bibliography created by librarian Steve Bergson, detailing the portrayal of Jews in comic books and comic strips.

National Foundation for Jewish Culture

ADDRESS: http://www.jewishculture.org

DESCRIPTION: This site details the goals of the group, its membership benefits, and its support for theater, film, museums, archives, libraries, and research projects. You can learn how to apply for a grant; check the group's newsletter, *CultureCurrents,* whose archives date back to 1998; and read selected articles from the foundation's magazine, *Jewish Culture News.*

World of Jewish Art Portraits

ADDRESS: http://www.jewish-portraits.com

DESCRIPTION: An online gallery of 119 portraits painted by European artists. The site sponsors a listserv and will accept commissions of work.

CLIP ART

Bitsela Artz Clip Art

ADDRESS: http://www.bitsela.com

DESCRIPTION: Bitsela Artz is a company that produces and sells Judaic graphics CD-ROMs. Its site offers some examples of its work for free, along with links to other Jewish clip art resources.

Jewish Art Source Clip Art

ADDRESS: http://www.jewishartsource.com

DESCRIPTION: Categorized collection of clip art for Jewish themes and holidays.

GALLERIES

Artcnet.com

ADDRESS: http://www.artcnet.com

DESCRIPTION: Virtual gallery of work by Israeli and Jewish artists. Hypertext directory of members is provided. The site sponsors a listserv, as well as an art tour of Israel.

Artistic Judaic Promotions

ADDRESS: http://www.ajp.com

DESCRIPTION: Virtual gallery selling Judaica produced by a large variety of American and Israeli artists. Site provides suggestions for gift purchases, a gift registry, fundraising ideas, and a hypertext list of contributing artists. The entire site is searchable.

Engel Galleries

ADDRESS: http://www.engel-art.co.il/main.html

DESCRIPTION: Displays of Israeli masterpieces and contemporary art from this Israeli gallery are accompanied by an annual online auction.

Inter ART Israel

ADDRESS: http://www.interart.co.il/

DESCRIPTION: The gallery sells Judaica and Israeli art in a variety of media. The site publishes an online newsletter called *The Arts Gazette* and provides information on new art books published in Israel. Of particular note is the hypertext list of selected art galleries in Israel.

Jerusalem Anthologia

ADDRESS: http://www.antho.net

DESCRIPTION: A virtual museum of contemporary Israeli artists and writers, along with a hypertext index of members. Site is in English, Hebrew, and Russian.

Stern Fine Art Gallery

ADDRESS: http://www.sternart.com

DESCRIPTION: This Israeli-based gallery sells classic and contemporary Israeli art and Judaica. The site includes an essay about the history of Jewish art and tips on caring for an art collection. Also of interest is the extensive material on the Pissarro family of artists, represented by the Stern Gallery in London.

BOOKS

Dfus-Graph

ADDRESS: http://www.index.co.il/dfus/

DESCRIPTION: A Hebrew language guide to 8,000 companies and businesses in the publishing industry in Israel. Arrangement is geographic, and the site has a clickable map of the country.

Virtual Judaica

ADDRESS: http://www.virtualjudaica.com

DESCRIPTION: A rare book resource that provides a database of over 15,000 Hebrew book titles printed prior to 1800, with auction prices dating back two decades, a searchable antiquarian book service with Hebraica and Judaica, an exhibit of material from the 16th to 18th centuries that is updated weekly, and an auction service for fundraising. The site also features live specialists who will answer questions and an appraisal service for antiquarian Hebraica and Judaica.

BOOKSELLERS

A. I. Weinberg Hebrew Books

ADDRESS: http://www.aiweinberg.com

DESCRIPTION: This Israeli provider of Hebrew titles has a browsable and searchable catalog online and services many large libraries, as well as individuals.

Books International

ADDRESS: http://www.booksinternational.com

DESCRIPTION: The online catalog of this distributor, dealing in academic, general, and religious books in a variety of languages published in Israel, features books from the Academon of Hebrew University and publications of Israeli museums. It also provides a monthly e-mail newsletter for libraries.

Broder's Rare and Used Judaica

ADDRESS: http://members.aol.com/bookssss/judaica.html

DESCRIPTION: Rare and used Judaica arranged by subject area. You can sign up for a free e-mail newsletter, with new offerings sent monthly.

Dbook Hebrew Bookstore

ADDRESS: http://www.dbook.co.il

DESCRIPTION: Amazon.com-like site for Hebrew books of all kinds. Each title has a long annotation and a picture of the cover. Most books are discounted and can be shipped worldwide. Site lists best sellers and has a cafe where titles are discussed. You can search the site using Dapey Reshet's virtual Hebrew keyboard, which appears on the screen. Some titles are available for listening in MP3 format as well.

Eichler's Bookstore

ADDRESS: http://www.eichlers.com

DESCRIPTION: A searchable and browsable site for this Brooklyn-based store that describes itself as "the largest Judaica store in the world." Browse through categories that include Books, Gifts, Software, and Children's Items.

English Online

ADDRESS: http://www.eol.co.il

DESCRIPTION: Browsable and searchable site for English-language books and CDs, both new and used, from the United States and the U.K. This site emphasizes its reduced shipping costs to Israel and its full customer service desk in Israel.

Gozlan's Sefer Israel

ADDRESS: http://www.seferisrael.com

DESCRIPTION: This New York-based company imports and distributes Hebrew teaching aids for adults and college students and *Tanach* and Hebrew material for Jewish day schools.

Henry Hollander

ADDRESS: http://www.hollanderbooks.com

DESCRIPTION: Catalogs from this antiquarian Judaica dealer based in San Francisco. Out-of-print book searches are also performed. Of particular note is the glossary of book-collecting terms.

Israel Book Center

ADDRESS: http://www.israelbookshop.com/merchant.mv

DESCRIPTION: Browsable and searchable site of this Boston-based Judaica shop, featuring books, music, videos, software, and *tallesim.*

IsraelShop—Online Jewish Bookstore

ADDRESS: http://www7.bcity.com/israelshop

DESCRIPTION: An Amazon.com affiliate, featuring a searchable selection of Jewish titles in 20 categories.

J. Levine Company

ADDRESS: http://www.levine-judaica.com

DESCRIPTION: Searchable site of this large Judaica store in New York City that sells a wide range of books, music, ritual objects, artwork, and multimedia. Drop-down menus offer suggestions for gifts or help you locate material for children or for specific study areas.

Jerusalem Post Store

ADDRESS: http://jpoststore.com

DESCRIPTION: Online shopping for books, music, videos, software, flowers, travel, and gifts distributed through this site associated with *The Jerusalem Post.*

Jewish Book Maven

ADDRESS: http://www.abebooks.com/home/JEWISHBOOKMAVEN

DESCRIPTION: Browse or search the catalog of this Albany, New York-based independent used bookstore, specializing in scholarly Judaica.

Libreria Cultural Maimonides

ADDRESS: http://www.libreriamaimonides.com/

DESCRIPTION: Browsable collection of Judaica in Spanish from this Caracas, Venezuela–based bookstore. Prices are in U.S. dollars and shipment is worldwide.

Mount Zion/Sifrei Har Tzion Books

ADDRESS: http://www.jerusalembooks.com and http://www.zionbooks.com/

DESCRIPTION: Describing itself as "the largest Jewish bookstore on the Web," this company specializes in *sifrei kodesh* in English, Hebrew, French, and Russian and ships worldwide. The site provides a Jewish music listening room, sells cassettes and CD-ROMs, and offers book reviews. Several full textbooks are available for download for free.

My Jewish Bookstore

ADDRESS: http://www.myjewishbooks.com and http://www.sefersafari.com/

DESCRIPTION: This joint project with Sefer Sefari provides an annotated list of English-language Judaica, arranged by subject and searchable. This site is a front end to Amazon.com, which fulfills the book orders. Each quarter the site's commission proceeds are donated to charity. An excellent list of Jewish and general charities is also available.

Nunbet Books

ADDRESS: http://www.nunbetbooks.co.il

DESCRIPTION: The home page of this Israeli company, which sells Judaica and Yizkor books in a number of languages, has a browsable catalog.

Opus Books

ADDRESS: http://www.opus.co.il/index.htm

DESCRIPTION: An Israeli bookstore that specializes in Hebrew-language materials about computers and the Internet, as well as Hebrew-language titles in fantasy literature. The site is searchable and has an Amazon.com-like shopping basket. It also hosts forums for members.

Robinson Books

ADDRESS: http://www.robinson.co.il/

DESCRIPTION: The Hebrew and English searchable site of this Tel Aviv-based bookstore that specializes in rare Judaica and rabbinica has a stock of 100,000 books, 80 percent of which are out of print and 90 percent of which are in Hebrew. It also has a large collection of Yizkor books and privately printed titles.

Rosenblum's World of Judaica

ADDRESS: http://www.rosenblums.com/ and http://www.alljudaica.com

DESCRIPTION: The browsable and searchable site of this Chicago-based store, describing itself as "the oldest and largest full service Jewish bookstore in the midwest," offers books, ritual objects, gifts, and multi-media for online purchase. An "ask the expert" feature and e-mail newsletter are also available.

Schoen Books

ADDRESS: http://www.schoenbooks.com

DESCRIPTION: Catalogs from this antiquarian Judaica dealer, who houses 25,000 titles in South Deerfield, Massachusetts.

Shemaria Judaica

ADDRESS: http://www.shemariajudaica.com

DESCRIPTION: Based in the U.K., this bookseller deals with rare and out of print Judaica and Hebraica titles. This site is browsable and searchable.

Sifrantica

ADDRESS: http://www.brijnet.org/sifrantica

DESCRIPTION: Based in the U.K., this Jewish antiquarian bookstore deals with rare and out-of-print titles in Judaica and rabbinic literature. Site is browsable.

Steimatzky

ADDRESS: http://www.steimatzky.co.il

DESCRIPTION: Despite the fact that Steimatzky is the largest English-language bookseller in Israel, most of this site is in Hebrew. English-language books on Israel are listed. Books are divided in categories, including children's titles, best sellers, textbooks, and new books, and the site is searchable. The site has a cafe where titles are discussed. There is also a link that allows you to subscribe to a number of English-language magazines.

Virtual Geula

ADDRESS: http://www.virtualgeula.com

DESCRIPTION: A bookseller providing over 20,000 titles in traditional Jewish studies, including *seforim* that are out of print.

PUBLISHERS

Association of Jewish Publishers

ADDRESS: http://www.avotaynu.com/ajbp.html

DESCRIPTION: This directory provides a hypertext list of member publishing houses, last updated in February 1997.

Art Scroll Books

ADDRESS: http://www.artscroll.com

DESCRIPTION: Searchable, browsable site of this major Judaica publisher. Additional sections include Best Sellers, Forthcoming Titles, and Recent Releases. You can also sign up for an online newsletter.

Behrman House

ADDRESS: http://www.behrmanhouse.com

DESCRIPTION: News, educational services, and the history of this leading publisher of educational materials for Jewish religious schools in North America. The online catalog is browsable and searchable.

Feldheim Publishers

ADDRESS: http://www.feldheim.com

DESCRIPTION: Searchable, browsable online catalog from this Judaica publisher. Site features an in-depth interview with an author, new releases, a newsletter available through e-mail, and the opportunity to download a chapter from one of the publisher's titles. Book selection by age is facilitated through the graphic of a house. Clicking on various rooms brings up related subjects. You can also find the publications of Targum Press at this site.

Gefen Publishing

ADDRESS: http://www.israelbooks.com/

DESCRIPTION: Browsable site of English-language books published in Israel.

Jason Aronson Publishers

ADDRESS: http://www.aronson.com

DESCRIPTION: Browsable and searchable catalog of this Judaica publisher. Free books are also included in each order. Free subscriptions to *Jewish Book News* are available. Information for prospective authors is provided, as well as interviews with authors published by the company.

Jewish Lights Bookstore

ADDRESS: http://www.jewishlights.com/

DESCRIPTION: Browsable catalog of this Vermont-based publisher that emphasizes titles in Jewish spirituality.

Jewish Publication Society

ADDRESS: http://www.jewishpub.org

DESCRIPTION: Browsable and searchable catalog of this veteran American Jewish publisher based in Philadelphia. The site includes short book reviews, a discussion *kumsitz* area, press releases, and information about becoming a member.

Jonathan David

ADDRESS: http://www.jonathandavidonline.com/

DESCRIPTION: Information about the company's print catalog entitled *Judaica Book Guide,* as well as an interview with an author, notes about forthcoming titles and new releases, and details about submitting manuscripts. Orders for books are fulfilled through other online bookstores.

Judaica Press

ADDRESS: http://www.judaicapress.com

DESCRIPTION: Browse by title or category through the online catalog of this Judaica publisher. The site also offers information on new books, author highlights, and press releases.

Kar-Ben Copies

ADDRESS: http://www.karben.com

DESCRIPTION: Browsable catalog of this publisher of children's Judaica. Information on holding a book fair and submitting manuscripts is also provided. The site also has a five-year calendar of Jewish holidays.

Keter Books

ADDRESS: http://www.keterbooks.co.il/default.html

DESCRIPTION: An affiliate of Dbook, this is the Hebrew-language site of the publishers of *The Encyclopedia Judaica.*

KTAV Publishing House

ADDRESS: http://www.ktav.com

DESCRIPTION: Browse or search the online catalog of this company featuring religious titles, scholarly books, and textbooks.

Littman Library of Jewish Civilization

ADDRESS: http://www.littman.co.uk

DESCRIPTION: This company, based in the United Kingdom, publishes scholarly works that explain and perpetuate the Jewish heritage and publishes translations of Hebrew and Aramaic classics. From its searchable Web site you can check the author and title indices and browse by subject category. Books may be ordered online. There are listings for forthcoming titles, special offers, and out-of-print titles as well.

Modan Publishing

ADDRESS: http://www.modan.co.il

DESCRIPTION: Hebrew-language site of this Israeli book and CD publisher. Site is browsable and searchable and accepts online purchases.

Modern Hebrew Literature in Translation

ADDRESS: http://www.blueandwhitebooks.com/

DESCRIPTION: The bookshop specializes in English-language books on the subjects of modern Hebrew literature in translation, Israel, the Holy Land, and Jewish subjects.

Rubin Mass

ADDRESS: http://www.age.co.il/mas/index.htm

DESCRIPTION: Basic information from this Israeli book publisher and distributor who can supply any book or periodical, in any language, published in Israel by any publisher. The company also distributes the publications of Yad Vashem and the maps and guides of Carta, the Israel Map and Publishing Company. You can sign up to receive a free bimonthly catalogue entitled "Recent Publications from Israel," highlighting about 300 titles.

Sephardic House

ADDRESS: http://www.sephardichouse.org/

DESCRIPTION: List of books, videos, music, and photos published by this organization devoted to Sephardic cultural history. Site includes a calendar of Sephardic events in the New York area and links to Web sites of Sephardic interest.

Soncino Press

ADDRESS: http://www.soncino.com

DESCRIPTION: Online listing with detailed descriptions of the books published by Soncino, best known for its translations of classic Jewish texts.

Torah Aura Productions

ADDRESS: http://www.torahaura.com/

DESCRIPTION: Browsable, searchable catalog of instructional materials, including books and toys. This is a rich instructional site that has a "Learn Torah With" electronic newsletter, sample pages from the Family Bet Din series that invites follow-up discussion online, and sample current events pages to stimulate online and offline debate.

CALENDARS

Hebcal Interactive Jewish Calendar

ADDRESS: http://www.sadinoff.com/hebcal/

DESCRIPTION: Created by Danny Sadinoff, this software available for download is a full-service calendar program that can be used by many computer platforms. The site also lists Web sites and books about the Jewish calendar, as well as references to other sites powered by Hebcal.

Kaluach

ADDRESS: http://members.tripod.com/~kaluach

DESCRIPTION: Created by Yisrael (Russ) Hersch, this award-winning calendar displays an entire month on the screen with holidays, *parshiot,* and halachic times. The author describes the software as "careware, not freeware" and requests a donation be made to his synagogue after downloading the program. Users can add personal data such as birthdays, anniversaries, and *yahrzeits.*

Perpetual Calendar

ADDRESS:http://www.uwm.edu/cgi-bin/corre/calendar

DESCRIPTION: Onscreen calculator that will translate a year on the civil calendar to the Hebrew calendar.

COMPUTERS

SOFTWARE

Davka Corporation

ADDRESS: http://www.davka.com/

DESCRIPTION: The browsable and searchable site of this major Judaic software producer is divided into subject categories, including Hebrew Instruction, Word Processing, Jewish Life and History, Israel, Jewish Clip Art, Hebrew Fonts, Educational Games, and Helpful Utilities. There are sections for Sale Items, Raffles, Technical Support, and links to sites of Jewish interest. Online purchases are accepted.

Dor L'Dor

ADDRESS: http://www.radix.net/~dor_l_dor/

DESCRIPTION: This producer of Jewish educational software also lists T-shirts and mouse pads among its categorized offerings. Some samples are available for downloading, and a tech support page is provided as well.

Hebrew Software Digest

ADDRESS: http://www.gy.com/www/he.htm

DESCRIPTION: This site distributes Hebrew software from a variety of companies. It provides an excellent collection of links to sites offering comparison shopping for Hebrew software, both software for learning the language and utilities for using Hebrew text online.

Infomedia Judaica

ADDRESS: http://www.imjl.com

DESCRIPTION: Markets 150 Judaic instructional software titles and audio visual materials. The company's catalog is browsable by subject area and media format.

Jewish Software Center

ADDRESS: http://users.aol.com/jewishsoft/

DESCRIPTION: This software distributor has a categorized list of titles divided into 22 subject areas.

Kabbalah Software

ADDRESS: http://www.kabsoft.com/

DESCRIPTION: This distributor of Judaic software has a browsable catalog with titles in reference materials, Jewish calendar programs, utilities, word processors, Torah study, and educational software. Information on clip art and fonts is also available.

Lev Software

ADDRESS: http://www.levsoftware.com/

DESCRIPTION: Producer of several titles designed to teach Hebrew reading and Bar mitzvah preparation.

PilotYid

ADDRESS: http://www.pilotyid.com

DESCRIPTION: For each piece of software in this archive, created by Ari Engle, PilotYid provides a short description of the software, a link to the author's Web site, and, when possible, a link to download the actual file. Only the software that is useful to the Jewish or Hebrew-speaking PalmOS user is listed here. Software is divided into categories by language and subject. If you use a PalmPilot, this is a must-see site.

Reviews of Jewish Software

ADDRESS: http://www.join.org.au/reviews/reviews.htm

DESCRIPTION: Ronnie Figdor of Australia writes incisive reviews of many commercial Judaica software packages and software to teach Hebrew.

Right to Left Hebrew Software

ADDRESS: http://rtlsoft.com/hebrew

DESCRIPTION: Browsable catalog of this distributor of Hebrew- and Jewish-related software. The site includes tips on Hebrew word processing, detailed description with screen shots of commercial software programs, and shareware programs that you can download.

TES Software (Torah Education Software)

ADDRESS: http://www.torahscholar.com and http://www.jewishsoftware.com/

DESCRIPTION: Describing itself as "the world's largest supplier of Judaic educational software," the home page of this company is divided into subject categories that include Hebrew Instruction, Hebrew English Word Processing, Bible Software, Torah Educational Games, Jewish Clip art, Hebrew Fonts, Judaic Encyclopedias and Reference, and Talmud Learning Aids. It has sections for Schools and Teachers, a free software contest, and accepts online orders. It also offers technical assistance and an FAQ section.

Torah Productions

ADDRESS: http://www.torahproductions.com/

DESCRIPTION: Producer of software related to Torah study that can be used by "those who are somewhere between Sunday school and scholarship." Each of the *parshiot* is available for sale individually, as are titles in the categories of People, Places, Things, Values, and Issues. A sample article in the *parsha* is available and updated weekly, and samples of a number of programs can be downloaded.

Zig Zag World

ADDRESS: http://www.zigzagworld.com/

DESCRIPTION: The home page of these producers of Hebrew and Judaic educational software also features a number of programs you can download for free. Of particular note are the Java applets that offer Hebrew keyboard instruction and other educational content.

FONTS

Hebrew Font Source

ADDRESS: http://www.digirain.com/hfs/

DESCRIPTION: Designed by Barak Floersheim, these free fonts provide the Web-page designer with a variety of Hebrew styles for noncommercial Web sites. The site includes an FAQ, tutorial, and mailing list for support.

Hebrew Keys

ADDRESS: http://www.hebrewkeys.com

DESCRIPTION: Hebrewkeys is a program that adds Hebrew support to Windows 95/98/NT. After downloading and installing it, you can type in Hebrew from right to left directly in most applications, such as Notepad, Wordpad, Internet Explorer, and Netscape. Installation instructions are included at the site. This is an excellent tool for Windows users who want to search Hebrew-language sites by typing in terms.

Jonathan (Jony) Rosenne's Hebrew Page

ADDRESS: http://www.qsm.co.il/Hebrew/

DESCRIPTION: This useful page of links to Hebrew utilities and explanations about their use includes details about displaying vowels, cutting and pasting in word processing, directional issues, the Hebrew keyboard and standard codes, fonts for the Internet, and the difference between logical and visual Hebrew displays.

THE INTERNET

Babylon

ADDRESS: http://www.babylon.com

DESCRIPTION: Download and install this free program, and you can translate any word on any English Web page and get its equivalent in Hebrew. You can also get an instant translation at the site. A companion free program, Babylonet, translates English written content for non-English speaking users. The site offers partnerships, forums, and support.

Captain Internet

ADDRESS: http://www.iol.co.il/captain

DESCRIPTION: A Hebrew-language weekly supplement about the Internet from the Israeli newspaper *Haaretz*. The site includes a searchable archive, reviews of new and interesting sites, letters from readers, and highlights of new multimedia products. A must read for Hebrew speakers interested in the Internet.

Hebrew HTML

ADDRESS: http://www.sigall.co.il

DESCRIPTION: Created by Sigall Bachman, this site offers a full-text, online explanation in Hebrew of how to build a site. Topics include HTML and using Hebrew, Java, JavaScript, and cascading style sheets. The entire site is searchable.

Hebrew Internet Guide for Webmasters

ADDRESS: http://www.internet-guide.co.il

DESCRIPTION: Full-text Hebrew and English guide to creating sites on the Internet in Hebrew. Includes an FAQ, links to dictionaries, and Hebrew support sites.

Israeli Domain Names

ADDRESS: http://www.isoc.org.il/domains.html

DESCRIPTION: This is an extensive list of domain names in Israel and the names of their owners. As of this writing, the list was last updated in July of 1999.

Kosher Net

ADDRESS: http://www.thekoshernet.com/

DESCRIPTION: Kosher Net provides two filters through which to view the Internet. The Business Version filters out undesirable sites. The Family Version allows children to view only preselected sites. Information on registering for the service, a list of access numbers, and a help desk are provided here.

LingoMAIL

ADDRESS: http://www.lingomail.co.il

DESCRIPTION: The program is a fully functioning stand-alone e-mail client that supports more than 30 languages in the same e-mail message. The message is sent with a small viewer as an attachment so the recipient can read it. A free demo is available at the site, along with support and screen shots.

New Mail

ADDRESS: http://www.newmail.co.il

DESCRIPTION: This site describes itself as "the first free international Web-based e-mail with POP access." You can send Hebrew e-mail to and from Hebrew-enabled computers using standard e-mail packages such as Microsoft Outlook and Eudora.

State of Israel Internet Policies

ADDRESS: http://www.itpolicy.gov.il/

DESCRIPTION: Publications of the Israeli Committee on Technology. Includes information about legal issues, filtering, and training programs. Most of the site is in Hebrew, but some material is also available in English.

Tiras

ADDRESS: http://www.tiras.co.il

DESCRIPTION: Tiras is a rating site that ranks Israeli sites by usage. Its home page lists the leading sites and provides additional statistics about them. Tiras also ranks sites in 25 subject areas.

DIRECTORIES

INTERNATIONAL DIRECTORIES

All Rabbis

ADDRESS: http://www.allrabbis.com/

DESCRIPTION: Short, encyclopedia-style articles about great rabbis of the past, as well as contemporary rabbis. Site is browsable and searchable.

Global Jewish Directory

ADDRESS: http://www.jewishdirectory.com/ and http://www.jewishglobe.com

DESCRIPTION: Created by Jewish Express, this searchable site provides a complete hypertext listing for over 2,700 Jewish institutions worldwide, a photo gallery of rabbis, links to Jewish news and greeting card services, and some music clips.

International Survey of Jewish Monuments

ADDRESS: http://www.isjm.org/

DESCRIPTION: Information about the organization, publications, calendar, awards, and projects of this group devoted to the preservation of Jewish historic sites worldwide. The American database may be browsed by location, architectural style, date of construction, landmark status, current use, and architect, while the worldwide index provides browsing by country, with a good selection of links about relevant sites. The full text of *Jewish Heritage Review,* dating back to March 1997, is available.

Jewhoo: The Jewish Celebrity Consortium

ADDRESS: http://www.jewhoo.com

DESCRIPTION: Begun as a "parody with a purpose," this site provides biographies of famous Jews in all walks of life, arranged by subject in a Yahoo look-a-like style. Additional areas include Today's Web Events, an FAQ, Personals, Classifieds, Locate the Landsmen, Free Personal Reminders, Jewish Holiday Guide, "News & Notes," Recipes, Chat, News, and Shopping. World Jewhoos and Metro Jewhoos bring up searches in Yahoo about Jews and Judaism for various areas.

Jewish Email Directory

ADDRESS: http://www.jewsearch.com

DESCRIPTION: This is a browsable directory of individuals who have entered their e-mail addresses. The site is searchable by name, address, occupation, interests, date of birth, and e-mail address and provides a place where individuals can post an annotated listing of their home pages.

Synagogues Worldwide

ADDRESS: http://www.synagogues.com

DESCRIPTION: Created by Jewish Express, this searchable site provides a complete hypertext listing for over 2,300 synagogues worldwide.

Worldwide Mikvah List

ADDRESS: http://www.kosher.co.il/mikvaot/

DESCRIPTION: Browsable database created by United Kashrut Authority, listing the name, address, and telephone number, along with relevant comments about *mikvaot* throughout the world.

ISRAELI AND REGIONAL DIRECTORIES

Cemeteries in New York

ADDRESS: http://www.geocities.com/Heartland/Woods/4900/JewishCemeteries.htm

DESCRIPTION: Created by Edward L. Rosenbaum, this browsable directory contains information for 135 area cemeteries and includes driving directions and links to Yahoo maps. The site also contains links to geneaology sites.

Dapei Reshet

ADDRESS: http://dapey.reshet.co.il

DESCRIPTION: A Hebrew-language Israeli Internet address directory arranged by subject.

Dfus-Graph

ADDRESS: http://www.index.co.il/dfus/

DESCRIPTION: A Hebrew-language guide to 8,000 companies and businesses in the publishing industry.

Israeli Phone Directory

ADDRESS: http://144.bezek.com/

DESCRIPTION: Search in Hebrew for an individual by name, address, city, or area code. The site also provides English-language access to telephone directories worldwide.

Israeli Yellow Pages

ADDRESS: http://www.yellowpages.co.il and http://dapaz.yellowpages.co.il and http://www.gold.net.il/

DESCRIPTION: Yahoo-like arrangement of services and businesses in Israel in both Hebrew and English. Site is searchable by subject, business, town, and area code. The site also offers a chat forum, bulletin boards on a variety of topics, basic computer information, and access to searchable maps of the country. Of particular note is the access to telephone directories throughout the world, provided by the page. The site also allows searching for people by name in Hebrew and provides links to a large number of government sites and officials.

Israeli Yellow Pages for New York and New Jersey

ADDRESS: http://www.porty.com/

DESCRIPTION: This yellow pages is a complete updated online edition of the book by the same title. Users can receive a consumer discount card, for a 10 percent discount at any business listed. Categories include Business, Computers, Discount Services, Education, Entertainment and Culture, Essential Services, Government, Health, Jewish and Israeli Communities, News, and Sports.

Jewish American Yellowpages for Detroit

ADDRESS: http://ja-yellowpages.com

DESCRIPTION: Developed by Mazel Publishing Company, this site offers listings of community and cultural institutions, as well as some basic Jewish reference material.

Jewish Entertainment Resource Guide

ADDRESS: http://www.jewishentertainment.net

DESCRIPTION: "Jewish Entertainment Resources is a worldwide network of entertainers who make all or part of their living through the performance or presentation of Jewish material." You can search the database by performer's name or category. The site provides instructions on how to place a listing in the database as well.

Kosher Caterers

ADDRESS: http://www.koshercaterers.com

DESCRIPTION: Search for a caterer, florist, photographer, musicians, tuxedo, and limo by state at this site. Included are those who have chosen to advertise through this directory.

Latinex: A Directory of Israeli Companies and Services in Spanish and Portuguese

ADDRESS: http://www.latinex.com

DESCRIPTION: Spanish and Portuguese browsable and searchable directory of over 2,000 Israeli companies, divided into 23 categories and developed to serve the marketing efforts of Israeli exporters interested in penetrating or expanding their businesses in Spanish- and Portuguese-speaking countries. The site includes a section on financial indicators.

Non-Orthodox Synagogues in Israel

ADDRESS: http://pw1.netcom.com/~bonnieg/isrcong.html

DESCRIPTION: A hypertext list of Reform and Conservative congregations in Israel, listed by denomination and geographical location. The site also includes a set of links to similar resources.

Sephardic Yellow Pages

ADDRESS: http://www.syny.com

DESCRIPTION: The beginnings of a Yahoo-style directory of businesses and services, community information, and links to sites of Jewish interest.

DIVREI TORAH

Audio Divrei Torah

ADDRESS: http://www.613.org/parasha.html

DESCRIPTION: This site houses what it describes as "the largest collection of *parsha* audio/video in the history of the Internet" and features over 250 speakers. The site is browsable by *parsha*. This is an excellent starting point for audio *divrei* Torah.

Shamash Divrei Torah

ADDRESS: http://shamash.org/tanach/dvar.html

DESCRIPTION: Founded and maintained by Seth Ness, this is the largest collection of *divrei* Torah on the Internet. The site is searchable and you can also browse by author. An essential first stop for anyone looking for *divrei* Torah.

Academic Articles on the Weekly Torah Reading

ADDRESS: http://www.biu.ac.il/JH/

DESCRIPTION: Sponsored by Bar Ilan University, the *divrei* Torah here combine traditional Jewish sources with material from the secular world. Essays are available in Hebrew and English and may be received through a free e-mail subscription or retrieved through the searchable archives. Additional *divrei* Torah from Bar Ilan's Yaacov Silverstein are located at http://faculty.biu.ac.il/~hm16.

TorahWeb

ADDRESS: http://www.torahweb.org

DESCRIPTION: Offers browsable access to *divrei* Torah from the leading Torah scholars of Yeshiva University. Access is by author, *parsha,* and holiday and the entire archives are keyword searchable. A free mailing list is also available.

ELECTRONIC PUBLICATIONS

American Jewish Press Association

ADDRESS http://www.ajpa.org/

DESCRIPTION: Browsable directory arranged by state of the 150 members of this organization. Information provided includes name, address, contact information, Web site, and annotation. The site also has a job bank and lists its annual awards.

ELECTRONIC MAGAZINES

Alliance

ADDRESS: http://www.alliancefr.com

DESCRIPTION: A French-language magazine featuring a discussion on Judaism and links to news from Arutz 7, Bnai Brith of France, the Israeli consulate in Canada, and radio programs from RCJ and Radio Beth El Valle. Site has browsable archives.

Answer Aliza

ADDRESS: http://www.AnswerAliza.com

DESCRIPTION: Part of the Jewish Family & Life magazine group, this publication provides a schmooze section, as well as articles about Judaism, morality, family, life, and a bibliography. Site is searchable.

Azure

ADDRESS: http://www.azure.org.il

DESCRIPTION: A publication of the Shalem Center, this magazine presents articles on Jewish and Israeli thought from a range of perspectives and is presented in both Hebrew and English. Full-text news reports, editorials, book reviews, and essays are available. Archives date back to 1996 and are browsable. Links to related periodicals and research institutes are also provided and the entire site is searchable.

Bridges: The Jewish Feminist Journal

ADDRESS: http://www.pond.net/~ckinberg/bridges/

DESCRIPTION: Selected full-text essays dating back to 1990 from this journal that explores Jewish feminist culture. The site also provides a community bulletin board and links to sites of interest to Jewish women.

Commentary Magazine

ADDRESS: http://www.commentarymagazine.com/

DESCRIPTION: Selected full-text articles dating back to 1996 from the back issues of this national news and opinion journal. Site is searchable.

Cross-Current: A Journal of Torah and Current Affairs

ADDRESS: http://www.cross-currents.com

DESCRIPTION: Browsable archives of this publication, which presents essays designed to put current events in a Torah perspective.

Eretz

ADDRESS: http://www.eretz.com

DESCRIPTION: Selected full-text articles from the current and back issues of this geography magazine that highlights places of interest in Israel. Access is also provided to the Hebrew-language publications of this company, including *Metropolis*, discussing travel outside of Israel; *Pashosh*, a children's nature magazine; and *Eretz VaTeva*, the Hebrew version of *Eretz*. The site also has a section called "A Pilgrim's Companion," aimed at Christian travelers to Israel.

Generation J

ADDRESS: http://www.generationj.com

DESCRIPTION: Part of the Jewish Family & Life magazine group, this publication focuses of issues of interest to Jews in the 25 to 45 age group.

Innernet Magazine

ADDRESS: http://www.innernet.org.il/

DESCRIPTION: Sponsored by Heritage House, this journal is published monthly as an online digest of articles from the Jewish world. Topics include relationships, spirituality, personal growth, philosophy, and special editions for the Jewish holidays.

Interfaith Family Magazine

ADDRESS: http:www.interfaithfamily.com

DESCRIPTION: A publication of Jewish Family & Life, this biweekly magazine "offers a Jewish perspective, respecting the faith of individuals from all religious backgrounds as well as appreciating differences in nationality, race, and culture." Its searchable site offers personal stories, dialogue and debate, and an interfaith celebrity profile. You can sign up for a number of discussion forums and newsletters and check the resources for interfaith families.

Israel Internet

ADDRESS: http://israel.internet.com

DESCRIPTION: Part of the Internet.com international channel, this online magazine follows business and computer stories in Israel. The site is searchable, and you can sign up for an e-mail newsletter.

Jbooks

ADDRESS: http://www.Jbooks.com/

DESCRIPTION: Part of the Jewish Family & Life magazine group, this publication provides a schmooze section, as well as articles about adult books, children's books, books for young adults, and a bibliography. Site is searchable.

Jerusalem Letter

ADDRESS: http://www.jerusalemletter.co.il/

DESCRIPTION: Monthly publication produced by Yad Yosef, providing a commentary on current events from a Torah perspective. Browsable archives of issues back to 1997 are available.

Jerusalem Report

ADDRESS: http://www.jrep.com

DESCRIPTION: Full-text articles from the current issue, covering news and feature articles about Israel, the Palestinians, the Jewish world, business, the arts, book reviews, food, letters, and opinion pieces. Previous articles available for a fee.

Jewish Blessings

ADDRESS: http://www.JewishBlessings.com/

DESCRIPTION: Part of the Jewish Family & Life magazine group, this publication provides a schmooze section, as well as articles about family occasions, holidays, Shabbat, and a bibliography. Site is searchable.

Jewish Culture

ADDRESS: http://www.JewishCulture.com

DESCRIPTION: Part of the Jewish Family & Life magazine group, this publication provides a schmooze section, as well as articles about films, style, music, family, and the Web. Site is searchable.

Jewish Health

ADDRESS: http://www.Jewishhealth.com

DESCRIPTION: Part of the Jewish Family & Life magazine group, this publication provides a schmooze section, as well as news and articles about eating well, holidays, your life, your child, and a health quiz. Site is searchable.

Jewish Heritage Online Magazine

ADDRESS: http://www.jewishheritage.com/ and http://jhom.com/

DESCRIPTION: A publication of the Memorial Foundation for Jewish Culture, this magazine represents a broad spectrum of thought and opinion and is devoted to the enrichment of Jewish culture worldwide. Articles include a community calendar, topics on the arts, the Torah portion, travel, book reviews, and a readers exchange. The site is searchable and offers free clip art and free Jewish greeting cards.

Jewish Holidays

ADDRESS: http://www.Jewishholidays.com/

DESCRIPTION: Part of the Jewish Family & Life magazine group, this publication provides a schmooze section, as well as articles about secular and Jewish holidays. Site is searchable.

Jewish Home

ADDRESS: http://www.Jewishhome.com/

DESCRIPTION: Part of the Jewish Family & Life magazine group, this publication provides a schmooze section, as well as articles about arts and crafts, education, books, food, health, holidays, and a bibliography. Site is searchable.

Jewish Internet

ADDRESS: http://www.jewishinternet.com/

DESCRIPTION: An online forum for discussion of a wide range of topics of Jewish interest.

Jewish Magazine

ADDRESS: http://www.jewishmag.co.il/

DESCRIPTION: Monthly articles in full text on Israel, Judaism, Zionism, and Jewish and Israel living, from mysticism to Jewish humor. The site is searchable and provides archives back to 1997.

Jewish Parenting

ADDRESS: http://www.jewishfamily.com

DESCRIPTION: Part of the Jewish Family & Life magazine group, this publication provides a schmooze section, as well as articles about values, books, holidays, hands-on projects, and a bibliography. Site is searchable.

Jewish Sports

ADDRESS: http://www.Jewishsports.com/

DESCRIPTION: Launched in 1998, this magazine, part of the Jewish Family and Life group and devoted to "competition with values," provides a schmooze section, news, and profiles of Jewish athletes. Of particular note are the sections on Jews in the MLB, NBA, NCAA, NFL, and NHL. Also, the site is searchable.

Jewish Travel

ADDRESS: http://www.Jewishtravel.org

DESCRIPTION: Part of the Jewish Family & Life magazine group, this publication provides a schmooze section, as well as articles about family, Israel, teen travel, and a bibliography. Site is searchable.

JFood

ADDRESS: http://www.JFood.com

DESCRIPTION: Part of the Jewish Family & Life magazine group, this publication provides a schmooze section, as well as articles about nutrition, recipes, children, cookbooks, holidays, and a bibliography. Site is searchable.

Juedisch Rundschau

ADDRESS: http://juedische.rundschau.ch/

DESCRIPTION: Based in Switzerland, this German-language publication presents feature articles and news. It also provides a searchable archive.

JVibe

ADDRESS: http:www.jvibe.com

DESCRIPTION: Part of the Jewish Family and Life series, this title is aimed at teenagers and includes columns on pop culture, real life, action, and games. You can join a chat group, write for the magazine, and check the message boards.

L'Arche, Le Mensuel Du Judaïsme Français

ADDRESS: http://www.col.fr/arche/

DESCRIPTION: French-language news and commentary magazine with browsable archives dating back to 1997.

La Tribune Juive

ADDRESS: http://www.col.fr/tj/

DESCRIPTION: Table of contents and editorial of this French-language publication. Archives of the same material are available back to 1997.

LeChaim

ADDRESS: http://www.fjc.ru/lechaim/index.htm

DESCRIPTION: A monthly Jewish magazine in Russian.

Lilith

ADDRESS: http://www.lilithmag.com

DESCRIPTION: Selected articles from the current and back issues of this quarterly independent Jewish women's magazine.

Response

ADDRESS: http://www.responseweb.org/

DESCRIPTION: Selected articles from read excerpts from this journal covering Jewish identity, community, culture, politics, and religion. Back issues are available. Site is being updated.

Scribe

ADDRESS: http://www.dangoor.com/scribe.html

DESCRIPTION: Full-text articles from this journal of Babylonian Jewry cover news, editorials, history, book reviews, obituaries, letters, and traditions of the community. Site is searchable.

Shabbat Shalom

ADDRESS: http://www.ShabbatShalom.com

DESCRIPTION: Part of the Jewish Family & Life magazine group, this publication provides a schmooze section, as well as articles about food, a how-to section, and a bibliography. Site is searchable.

Shma Magazine

ADDRESS: http://www.shma.com

DESCRIPTION: A publication of Jewish Family & Life, "Sh'ma serves as a gathering place for independent dialogue." The journal offers full-text articles, book reviews, and letters to the editor, along with access to the group's radio and TV programming. Information on internships is available, and you can browse older issues of the publication back to 1999. Of particular note are the Torah commentaries of Nechama Leibowitz and Socialaction.com, which are provided here.

Simcha

ADDRESS: http://www.Simcha.com

DESCRIPTION: Part of the Jewish Family & Life magazine group, this publication provides a schmooze section, as well as articles about bar/bat mitzvahs, weddings, births, and a bibliography. Site is searchable.

Social Action

ADDRESS: http://www.socialaction.com

DESCRIPTION: Part of the Jewish Family & Life magazine group, this publication provides sections on Teachings, Holidays, Changemakers, Life-Cycle Events, Issues, Communities, and Resources in the Field of Social Action. Site is searchable.

Southern Shofar

ADDRESS: http://www.bham.net/shofar/

DESCRIPTION: Based in Alabama, this site features monthly Alabama news and some articles and editorials from the current issue. The archives date back to 1995 for full text and selected articles back to 1990. CyberShofar libraries provide links to Alabama and general Jewish sites.

Sparks!

ADDRESS: http://www.sparksmag.com

DESCRIPTION: Aimed at children ages 9–13, this magazine includes a forum for discussions, nature, sports, a look back in history, and a "What's Hot" section. The site is searchable and publishes children's writing.

Tikkun

ADDRESS: http://www.tikkun.org

DESCRIPTION: Selected full-text articles from this bimonthly Jewish critique of politics, culture, and society.

Torah from Dixie

ADDRESS: http://www.tfdixie.com

DESCRIPTION: Comments on the weekly Torah portion from this Atlanta-based publication that also has browsable archives arranged by *parsha* and holiday. The site is searchable. Links are available to audio and video classes produced by local rabbis and housed on a variety of Web sites.

Women in Judaism

ADDRESS: http://www.utoronto.ca/wjudaism/

DESCRIPTION: This site provides access to two publications—an interdisciplinary journal on women in Judaism and a collection of contemporary articles and fiction by and about them. Full-text articles from issues dating back to 1997 are provided.

ELECTRONIC NEWSPAPERS

Atlanta Jewish Times

ADDRESS: http://www.atljewishtimes.com/

DESCRIPTION: Table of contents and full text of the cover story from this weekly are provided online. Browsable archive dating back to 1998 is available as well.

Baltimore Jewish Times

ADDRESS: http://www.jewishtimes.com

DESCRIPTION: The online version of this print paper offers sections on News, Opinion, Books, Computers, Restaurants, Food, Holidays, Personals, and Ads. Archives are searchable and browsable. The Community Links and Sourcebook sections serve as a portal to Jewish Baltimore.

Boston Jewish Advocate

ADDRESS: http://www.thejewishadvocate.com

DESCRIPTION: Serving the greater Boston area, the online version of this print publication features news, letters, editorials and op-ed pages, a personals column, and organizational information. Archives are browsable and date back about one year. You can receive the online version by e-mail.

Canadian Jewish News

ADDRESS: http://www.cjnews.com/

DESCRIPTION: A selection of stories from the print edition of this newspaper. Topics include news, travel, health, sports, kids, campus, seniors, books, and food. Archive of past issues is also available.

Chicago Jewish News

ADDRESS: http://www.chijewishnews.com

DESCRIPTION: Access to the cover stories, editorial, and a weekly feature article.

Detroit Jewish News

ADDRESS: http://www.detroitjewishnews.com/

DESCRIPTION: This searchable site provides the full-text of news articles, community events, personals, entertainment, editorials, and letters. Death notices are updated daily online, are searchable by last name, and are archived back to January 1998. A directory of Jewish resources in the Detroit area is also available.

Dry Bones

ADDRESS: http://drybones.org.il/GALLERY.HTML

DESCRIPTION: A collection of political cartoons from Israel. Several hundred samples are available, dating back to 1976.

Forward

ADDRESS: http://www.forward.com

DESCRIPTION: Full text of this major national Jewish newspaper, with coverage in news, arts, and editorials. The "Looking Back" column highlights stories covered by *The Forward* 100, 75, and 50 years ago, when it was the premier Yiddish newspaper of the United States. Archives are searchable and browsable and date back to 1998. You can subscribe to weekly e-mail updates. There is also an extensive collection of links to sites for Jewish and general news.

Intermountain Jewish News

ADDRESS: http://www.ijn.com/

DESCRIPTION: Based in Denver, this 87-year-old publication includes news, editorials, feature articles, classifieds, community events, and personals.

International Jewish Gazette

ADDRESS: http://aha.ru/~tankred/

DESCRIPTION: A weekly Russian- and English-language newspaper based in Moscow that reports on regional news and anti-Semitism.

Jerusalem Post

ADDRESS: http://www.jpost.co.il

DESCRIPTION: The major English-language newspaper of Israel provides full-text articles in news, business, real estate, opinion and feature columns, sports, the arts, books, tourism, computers, and health. Archives going back one year are available and searchable for free, but articles retrieved cost $1.95 to read.

Jewish Bulletin of Northern California

ADDRESS: http://www.jewishsf.com

DESCRIPTION: News, feature articles, letters and editorials, arts, cooking, community events, Torah thoughts, personal announcements, and classified ads are covered. Searchable archives are available. There is also full-text access to a guide to Jewish life in the Bay area.

Jewish Chronicle

ADDRESS: http://www.jchron.co.uk

DESCRIPTION: This site, the voice of London Jewry, requires registration, but registering is free. Searchable archives are available, along with international and national news, a community chronicle, Arts and Leisure section, events for singles, campus and youth activities, travel, cooking, and editorials. The paper prides itself on its editorial independence and represents the full spectrum of Jewish opinion and religious orientation.

Jewish Exponent

ADDRESS: http://www.jewishexponent.com/

DESCRIPTION: This weekly from Philadelphia provides full-text news articles, editorials, community events, young adult pages, campus life, a food column, personal announcements, and columns on art, health, business, jobs and the Federation. To search the archives, you must put in an e-mail address.

Jewish Herald-Voice

ADDRESS: http://jewishherald-voice.com/

DESCRIPTION: Information about subscribing to the print version of this Houston-based newspaper is all that is currently available.

Jewish Journal of Greater Los Angeles

ADDRESS: http://www.jewishjournal.com/

DESCRIPTION: Full-text articles on news, the arts, editorials, letters, personals, classified ads, community events, the Torah portion, and a women's column. Archives are available and searchable.

Jewish Post of New York

ADDRESS: http://www.jewishpost.com

DESCRIPTION: News, editorials, and human interest stories from this New York-based publication. The business section includes a thumbnail from the Wall Street Journal Interactive Edition, and the Judaica Online section has many links to Web sites about holidays and software.

Jewish Press

ADDRESS: http://www.the jewishpress.com

DESCRIPTION: The Web site of this paper, which bills itself as "the largest Anglo-Jewish weekly," provides access to the headlines, op-ed pieces, polls, *divrei* Torah, advice, and food columns from the current issue.

Jewish Review

ADDRESS: http://www.jewishreview.org

DESCRIPTION: Published by the Jewish Federation of Portland, this is the first Jewish online newspaper and covers Oregon and Southwest Washington. It features world and national news, local events, and information about the Federation.

Jewish Week

ADDRESS: http://www.thejewishweek.com

DESCRIPTION: Full text of this Federation-sponsored newspaper covering the greater New York area. Regional additions are available for the five boroughs and Long Island. You can search the archives with a password, participate in a chat room, and read the newspaper's poll results on topical issues. Of particular note is the section called "Directions," which offers an extensive guide to Jewish life and facilities in New York.

Jewish World Review

ADDRESS: http://www.jewishworldreview.com

DESCRIPTION: Published five times a week, this extensive online paper offers a view of Jewish culture and politics and includes articles on health, arts and letters, and political cartoons, as well as short stories, commentary on politics, geopolitics, and society.

Jewishwest.com

ADDRESS: http://jewishwest.com

DESCRIPTION: Features news, community events, arts and entertainment, letters, editorials, a travel section, and a business directory for Jewish communities in 12 states west of the Mississippi. The publication is aimed at the observant community. The Travel West has a useful hypertext list of Jewish resources for the traveler in these communities.

Kansas City Jewish Chronicle

ADDRESS: http://www.sunpublications.com/jchron/jchron.html

DESCRIPTION: Full text of news, feature articles, editorials, community calendar, arts, business, obituaries, and columns.

London Jewish News

ADDRESS: http://www.ljn.co.uk/ljn

DESCRIPTION: Current issue and previous issue of this London paper that covers news and personal ads.

Maccabiah Press from Atlanta

ADDRESS: http://www.mindspring.com/~maccabi/

DESCRIPTION: Full text of this monthly paper distributed for free in the Atlanta area. Topics covered include news, business, sports, teens, community activities, personal announcements, and obituaries. There are also organizational and synagogue directories for Atlanta and Georgia.

New Jersey Jewish News

ADDRESS: http://www.njjewishnews.com/

DESCRIPTION: Full text of articles covering the week in review, news and commentary, feature articles, arts, community events, and personal announcements for each of three areas—Metrowest, Central, and Princeton; Mercer; and Bucks counties. Archives back to 1998 are available. The section on 100 years of Jewish life in New Jersey features prominent individuals, synagogues, and events.

USAJewish.com

ADDRESS: http://www.usajewish.com

DESCRIPTION: Created by Yori Yanover, this online newspaper appears daily and includes articles from many sources, Jewish and secular. While the first page is structured like a tabloid, the ensuing articles are from reputable sources. In addition to the news and sections on Israel, culture, Jews, Arabs, and anti-Semites, there are forums, classified ads, and a list of resources. Browsable and searchable archives date back to April 1999.

Yated Neeman

ADDRESS: http://www.yated.com/ and http://www.yatedneeman.com/

DESCRIPTION: This Orthodox weekly paper based in New York does not provide an online version but does have an edition you can download to read on a PalmPilot and a selection of articles that can be received by e-mail subscription.

HEBREW-LANGUAGE PUBLICATIONS

Hebrew Language Newspapers Online

ADDRESS: http://itonim.vr9.com/

DESCRIPTION: A complete listing of Hebrew-language newspapers and magazines online, arranged by subject. Each title is annotated and rated for content, ease of use, and currency.

Haaretz

ADDRESS: http://www.haaretz.co.il

DESCRIPTION: *Haaretz* is the premier Hebrew-language newspaper of Israel. This site provides articles on news, business, sports, political opinion, culture, book reviews, real estate, health, classified ads, and computers. Archives are available for a fee, but the entire site is searchable. The daily edition can be downloaded for reading on a PalmPilot. An English version of the paper is also available here.

Hebrew Journals

ADDRESS: http://www1.snunit.k12.il/heb_journals/all_journals.html

DESCRIPTION: Provides access to 25 Hebrew journals in a variety of academic subjects, which are housed on servers at the Hebrew University.

Maariv

ADDRESS: http://www.maariv.co.il

DESCRIPTION: *Maariv* is one of the leading Hebrew-language newspapers of Israel. This site provides articles on news, business, sports, political opinion, culture, book reviews, real estate, health, classified ads, and computers. There are numerous magazine supplements available, including a section for children.

Masa Aher

ADDRESS: http://www.masa.co.il

DESCRIPTION: This site offers selected articles from current and back issues of this travel magazine, a quiz, discussion groups, tours, travel information, an online store, and articles on ecology.

Pnai Plus

ADDRESS: http://www.pnaiplus.co.il

DESCRIPTION: This online *TV Guide*–style magazine, produced by the newspaper *Yediot Aharonot,* covers the popular entertainment scene in Israel, with sections on Movies, Music, Television, Children, and Stars. The site is searchable.

Rosh 1

ADDRESS: http://www.rosh1.co.il

DESCRIPTION: Online version of this weekly magazine for young people, published by the newspaper Yediot Aharonot. Includes sections on Love, Fashion, Entertainment, Astrology, Stories, Letters, and feature articles.

TAM

ADDRESS: http://www.tam.co.il

DESCRIPTION: Full-text articles from the current and back issues of this Tel Aviv newspaper, covering news, sports, culture, feature articles, and letters. Archive dating back to 1997 is browsable by date and subject.

Teva Hadvarim

ADDRESS: http://www.tevahadvarim.co.il/index1.html

DESCRIPTION: This publication in the style of *National Geographic* focuses on nature and cultures of the world. Its site provides full-text articles and browsable archives dating back to 1999. The site also hosts a variety of interactive programs, including a photography course, ecology news, and nature videos.

Yedtichon

ADDRESS: http://www.yedtichon.co.il

DESCRIPTION: A searchable site for young adults from the newspaper Yediot Aharonot. Topics covered include students and teachers, fashion, culture, sports, politics, personal issues, and health. The site also contains an excellent set of links to sites related to young adults, education, the army, and university study, and information about life outside and after school. You can also find documents about the Bagrut exams in Hebrew Word document format.

Yofi

ADDRESS: http://www.yofi.co.il

DESCRIPTION: Israel's online magazine for women provides articles on cosmetics, health, style, tourism, computers, horoscopes, art, food, people, education, and women in the world. Archives of earlier issues are also provided.

GAMES AND RECREATION

Jewish Sport.com

ADDRESS: http://www.jewishsport.com/

DESCRIPTION: Subtitled "news, reports, and stats from the Jewish world of sport," this searchable site follows soccer, U.S. sports, Israeli basketball, Maccabiah games, golf, tennis, and other sports. There is a section on Jewish sportsmen, arranged by sport, as well as a hypertext index. Also available are extensive links to sites covering all sports areas worldwide, with an emphasis on Israel. This is an excellent starting point for information on Jews in sports.

Crosswords

ADDRESS: http://members.aol.com/jewxword/index.html

DESCRIPTION: Sample copy of a Jewish crossword puzzle, with information on ordering a book of them by Kathy and Gary Handler.

Haikus for Jews

ADDRESS: http://www.haikusforjews.com

DESCRIPTION: Several samples from this book by David Bader, along with ordering information and an FAQ about haikus.

International Jewish Sports Hall of Fame

ADDRESS: http://www.jewishsports.net/subindex.html

DESCRIPTION: Based at the Wingate Institute for Physical Education and Sports in Netanya, this organization honors Jewish men and women worldwide who have made contributions to the world of sports. The site has an alphabetical list of honorees, with their country, area of expertise, and date inducted. Links to regional sports halls of fame are also provided.

Israel Coins and Medals Corporation

ADDRESS: http://www.coins.co.il

DESCRIPTION: Information on commemoratives, latest issues, membership in a variety of purchasing clubs, a list of authorized dealers, general information and FAQs, as well as links to other sites handling Israeli coins. Information is provided in both English and Hebrew.

Israeli Amateur Radio Club

ADDRESS: http://w3.iarc.org

DESCRIPTION: News, awards, contests, and links to discussion forums for those interested in ham radio in Israel and the Jewish world.

JCC Maccabi Games

ADDRESS: http://www.jccmaccabi.org

DESCRIPTION: "The JCC Association, formerly the National Jewish Welfare Board (JWB), is the umbrella organization for Jewish Community Centers and YW/YMHAs throughout the United States and Canada." Its home page describes the athletic program, profiles all the participants, and details how to participate in the games.

Jewish Jugglers

ADDRESS: http://www.juggling.org/~jews/index.html

DESCRIPTION: Maintained by Scott Seltzer, this site provides information on the role of juggling in Jewish life. Material includes articles on juggling in biblical times and in post-biblical sources by Raphael Harris, occasions to juggle, juggling mitzvahs, juggling Jews, photos of Jewish performers, juggling in Israel, Jewish juggling tricks, and links to Jewish and juggling sites.

JewishSports.com

ADDRESS: http://www.JewishSports.com

DESCRIPTION: Launched in 1998, this magazine, part of the Jewish Family and Life group and devoted to "competition with values," provides a schmooze section, news, and profiles of Jewish athletes. Of particular note are the sections on Jews in the MLB, NBA, NCAA, NFL, and NHL. Also, the site is searchable.

Lori's Mish Mash Jewish Humor Page

ADDRESS: http://come.to/jewishjokes

DESCRIPTION: Created and maintained by Lori Sheiman, this is an extensive collection of Jewish jokes and humor found on the Internet and organized alphabetically. The site also contains a special section on holiday humor, links to other Jewish and jokes sites, and an update list you can sign up to receive by e-mail.

Maccabi USA

ADDRESS: http://www.maccabiusa.com

DESCRIPTION: Details about this organization devoted to encouraging Jewish sports activities worldwide. The site includes information about the Pan Am Games, Maccabiah Games, and golf tournaments; a calendar of events; alumni; and sponsors, as well as the group's newsletter, *SportScene*. Links to sites about Jewish and Israeli sports on the Web are also available.

Mosaic: The Jewish Outdoor Clubs

ADDRESS: http://www.mosaics.org

DESCRIPTION: Mosaic Outdoor (Mountain) Clubs is a network of nonprofit organizations dedicated to organizing outdoor, active, and/or environmental activities for Jewish adults. There are approximately 20 clubs located throughout the United States, Canada, and Israel. The site provides information about upcoming events, a listing of local clubs and forums, the history and bylaws of the group, as well as links to other Jewish and outdoor organizations. You can also sign up to receive an e-mail newsletter.

Society of Israel Philatelists

ADDRESS: http://www.israelstamps.com

DESCRIPTION: This organization is devoted to the study and collection of Israeli stamps and stamps of Judaic interest. The site includes chapters news by region, information on the educational fund, research projects, monthly news, and membership and also sponsors a kid's room. Access to portions of the group's IP Magazine is also provided.

GENEALOGY

Avotaynu

ADDRESS: http://www.avotaynu.com/

DESCRIPTION: Avotaynu is the leading publisher of material relating to Jewish genealogy and Jewish family history. This includes the journal *Avotaynu,* books, and microfiche. An index to the last 14 years of the journal, dating back to 1985, is available. In addition, Avotaynu offers books, maps, and videotapes published by other companies and provides a free biweekly e-mail newsletter. Of particular interest is the Consolidated Jewish Surname Index (CJSI), a searchable gateway to information about more than 230,000 Jewish surnames that appear in more than 28 different databases. These databases, combined, include more than 1,000,000 entries.

Jewish Genealogical Society of Great Britain

ADDRESS: http://www.jgsgb.ort.org/

DESCRIPTION: From this page you can learn about the activities, seminars, and membership benefits of this organization. Access is provided to selected current and back issues of the quarterly journal *Shemot.* Of particular note are the searchable library catalog, the family finder index, and the extensive set of links and information sources. You can search by surname or town. This is an excellent starting point for genealogical research, especially for material related to Great Britain.

Jewish Genealogy Links

ADDRESS: http://jewish.genealogy.org

DESCRIPTION: Created and maintained by Michael Meisel, this site provides an extensive list of more than 200 links divided into the following categories: archives, books, cemeteries, newsgroups and Web rings, databases, family pages, genealogical societies, Holocaust material, orphanages, *Sephardim,* surname directories, telephone directories, and *yizkor* books. There is also a news section and an FAQ about Jewish genealogy. You can receive e-mail when the page is updated.

Jewish Sephardic Genealogy Sources

ADDRESS: http://www.orthohelp.com/geneal/sefardim.htm

DESCRIPTION: Maintained by Jeff Malka, this extensive collection of links includes sections on Sephardic Jewish Web sites, newslists, archival sources, books, and forums, as well as an area where you can search for Sephardic names. The site is divided by geographic area, and you can receive e-mail updates when new material is added.

Jewish Gen: The Home of Jewish Genealogy

ADDRESS: http://www.jewishgen.org/

DESCRIPTION: "JewishGen is the primary Internet source connecting researchers of Jewish genealogy worldwide. Its most popular components are the JewishGen Discussion Group, the JewishGen Family Finder (a database of over 150,000 surnames and towns), the comprehensive directory of InfoFiles, ShtetLinks for over 200 communities, and a variety of databases such as the ShtetlSeeker and Jewish Records Indexing—Poland. JewishGen's online Family Tree of the Jewish People contains data on over one million people." Its searchable database is divided into sections on Learning, Researching, Discussion Groups, Projects, Fundraising, Hosted Organizations, and General Information.

Generations Press Books and Maps

ADDRESS: http://www.generationspress.com

DESCRIPTION: Based in Southern California, this company distributes new and used books and reproduction maps of interest to those researching Jewish genealogy. Material can be ordered online. You can also contact Ted Gostin, a professional genealogist and owner of the company, for information about his personal services.

Hebrew National Orphan Home

ADDRESS: http://www.scruz.net/~elias/hnoh/

DESCRIPTION: Marge Spears-Soloff, the creator of this site, provides a wealth of information about children who passed through the Jewish orphanage system. Included at the site are sections on the history of the organization and Jewish orphanages, details on alumni, memorials, photo albums, archives, alumni reunions, an online bookstore, and links to other Jewish genealogy resources. There is also information about the holdings of orphanage directories, federal census holdings, and the records of foundling burials from 1880 to 1920.

Jewish Genealogy Home Page

ADDRESS: http://www.genhomepage.com/jewish.html

DESCRIPTION: Stephen Wood provides an FAQ and a number of links to family Web sites and genealogical societies and discussion groups.

Jewish Roots Ring

ADDRESS: http://pw1.netcom.com/~barrison/jewgenwebring.html

DESCRIPTION: Owned by Miriam Barrison, this is the entry point for the Jewish Genealogy Web ring. Those hosting a site in this area may sign up to become part of the ring.

Sephardim.com

ADDRESS: http://www.sephardim.com/

DESCRIPTION: This site by Harry Stein offers several sections of interest to those researching Sephardic Jewish genealogy, including Sephardic Names, Recipes, Facts and Lore, Heraldry, and links to comparable sites.

HEBREW

Mining Company's Hebrew Page

ADDRESS: http://hebrew.about.com

DESCRIPTION: About.com's major collection of links is a good introduction to sites on the Web about the Hebrew language. Of particular note are the Hebrew slang dictionary, the collection of resources for Hebrew 101, the "verb of the week," and the conversational language lessons. The entire site is also searchable.

Babylon

ADDRESS: http://www.babylon.com

DESCRIPTION: Download and install this free program, and you can translate any word on any English Web page and get its equivalent in Hebrew by simply right clicking on it. You can also type a word onto the site and get an immediate translation in any of 12 languages. The site also has forums and offers technical support. This is an excellent add-on to any computer.

Davar Hebrew Dictionary

ADDRESS: http://members.xoom.com/freedavar/davar.htm

DESCRIPTION: Created in the Czech Republic, this free downloadable dictionary for Windows has versions for modern and biblical Hebrew. You can also add and delete words from it.

My Hebrew Dictionary

ADDRESS: http://www.dictionary.co.il

DESCRIPTION: Created by Jacob Richman, this site provides a browsable collection of Hebrew words in a large number of categories, with an emphasis on computer terminology.

Academy of the Hebrew Language

ADDRESS: http://sites.huji.ac.il/ivrit/english.html

DESCRIPTION: This Hebrew and English Web site comes from the official organization charged with the creation of new Hebrew words. Information on the decisions of the academy, its goals and projects, the Mazia Institute, the Ben Yehudah Museum, and the academy's publications is provided. The site is searchable in Hebrew. Of particular interest is the list of new words that the academy has added to the Hebrew language.

Discovering Hebrew

ADDRESS: http://www.ort.org/ort/hebrew/start.htm

DESCRIPTION: "This is an interactive series under development for teaching modern Hebrew. The 60 units, when complete, will develop basic reading, listening and speaking skills in Hebrew." As of this writing, there is some basic information about the Hebrew alphabet and some introductory vocabulary.

Dor L'Dor

ADDRESS: http://www.radix.net/~dor_l_dor/

DESCRIPTION: This producer of Jewish educational software also lists T-shirts and mouse pads among its categorized offerings. Some samples are available for downloading, and a tech support page is provided as well.

Guide for Editors and Translators of English Sefarim

ADDRESS: http://binyomin.home.gs.net/

DESCRIPTION: Written by Binyomin Kaplan, this online guide provides general suggestions and transliteration rules for translators of traditional Jewish texts from Hebrew to English.

Hebrew Acronyms

ADDRESS: http://infoshare1.princeton.edu/katmandu/hebrew/open.html

DESCRIPTION: Compiled by Princeton University Library cataloger Rachel Simon, this browsable alphabetical list of Hebrew abbreviations should be invaluable to librarians and researchers alike. Ms. Simon provides the romanization and the spelled-out form of each abbreviation. The site is part of the Hebrew Cataloging page that includes material on chapters of the Talmud, a Hebrew transliteration table, Hebrew diacritics, and a romanization FAQ.

Hebrew Font Source

ADDRESS: http://www.digirain.com/hfs/

DESCRIPTION: Designed by Barak Floersheim, these free fonts provide the Web page designer with a variety of Hebrew styles for noncommercial Web sites. The site includes an FAQ, tutorial, and mailing list for support.

Hebrew for Me

ADDRESS: http://www.zigzagworld.com/hebrewforme/

DESCRIPTION: These free Java applets provide a wonderful interactive way of learning the language online. An e-mail newsletter and discussion group are also provided.

Hebrew Institute of Boston

ADDRESS: http://www.hebrewinstituteofboston.org

DESCRIPTION: "Hebrew Institute of Boston is a nonprofit corporation providing the following services: translation and notarization, customized *ketubbot,* consultation on Hebrew teaching techniques and program developments, Hebrew courses for professionals, Hebrew kindergarten and the *bagrut,* the Israeli matriculation exams."

Hebrew Keyboard Tutor

ADDRESS: http://www.zigzagworld.com/HKTutor

DESCRIPTION: Part of the offerings of the computer company Zig Zag World, this is a free, interactive Java applet that offers practice in touch typing in Hebrew.

Hebrew Poetry on the Net

ADDRESS: http://members.tripod.com/~rongill/hebpoems.html

DESCRIPTION: Begun in 1997, this site now contains links to sites about Hebrew poetry, poetry on personal pages, online anthologies, discussion groups, and poetry set to music.

Hebrew Resources

ADDRESS: http://www.hebrewresources.com

DESCRIPTION: This site provides access to a variety of resources, including a Hebrew Windows-based computer tutorial, online Hebrew class, a free e-mail subscription to a Hebrew word of the day, cantillation overviews, prayers, calendars, audio and video Hebrew sites, Bible research tools, and a number of discussion forums.

Hebrew Software Digest

ADDRESS: http://www.gy.com/www/he.htm

DESCRIPTION: This site distributes Hebrew software from a variety of companies. It provides an excellent collection of links to sites offering comparison shopping for Hebrew software, both software for learning the language and utilities for using Hebrew text online.

Hebrew Trans

ADDRESS: http://www.hebrewtrans.com/

DESCRIPTION: Rina Ne'eman offers a wide range of Hebrew translation services. Samples of her projects are included.

Hebrew Translator's Home Page

ADDRESS: http://www.geocities.com/SiliconValley/Park/1602/

DESCRIPTION: This personal page, created by Yosi Rozenman, has not been updated since 1997 but still contains some useful material. He provides a hypertext list of translators, as well as a "black list" of people to avoid. There are links to sites of interest to translators and a short dictionary of some terms in Hebrew and English.

Hebrew Tutoring Software

ADDRESS: http://janeway.tilda.com.au/ben_s/RosettaStone.html

DESCRIPTION: Provided by Ben Stitz, RosettaStone is a free computer application and support materials designed to teach a 4,000-word Hebrew vocabulary. Educators may contact the author and have their own vocabulary added to the application. You can also sign up to be part of an e-mail discussion group. There are a good number of links to sites about Hebrew and other areas of Jewish and general interest.

Hebrew Words

ADDRESS: http://www.gallery.co.il/hebrew/

DESCRIPTION: Subtitled "pearls of Hebrew," this site provides a browsable, alphabetical list of strange and offbeat Hebrew words.

Histadruth Ivrith of America

ADDRESS: http://www.hist-ivrit.org

DESCRIPTION: The history and goals of this group, the oldest organization in America devoted to the promotion of Hebrew, are presented here, along with details of news and services. There is a section on each of the organization's publications, along with a sample of the first page of the current issue. The entire site is searchable.

Jonathan (Jony) Rosenne's Hebrew Page

ADDRESS: http://www.qsm.co.il/Hebrew

DESCRIPTION: This useful page of links to Hebrew utilities and explanations about their use includes details about displaying vowels, cutting and pasting in word processing, directional issues, the Hebrew keyboard and standard codes, fonts for the Internet, and the difference between logical and visual Hebrew displays.

Lamed Leshonkha

ADDRESS: http://www.geocities.com/SiliconValley/Park/1602/lamed.html

DESCRIPTION: This site contains full-text copies of booklets published by the Academy of the Hebrew Language, with new words adopted by the academy. There are booklets from 1995 and 1996 and a browsable index in English.

Learn Hebrew

ADDRESS: http://www.learnhebrew.org.il

DESCRIPTION: Created by Eli Birnbaum and Robin Treistman of the Jewish Agency for Israel, this site is actually the archive for the listserv Passing Phrase, which you can sign up for here. Each day you will receive a Hebrew phrase in your e-mail that you can hear pronounced and whose definition and explanation are given. The archived list of phrases is available for browsing. The emphasis is on everyday, real spoken Hebrew.

Mikhtav

ADDRESS: http://www.hevanet.com/dshivers/mikhtav

DESCRIPTION: A collection of cross-platform tools for writing in Hebrew on the Internet. Includes downloadable utilities for Macintosh, Windows,

DOS, and UNIX machines, as well as links to sites with more information about the use of Hebrew fonts on these various computers.

National Center for the Hebrew Language

ADDRESS: http://www.ivrit.org

DESCRIPTION: This site provides an overview and information on the members of this New York–based group headed by Joseph Lowin and dedicated to the promotion of Hebrew. Areas on the site include a "What's New" section, a column on words and roots, a literary corner, reviews of some study and teaching tools, and a list of relevant links. Of particular note is the searchable *ulpan* directory for the United States and Canada.

Poetry and Prose of Yehudah HaLevi

ADDRESS: http://www.angelfire.com/ct/halevi/index.html

DESCRIPTION: This site contains samples of the medieval Spanish poet Yehudah HaLevi's work in English. Selected poems, as well as prose from his work *The Kuzari,* are included.

Right to Left Hebrew Software

ADDRESS: http://rtlsoft.com/hebrew

DESCRIPTION: Browsable catalog of this distributor of Hebrew- and Jewish-related software. The site includes tips on Hebrew word processing, detailed descriptions with screen shots of commercial software programs, and shareware programs that you can download.

Yamada Hebrew Guide

ADDRESS: http://babel.uoregon.edu/yamada/guides/hebrew.html

DESCRIPTION: This guide from the University of Oregon provides links to Hebrew fonts, mailing lists, and newsgroups, as well as to other relevant sites on the Web.

HISTORY

American Jewish History

ADDRESS: http://www.artists-in-residence.com/users/jewishistory/

DESCRIPTION: This is an "incomplete and subjective guide" to resources centering on the historical and anthropological aspects of Eastern European Jewish immigration to the United States from 1880 to 1920. Created by graduate student Dustin Wax, the site, which is searchable, presents a collection of sites the Webmaster has found useful in his research, as well as more general information on Jewish language, culture, and history, immigration, ethnic studies, anthropology, and contemporary Jewish life. Book reviews, essays, a bibliography, and links to relevant Web rings are also provided.

Internet Jewish History Sourcebook

ADDRESS: http://www.fordham.edu/halsall/jewish/jewishsbook.html

DESCRIPTION: Compiled and maintained by Paul Halsall of Fordham University, this page contains links to online sourcebooks in ancient, medieval, and modern Jewish history, augmented by additional text and Web site indicators. This is a well-organized and comprehensive site arranged by major theme.

Jewish History Resources

ADDRESS: http://members.theglobe.com/judaism/

DESCRIPTION: This Web site contains links to resources in Jewish history, including Centers, Societies, and Organizations; Museums and Virtual Exhibits; Research Libraries and Archives; General Links to Jewish Culture, Religion, and Genealogy; Journals, Newspapers, Magazines, and Listservs; and Other Sites of Potential Interest. This is an excellent starting point for locating Jewish history items.

Annotated Bibliography and Guide to Archival Resources on the History of Jewish Women

ADDRESS: http://www.library.wisc.edu/libraries/WomensStudies/jewwom/jwmain.htm

DESCRIPTION: Including books, articles, memoirs, and archives, this searchable, annotated bibliography by Phyllis Holman Weisbard was written in 1997 but is still an excellent resource for research in American Jewish women's history.

Beyond the Pale

ADDRESS: http://www.friends-partners.org/partners/beyond-the-pale/

DESCRIPTION: This in an online version of an exhibition that has toured Russia since 1995, depicting the history of anti-Jewish attitudes and the history of Jews in Europe and in Russia. The striking presentation, created by Joke Kniesmeyer and Daniel Cil Brecher, covers the period from the Middle Ages to the present and includes links to relevant Jewish and Russian Web sites. The site is available in English and Russian.

Bubbe's Back Porch

ADDRESS: http://www.bubbe.com

DESCRIPTION: Sit on the back porch with Bubbe and read through these stories on romance, birth, death, education, and journeys submitted by bubbes and their children around the world. Also included are recipes and grandmother stories.

Builders of America

ADDRESS: http://www.borisamericanjews.org

DESCRIPTION: A browsable online exhibit created by Florida Atlantic University, highlighting the role of Jews in the history and cultural life of America, from its earliest days to the present. Information on how to borrow the physical exhibit is also available.

Center for Educational Technology

ADDRESS: http://www.cet.ac.il/history.asp

DESCRIPTION: This Hebrew-language site provides some excellent resources, including the full text of Theodore Herzl's diary that he kept during his trip to Israel, reproductions of posters from early Zionist history, a collection about the development of the Israeli flag, and historical materials related to Terezin, the siege of Jerusalem, and the period of the Second Temple.

Chaim Herzog Memorial Site

ADDRESS: http://www.herzog.org.il

DESCRIPTION: This site presents a wealth of information about the life and accomplishments of this former president of Israel. It also details the work of the projects and institutes established in his memory. The site is available in Hebrew and English.

Dorledor

ADDRESS: http://www.dorledor.org/

DESCRIPTION: This site, created by Walter Field, provides the full text of his book *A People's Epic,* a summary of 4,000 years of Jewish history in 40 pages. He also provides links to short biographies of Jews who have won Nobel Prizes.

Eli Cohen

ADDRESS: http://www.elicohen.com/

DESCRIPTION: This site presents memorabilia, personal testimonies, a chronology, and a play about this Israeli spy who was caught and hanged in Damascus. Included are a history of spying and a petition for the return of Cohen's body and the establishment of a memorial in his name, as well as an interactive spying experience.

History of Belorussian Jewry

ADDRESS: http://beljewhist.virtualave.net

DESCRIPTION: Created by Alex Friedman, a student at the Belorussian State University, this site, in both Russian and English, provides information about Jewish life in Belorussia. Included are maps and details about people and places associated with the area. Of special note are the links to 1897 census figures for Jews.

History of Turkish Jews

ADDRESS: http://www.mersina.com/lib/turkish_jews/index.html

DESCRIPTION: This site details the history of Jews in Turkey, with a special look at the lives of Jews in Anatolia. Much of the material was written by Naim Guleryuz to commemorate the 500th anniversary of the community there.

Jerusalem Archives

ADDRESS: http://www.jerusalem-archives.org

DESCRIPTION: This site currently has maps and photographs showing the history of Jerusalem from 1838 to 1915 and during the War of Independence. Additional sections on the period from biblical history to1837, 1916 to 1947, 1948 to 1967, and 1968 to the present are planned, as well as a section on the Six-Day War and one on primary resource documents.

Jewish Culture and History

ADDRESS: http://www.igc.apc.org/ddickerson/judaica.html

DESCRIPTION: David Dickerson's site provides an annotated list of links to sites relating to Jewish history and culture.

Jewish Destiny

ADDRESS: http://www.jewishdestiny.com

DESCRIPTION: This site features the articles, columns, books, and audio tapes of author Rabbi Berel Wein and lists his upcoming lectures.

Jewish Folklore in Israel

ADDRESS: http://www.folklore.org.il

DESCRIPTION: Created by Gila Gutenberg of Ben Gurion University, this searchable site in English and Hebrew offers an essay on the study of Jewish folklore in Israel, access to the Israel Folktale Archives, and a listing of academic departments, conferences, periodicals, scholars, and institutions in this area.

Jewish Heroes and Heroines in America

ADDRESS: http://www.fau.edu/library/brodytoc.htm

DESCRIPTION: This site provides 150 biographies of famous American Jews, from colonial times to the present, taken from the book *Jewish Heroes and Heroines in America,* published by Seymour Brody.

Jewish Life during the Italian Renaissance

ADDRESS: http://www.medici.org/jewish/

DESCRIPTION: A description of the collection of materials about medieval Jewish Italian life that are stored at the Medici Granducal Archives, along with sample documents, is provided here. Documents cover the period from 1537 to 1743.

Jewish-American History

ADDRESS: http://www.jewish-history.com/

DESCRIPTION: "This site is dedicated to 19th-century Jewish-American history, poetry and fiction, polemics and philosophy." It has two major sections on Jews in the Civil War and in the Wild West, as well as an online bookstore, a library of primary source material, a Civil War clip art gallery, and a large collection of links to Jewish and historical sites and Web rings. The site is also searchable.

National Photo Collection

ADDRESS: http://147.237.72.31/topsrch/abcole.htm

DESCRIPTION: This site from the Israeli Government Press Office houses a searchable database of more than 500,000 photos assembled in honor of Israel's 50th birthday. The database can be searched by keywords in English and Hebrew, and all photos contain captions.

Zionism: The First Hundred Years

ADDRESS: http://www.israelemb.org/zionism/

DESCRIPTION: Despite its name, this hypertext chronology, created by the Israeli Embassy in Washington, D.C., traces the history of Zionism back to 70 C.E., with photographs and text written by Dr. Mark A. Raider of the State University of New York at Albany.

HISTORICAL ORGANIZATIONS

Dinur Center for Jewish History

ADDRESS: http://www.hum.huji.ac.il/dinur/

DESCRIPTION: This comprehensive site from the Hebrew University provides access to academic programs, conferences, institutes, databases, a listing of scholars, course syllabi, libraries, museums, news groups, Hebrew University dissertations, journals, bibliographies, publishers, and a set of basic reading lists, along with information on genealogical and archaeological resources. Also included are sections on biblical history, the Second Temple period, medieval history, the Holocaust, Zionism, American Jewish history, and Jewish communities worldwide. Finally, a chronology is also provided.

American Jewish Historical Society

ADDRESS: http://www.ajhs.org

DESCRIPTION: In addition to information about the events, membership, staff, library, archives, museum, prizes and fellowships, goals, and history of this organization, this site is rich with other material of interest to Jewish historians. First, you can access the full text of the weekly articles on American Jewish history that the organization publishes in *The Forward.* There are also searchable databases of speakers, faculty and departments in American Jewish history, regional Jewish historical councils and genealogical societies, and an extensive set of links to relevant organizations and publications in the subject area. Through e-mail, you can ask a reference question or subscribe to the electronic discussion group "amihistory."

Center for Iranian Jewish Oral History

ADDRESS: http://www.cijoh.org/

DESCRIPTION: Details about the past and future events of this group, as well as information about its awards and oral history project, are presented. There is a browsable archive of its publication, *Terua,* with summaries of articles in English and Farsi.

Center for Jewish History

ADDRESS: http://www.centerforjewishhistory.org

DESCRIPTION: The center, in New York City, houses the American Jewish Historical Society, the American Sefardi Federation, the Leo Baeck Institute, the Yeshiva University Museum, and the YIVO Institute for Jewish Research.

Historical Society of Jews from Egypt

ADDRESS: http://www.hsje.org

DESCRIPTION: This site provides information and press releases about this group. Of particular interest are the many primary source materials and photographs, including genealogical information about the Jewish community as it existed in Egypt and as it has reformed mainly in the United States. The genealogical section includes a list of registered family names. You can sign a guestbook and participate in a discussion forum. The site is also searchable.

International Survey of Jewish Monuments

ADDRESS: http://www.isjm.org

DESCRIPTION: This searchable site provides information about this organization, that is dedicated to the documentation, study, care, and conservation of historic Jewish sites throughout the world. Full-text access to all back issues of its journal, Jewish Heritage Report, is provided. Of particular note are the two large databases providing a country-by-country listing of Jewish monuments, and a database on American

Jewish monuments searchable by location, style, date, architect, landmark status, and current use.

Jewish Heritage Society

ADDRESS: http://www.jewish-heritage.org

DESCRIPTION: This site provides general information about the goals and programs of this group devoted to the study of Jewish life in Eastern Europe. The site is available in English and Russian and includes a list of relevant links. Of particular interest is the section on publications that provides full-text access to a variety of bibliographies, monographs, reprints, and syllabi from the society and from other scholarly publications in the CIS.

New Mexico Jewish Historical Society

ADDRESS: http://www.nmjewishhistory.org

DESCRIPTION: This site provides information about the goals and events of the group and provides an archive of its newsletter. There are links to relevant Jewish and New Mexico–related sites as well.

Southern Jewish Historical Society

ADDRESS: http://www.jewishsouth.org

DESCRIPTION: The society focuses on Jewish life in the American South from colonial times to the present. The site includes information about the conference, newsletter, archives, and grants of the group. Relevant book titles are highlighted and can be ordered through Amazon.com. Of particular interest is the traveler's guide that provides access to information about Jewish communities in the South.

THE HOLOCAUST

Academic Info Holocaust Studies

ADDRESS: http://www.academicinfo.net/histholo.html

DESCRIPTION: Part of the About.com series, this independent guide by Mike Madin provides a step-by-step research guide to the time period, including meta indexes and directories, digital libraries and museums, teaching material, and information about the camps and survivors.

Anne Frank Internet Guide

ADDRESS: http://www-th.phys.rug.nl/~ma/annefrank.html

DESCRIPTION: Created by Whee Ky (Wei Ji) Man, this is an extensive and well-organized collection of rated and annotated links to Internet sites relating to Anne Frank. Included are sections on organizations; her life, diary, and background; biographies only; the diary only; educational materials and exhibitions; articles, books, and other media.

Cybrary of the Holocaust

ADDRESS: http://remember.org/

DESCRIPTION: "The Cybrary of the Holocaust uses art, discussion groups, photos, poems, and a wealth of facts to preserve powerful memories and to educate scholars and newcomers alike about the Holocaust." Its research section includes a teacher's guide, interviews with survivors, an extensive, annotated links area divided into 14 subject categories, and an online bookstore with over 2,000 titles. There are also discussion forums, areas for feedback from students, and a section devoted to children of survivors. An FAQ is provided, and the entire site is searchable. This is a first stop for anyone looking for Holocaust material.

Holocaust Chronicle

ADDRESS: http://www.holocaustchronicle.org

DESCRIPTION: This full-textbook, created by Publications International, provides an in-depth timetable of the Holocaust. You can browse by year and read about significant events of that year. You can also search the entire text by page number or date range, and there is an alphabetical subject list. The site includes appendices with numerous tables of statistics and an extensive list of recommended reading. The book is available for sale in print format. This is an excellent starting point for students researching the time period.

Holocaust Teacher's Resource Guide

ADDRESS: http://www.holocaust-trc.org/

DESCRIPTION: This searchable site is maintained by the Holocaust Education Foundation and provides links to and information about lesson plans, curricula, essays, publications, and annotated bibliographies of material related to the teaching of the Holocaust. An excellent first site to check for instructional materials.

Simon Wiesenthal Center

ADDRESS: http://www.wiesenthal.com/

DESCRIPTION: Located in Los Angeles, this center monitors hate groups worldwide. There is an online exhibit from the Museum of Tolerance, as well as educational material produced by the museum. Details about the center's audio, visual, and written publications are provided, along with information about its library. Of special note is the section on Holocaust assets, detailing the latest information on reparations.

United States Holocaust Memorial Museum

ADDRESS: http://www.ushmm.org

DESCRIPTION: More than a museum, this searchable site provides a vast wealth of information about the Holocaust and the many projects and educational programs it houses. Along with its impressive online exhibits, the site provides access to the contents of its museum shop and information about its activities. Of particular value is the ability to search the museum's library online.

Yad Vashem

ADDRESS: http://www.yad-vashem.org.il

DESCRIPTION: Israel's official memorial to the Holocaust offers information about the time period, an online exhibit, excerpts from the foundation's publications, details about its archives and library, and a section on educational materials. There is also an online magazine. Of particular note is the section on "The Righteous among the Nations," which includes biographies of those who have been honored by Yad Vashem as rescuers of Jews.

AMCHA: Israeli Centers for Holocaust Survivors and Second Generation

ADDRESS: http://www.amcha.org.il

DESCRIPTION: From this Web site you can find out about the news and mission of the group, read its newsletter and calendar of events, check its publications lists, and browse its archives dating back to 1995. Of particular note are the two sections of resources on finding relatives and entering claims for reparations.

Anne Frank House

ADDRESS: http://www.annefrank.nl

DESCRIPTION: In German, Dutch, and English, this site provides information about the house in Amsterdam where Anne Frank hid and her diary. There is an FAQ about the house and its occupants, publications for sale, and a guestbook to sign. E-mail post cards featuring pictures from the house are provided. Details about educational activities and traveling exhibits are also available, as well as access to relevant links. The entire site is keyword searchable. Of particular interest is the Library section, that offers an extensive bibliography about Anne Frank.

Anne Frank On-Line

ADDRESS: http://www.annefrank.com/

DESCRIPTION: Sponsored by the Anne Frank Center of the United States, this site provides information about the life and times of Anne Frank, as well as information on the organization, its bookstore, the traveling exhibit, and educational programs.

Candles Holocaust Museum

ADDRESS: http://www.candles-museum.com/

DESCRIPTION: C.A.N.D.L.E.S., which stands for Children of Auschwitz Nazi Deadly Lab Experiments Survivors, is located in Indiana. Its Web site contains basic information about the Holocaust reproduced from Encarta, teacher lesson plans, and an extensive list of twins who were subjects of medical experiments.

Descendants of the Shoah

ADDRESS: http://www.descendants.org

DESCRIPTION: This organization seeks "to provide a means of communication for descendants of Holocaust survivors." Of particular note is its section providing an overview of claims and reparations.

Fortunoff Video Archive for Holocaust Testimonies

ADDRESS: http://www.library.yale.edu/testimonies/homepage.html

DESCRIPTION: This collection of over 4,000 videotaped interviews with witnesses and survivors of the Holocaust is housed at Yale University. Excerpts from the testimonies are provided, and the archive is searchable online.

Ghetto Fighters' House

ADDRESS: http://www.gfh.org.il

DESCRIPTION: This museum, located in Kibbutz Lochamei Hagetaot in Israel, has an English and Hebrew site featuring information about visiting hours, exhibits, the library, events, and educational programs. A catalog of publications, searchable by keyword or catalog item number, is also available. Of particular note are the database of material on the life and writings of Janusz Korczak, the famous Polish educator who perished with the orphans he cared for in the Warsaw Ghetto, and the biographies of partisan fighters.

Holocaust History Project

ADDRESS: http://www.holocaust-history.org

DESCRIPTION: Created by a team of volunteers, this site houses "a free archive of documents, photographs, recordings, and essays regarding the Holocaust, including direct refutation of Holocaust-denial." Links to other Holocaust sites are available, as is an e-mail reference service. The entire site is searchable.

Holocaust Names

ADDRESS: http://www.holocaustnames.com

DESCRIPTION: This site, created by Emil Mark, is designed to help people find survivors and relatives. The site is searchable by name and posts messages from those seeking relatives. At this writing, the collection seems rather limited. Links to Holocaust sites and news about the Shoah are also provided.

Holocaust Rescuers

ADDRESS: http://www.cs.cmu.edu/afs/cs.cmu.edu/user/mmbt/www/rescuers.html

DESCRIPTION: Written by Mary Mark, this lengthy hypertext bibliography of books by and about rescuers was last updated in 1998.

Holocaust Webring

ADDRESS: http://www.netbistro.com/electriczen/holoring.html

DESCRIPTION: This site outlines the requirements for linking one's site to the Holocaust Web ring.

Janusz Korczak

ADDRESS: http://www.galim.org.il/korczak

DESCRIPTION: Part of the Galim site aimed at children, this Hebrew-language Web page offers a biography of the Polish educator and orphanage director who perished with his children during the Holocaust. The site, in vocalized Hebrew, describes Korczak's life and work and has a bibliography.

Jewish Foundation for the Righteous

ADDRESS: http://www.jfr.org

DESCRIPTION: This site describes the programs and speakers' bureau of this group dedicated to supporting Holocaust rescuers. Stories of moral courage are highlighted, and you can purchase books on rescuers, the Holocaust, and Anne Frank through the site's link with Amazon.com.

L'Chaim: A Holocaust Web Project Home Page

ADDRESS: http://www.charm.net/~rbennett/l'chaim.html

DESCRIPTION: This is a personal Web project divided into three categories—memories, links, and a virtual tour of Dachau. As of this writing, the last of these items was not yet functional. There is a Holocaust glossary featured in the links section.

March of the Living

ADDRESS: http://www.motl.org/

DESCRIPTION: The March of the Living is an international, educational program that brings Jewish teens from all over the world to Poland to retrace the death march from Auschwitz to Birkenau and then to Israel. In addition to sections for Alumni and Parents, there is a chat room and an online curriculum for the program. Alumni may also participate in a virtual online conference.

Martef HaShoah: Chamber of the Holocaust

ADDRESS: http://www.mznet.org/chamber/index.htm

DESCRIPTION: Part of the Mount Zion Web site, "the Chamber of the Holocaust was founded together with the State of Israel by former Director-General of the Ministry of Religion and Curator of Mt. Zion, Rabbi Dr. S. Z. Kahana. It is maintained by the Diaspora Yeshiva on Mount Zion." The site features an online tour of the memorial. Of particular note is the alphabetical listing of 1,600 communities destroyed in the Holocaust.

Massuah: Institute for the Study of the Holocaust

ADDRESS: http://www.massuah.org

DESCRIPTION: Based in Kibbutz Tel-Itzhak, Massuah, whose name means "beacon," houses a pedagogic center, video archive, and museum whose exhibits, library, scholarships, and programs are described at this site. You can also participate in a number of online discussion groups.

Mazal Library

ADDRESS: http://www.mazal.org

DESCRIPTION: The private Mazal Library "contains upwards of 20,000 books, microfilm rolls, pamphlets, and ephemera related to the Holocaust, anti-Semitism, racism and bigotry. A complete catalogue of these books, documents and papers will soon be found under 'Library,' presently under construction. This cyber-library will contain the complete, searchable text of the 42 volumes of the International Military Tribunal, the so-called 'blue' series); the 15 volumes of the Nuremberg Military Tribunal (the so-called 'green' series); and the 11 volumes of Nazi Conspiracy and Aggression (the so-called 'red' series). Every text file will be linked through an icon to its original scanned graphic page."

Mechelen Museum of Deportation and the Resistance

ADDRESS: http://www.cicb.be/shoah/welcome.html

DESCRIPTION: Located in Belgium, this museum documents the deportation and resistance of the Jewish community there. Some of that material is presented online along with information on two organizations devoted to Jewish martyrs and their descendants.

Moreshet Memorial and Publishing House

ADDRESS: http://www.inter.net.il/~givat_h/givat/moreshet/moreshet.htm

DESCRIPTION: This site, the home of the Mordechai Anilevich Memorial Study Center for Teaching the Holocaust, lists the Hebrew and English publications of the organization and provides details about its archive and Arab teachers' training program at Givat Haviva.

Raoul Wallenberg

ADDRESS: http://www.raoulwallenberg.com/

DESCRIPTION: Created by the Raoul Wallenberg Committee of Jamestown, New York, this page provides a communication tool for those in the Free Wallenberg Movement, seeks to compile a bibliography of works about Wallenberg, and strives to educate people about his rescue work in Budapest during the Holocaust. Books are available for sale, and a set of relevant links is provided as well.

Shoah Visual History Foundation

ADDRESS: http://www.vhf.org

DESCRIPTION: This organization houses Steven Spielberg's archive of more than 50,000 stories by survivors. The site provides details of the oral history project, including a breakdown by country of the stories' origins. Links to other relevant resources are also available.

Swiss Bank Claims

ADDRESS: http://www.swissbankclaims.com

DESCRIPTION: Available in 20 languages, this is the official site for the Holocaust victim assets litigation against Swiss banks and other Swiss entities. Information about who is affected by the settlement, deadlines and key dates, questions and answers, proposals for allocation and distribution, and directions for receiving a mailed notice about disbursements are provided. One can search by country and zip code to find a local organization engaged in helping survivors stake their claims. In addition to the listed questions and answers, one can submit other questions by e-mail.

Teaching the Holocaust Using Postage Stamps

ADDRESS: http://web.macam98.ac.il/~ochayo//111.htm

DESCRIPTION: A teaching guide, dictionary of terms, and instructions accompany this educational activity created by Chaya Ostrower and designed to teach about the Holocaust through stamps, pictures, texts, and children's paintings. An English version of the page is located at http://web.macam98.ac.il/~ochayo//einvert.htm

Women and the Holocaust

ADDRESS: http://www.interlog.com/~mighty/

DESCRIPTION: Poetry, book reviews, personal reflections, academic essays, and tributes to rescuers are among the topics covered in this extensive site dedicated to the memory of women who died during the Holocaust. Of particular note are the extensive and very current bibliographies in three major areas—the period before and after the Holocaust, documenting the Holocaust, and gender issues.

REVISIONISM

Nizkor

ADDRESS: http://www.nizkor.org

DESCRIPTION: Nizkor, meaning "we will remember," is Ken McVay's major project to counter Holocaust deniers. This extensive site offers large numbers of documents dedicated to this end. There are primary source material and photos on the concentration camps, individuals of the period, revisionists, and bibliographies. Sections on the Nuremberg Trials and Holocaust organizations are also provided, as well as a review of the revisionist movement. This is a first stop for material about both revisionist history and the Holocaust.

Documentary Resources on the Nazi Genocide and its Denial

ADDRESS: http://www.anti-rev.org

DESCRIPTION: French and English site providing documentary resources on the denial of Nazi genocide. The site provides articles, testimonies, and poems in a searchable format.

ISRAEL—BASIC FACTS

Central Bureau of Statistics

ADDRESS: http://www.cbs.gov.il

DESCRIPTION: This English and Hebrew site offers selected statistical data about Israel, including last month's price indices, a census of population and housing, the *Monthly Bulletin of Prices* (in Hebrew), the *Monthly Bulletin of Statistics*, economic and financial indicators, and the *Statistical Abstract of Israel*. Of particular note is the section on selected data that provides a vast array of material from the number of road accidents to the number of school age children. It is also possible to construct a search to extract desired information about a given area or time period. This is a powerful site for those seeking statistical information about Israel.

Israel Ministry of Foreign Affairs

ADDRESS: http://www.israel.org/

DESCRIPTION: With more than 13,500 pages and 2,600 external links, this official site of the Israeli government provides key information about the country and its people. Sections on basic facts, foreign relations, Israeli history, government, law, famous personalities, the peace process, culture, the economy, and religion are provided, along with subscription forms for two listservs; Israeline, covering daily press releases; and Israel-Mid East, covering daily news items. Access to older information dating back to 1994 is also provided through the ministry's gopher service. The entire site is searchable, and there is an alphabetic index of materials in seven languages. Finally, you can personalize the page to retrieve items of interest to you. This is an extensive collection of material.

Background Notes

ADDRESS: http://www.state.gov/www/background_notes/israel_1298_bgn.html

DESCRIPTION: Provided by the United States Department of State, these background notes provide a thumbnail sketch of Israel, covering areas such as the history, government, economy, and political relationship with the United States. This site was last updated at the end of 1998.

CIA World Factbook on Israel

ADDRESS: http://www.odci.gov/cia/publications/factbook/is.html

DESCRIPTION: Taken from the print version of this book, this site provides a map of Israel, along with statistical information about the geography, people, government, economy, communications, transportation, and military might of Israel.

Etzel: The History of the Irgun

ADDRESS: http://www.etzel.org.il

DESCRIPTION: This Hebrew and English site provides information about the individuals and operations associated with this resistance movement that operated in Mandate Palestine. The entire site is searchable, and a hypertext index is available.

Facts about Israel

ADDRESS: http://www.israel-mfa.gov.il/facts/

DESCRIPTION: A subset of the Ministry of Foreign Affairs site mentioned previously, this site offers information in five languages about Israel, its history, education, culture, economy, society, land and people, health and social services, science and technology, and its place among the nations of the world. Like its larger sister page, the entire site is searchable, and there is an alphabetic index of materials in seven languages. Finally, you can personalize the page to retrieve items of interest to you.

Geobase

ADDRESS: http://geobase.huji.ac.il

DESCRIPTION: "Geobase is organized as a geographic data warehouse and consists of regularly updated annual and quarterly series on topics such as: economic activities, labor and wages, population, transportation, tourism, housing & construction and education. Its contents are extracted from sources such as statistical publications, local authorities databases, public services records, and summaries derived from individual level datasets. The main source of data is the Central Bureau of Statistics." The data is correlated with maps in a GIS format. There is a search demo provided, and the interface is available in English and Hebrew.

Hagana

ADDRESS: http://www.hagana.co.il

DESCRIPTION: This site describes in English the establishment of the Hagana, the ancestor of the current Israel Defense Forces, and the role it played in the establishment of the State. Other pages in Hebrew provide biographies of individuals who figured prominently in the Hagana's history, a list of programs and activities sponsored by organizations associated with the Hagana, and an annotated bibliography.

Israel Yearbook and Almanac

ADDRESS: http://www.iyba.co.il/iybahome.htm

DESCRIPTION: This Web site offers excerpts from the current and past issues of IYBA, dating back to 1995; a listing of the table of contents; and an order form for the print version of this 200-page annual publication that provides overview articles, graphs, tables, and chronologies about Israel. Of particular note is the Lexicon of Israeli English that defines terms, acronyms, and abbreviations often used in media coverage about the country.

Kibbutz Artzi

ADDRESS: http://www.kba.org.il/

DESCRIPTION: Created by Hashomer Hatzair, this site provides information about the 85 kibbutzim that comprise its Kibbutz Artzi Federation. Material provided in English includes an overview of the Federation and details about its program center and *ulpan* program. The more extensive information in the Hebrew section includes hypertext links to the home pages of all the member kibbutzim and news, bulletin boards, discussion groups, and events of the Federation. There is also material about the education, economy, and publications of the kibbutzim. The entire site is searchable in Hebrew.

ISRAEL—THE ENVIRONMENT

Society for the Protection of Nature in Israel

ADDRESS: http://www.spni.org/

DESCRIPTION: In English at this site you can find information about the organization, its nature tours, and newsletter. The Hebrew site offers this material plus access to descriptions of the group's projects and educational undertakings, explanations of trail markings, an online searchable store of camping equipment, and links to other relevant sites.

Ministry of the Environment

ADDRESS: http://www.environment.gov.il

DESCRIPTION: This English and Hebrew site offers general information about the work of the ministry and full-text access to its bulletins dating back to 1996. The Hebrew site provides this material, as well as sections on air quality and environmental activism.

Landmark Preservation Commission

ADDRESS: http://www.shimur.co.il

DESCRIPTION: This Hebrew site describes the work of the commission and provides a searchable database by geographic region detailing the buildings that have been granted landmark status.

ISRAEL—THE GOVERNMENT

Government Gateway

ADDRESS: http://www.info.gov.il

DESCRIPTION: This site is intended to be the entry point for services provided by the Israeli government through the Internet. The searchable site offers, in English and Hebrew, indices arranged by subject and government structure. In addition there are links to local authorities, the telephone directory, national institutes, and e-mail addresses of all government ministries. If you are looking to contact anyone in the government, this is a valuable resource.

Israel Defense Forces

ADDRESS: http://www.idf.il/

DESCRIPTION: This Web site provides information about the history, doctrine, organization, insignia, and armaments of the army. There are also sections on statistics, news, civil defense, and the IDF in pictures. All material is available in English and Hebrew.

Israel Navy

ADDRESS: http://members.xoom.com/israelnavy/

DESCRIPTION: From this unofficial site you can learn about the history, fleet, bases, craft, missions, and the Shin 13 commandos of the Israeli Navy.

Israeli Air Force

ADDRESS: http://www.iaf.org.il

DESCRIPTION: This official, searchable Hebrew-language site describes the history, aircraft, and campaigns of the Israeli Air Force. There is a chronology searchable by date. You can also read current issues of the Air Force's publications and search its archives. The members' club offers chats and discussions, along with links to other air force and Israeli sites.

Israeli Civil Service

ADDRESS: http://www.civil-service.gov.il/index.asp

DESCRIPTION: This Hebrew-only site provides information about the Civil Service Commission, including press releases and a searchable archive of its publications. A dictionary of terms is also planned.

Israeli Police

ADDRESS: http://www.police.gov.il

DESCRIPTION: This Hebrew-language site describes the history, organization, and programs provided by the Israeli police. It has a section devoted to safety tips for the public and information on how to respond to emergencies. You can learn how to join the force and read back issues of its publications in Adobe Acrobat format.

Jerusalem Municipal Information

ADDRESS: http://www.jerusalem.muni.il

DESCRIPTION: Available in English, Hebrew, and Arabic, this official site from the Municipality of Jerusalem provides information on tourism, events, and arts and culture in the city. Information about the government of the city and its services is also provided.

Judicial Authority

ADDRESS: http://www.court.gov.il

DESCRIPTION: This Hebrew-language site describes the organization of the judicial system in Israel, has a searchable database of verdicts, and provides an online tour of the new Supreme Court building.

Knesset

ADDRESS: http://www.knesset.gov.il/

DESCRIPTION: The Knesset is Israel's parliament. This multimedia site in English and Hebrew provides an introduction to the Knesset through a lexicon of terms defining the roles of government members and a selection of audio and video clips that can be viewed online. An online tour is also available. There are sections describing the Knesset's organization, members, committees, history, and press releases. There are also areas about the Israeli government, its laws, and the most recent elections. E-mail and telephone listings for Knesset members are available. The entire site is searchable and has an index.

Ministry of Agriculture

ADDRESS: http://www.moag.gov.il

DESCRIPTION: At this writing, this site was under construction.

Ministry of Communications

ADDRESS: http://www.moc.gov.il

DESCRIPTION: Information on the organizational structure, press releases, and policy documents of the ministry are provided in this Hebrew and English searchable site. An overview of the Israeli telecommunications market is available, along with a chronology documenting the last 50 years of development. You can sign up to receive press releases by e-mail.

Ministry of Construction and Housing

ADDRESS: http://www.moch.gov.il/

DESCRIPTION: In addition to information about the structure of and announcements from the ministry, this Hebrew-only site offers a searchable database of building projects by geographic area, information of interest to *olim* and native Israelis regarding housing subsidies, details on filing a complaint against a contractor, redevelopment projects, and e-mail contacts within the ministry.

Ministry of Defense

ADDRESS: http://www.mod.gov.il

DESCRIPTION: The structure, projects, publications, and functions of the ministry are described at this Hebrew-only site. Information for discharged soldiers and students in Nachal is provided.

Ministry of Education

ADDRESS: http://owl.education.gov.il

DESCRIPTION: Dubbed "OWL'" from its Hebrew initials for Internet and educational material, this extensive and searchable site provides information about the ministry and its activities, exams, and publications. Of particular use to those outside of Israel are the links to instructional material for the Jewish holidays.

Ministry of Health

ADDRESS: http://www.health.gov.il

DESCRIPTION: This Hebrew site provides information about the ministry, general health tips for the public, and statistics about the health situation in Israel.

Ministry of Industry and Trade

ADDRESS: http://www.israel-industry-trade.gov.il and http://www.tamas.gov.il

DESCRIPTION: The English section of this site is subtitled "The Investment Promotion Center" and offers facts and figures about and links to a variety of industries in Israel. Advantages of doing business in the country are also outlined. The more extensive Hebrew section provides additional material about the ministry and the state of trade in the country.

Ministry of Justice

ADDRESS: http://www.justice.gov.il

DESCRIPTION: This Hebrew-only site outlines the structure of the ministry and reproduces its press releases. Of particular note is the searchable database of patents and registered trademarks.

Ministry of Transportation

ADDRESS: http://www.mot.gov.il

DESCRIPTION: This Hebrew-only site has sections on weather, the seaports, and the airports, as well as detailed information on driving regulations and how to go about getting a driver's license.

National Insurance System

ADDRESS: http://www.btl.gov.il

DESCRIPTION: Bituach Leumi is Israel's social security system. This site, in Hebrew and English, provides general information about the system, including benefits and rates, collections, service locations, terms and definitions, and ministry publications.

Ports and Railway Authority

ADDRESS: http://www.israports.org.il

DESCRIPTION: This government site offers information about the structure of the authority and information and statistics on the cargo and passengers in the three ports in Haifa, Ashdod, and Eilat and the Israeli Railways.

Postal Authority

ADDRESS: http://www.postil.com

DESCRIPTION: This official site in English and Hebrew profiles the agency and offers information on its products, philatelic and electronic services, and postal rates. The authority sponsors a bank and has an online teller as well. You can also track packages sent through the mail here. On the Hebrew section of the page is a very useful zip code search engine.

Prime Minister's HomePage

ADDRESS: http://www.pmo.gov.il/

DESCRIPTION: This English and Hebrew site provides details about the prime minister, his office, and his cabinet. There is a section on past prime ministers that contains photos and a biography.

Research Institute of Municipal Tax

ADDRESS: http://www.arnona.co.il

DESCRIPTION: This site, in Hebrew only, provides information about the *arnona,* Israel's real estate tax, as well as other municipal taxes. Full-text essays offering a self-taught course on the topic of taxes are available. You may also sign up to receive the institute's online magazine *Arnona.*

Sherut Yeutz Laezrach

ADDRESS: http://shil.huji.ac.il/Develop/Hebrew/index.htm

DESCRIPTION: The Citizen's Advice Bureau, from the Ministry of Welfare and Works, provides information in Hebrew about social security, health, housing, education, family, taxes, work issues, welfare, the army, and *aliyah* relating to Israeli citizens. This extensive information site is fully searchable.

Union of Local Authorities in Israel

ADDRESS: http://www.ladpc.gov.il/shilton/eng/open.htm

DESCRIPTION: "The Union of Local Authorities in Israel is an umbrella organization of local authorities in Israel comprising 50 municipalities and 142 local councils including 65 municipalities from the Arab communities." This site, in Hebrew and English, describes the work of this nonprofit group. It is particularly noteworthy for its extensive set of links to the home pages of cities throughout Israel.

ISRAEL AND STUDENTS

Academic Web of Israel

ADDRESS: http://www.ac.il

DESCRIPTION: This site provides links to all of the universities and regional colleges and schools in Israel.

Israel Programs Foundation

ADDRESS: http://www.ipf.org/

DESCRIPTION: A listing of programs in Israel for high school and college students, young adults, and those with special needs.

Jeff Seidel's Guide to Jewish Student Information Services

ADDRESS: http://www.geocities.com/Athens/7613/

DESCRIPTION: Jeff Seidel's centers provide tours and home hospitality to students visiting Israel. His home page describes the services of the centers in Jerusalem and Tel Aviv and provides access to the centers' publications, posters, and tours. There is also a set of links to Israeli yeshivot popular with overseas students.

Jerusalem College of Technology: Machon Lev

ADDRESS: http://www.jct.ac.il

DESCRIPTION: This college integrates study of Torah with instruction in technological skills. Its Web site provides information about the courses of study, admission policies, research projects, and conferences sponsored by the college. Of particular note is the section on Judaic resources, which includes *divrei* Torah that incorporate scientific topics and material on German Jewish leaders and Moroccan Jewry. The site is available in Hebrew and English.

Jerusalem Fellowships

ADDRESS: http://www.jerusalemfellowships.org/jf.html

DESCRIPTION: This site provides information in Spanish and English on this program that offers college and graduate students the opportunity to study in Israel. In addition, there are a virtual tour, a weekly newsletter and discussion group for alumni, and an online application request form.

Ramah in Israel

ADDRESS: http://www.ramah.org.il/

DESCRIPTION: Part of the Conservative movement in the United States, Ramah offers a number of study programs in Israel that are detailed at this site. There is information about the programs, a photo gallery, and some educational material, as well as a place where alumni can register for the database the group is compiling.

Yad HaRav Nissim

ADDRESS: http://www.yadnissim.internet-zahav.net

DESCRIPTION: Founded originally to train rabbis and rabbinical judges, this institute offers lectures and publications to the public as well. The site provides a biography of the institute's founder, Rav Yitchak Nissim; information about its lectures; and a product catalog in English. The Hebrew portion of the site includes the table of contents for the institute's yearbook, *Asufot,* and some responsa material.

PROGRAMS IN ISRAEL

Birthright Israel

ADDRESS: http://www.israelexperience.org

DESCRIPTION: This Web site provides information on free trips for first-time student visitors to Israel. There are a virtual tour, stories from participants, a message board and a sign up for an e-mail newsletter. Of particular note is the searchable database of programs that allows you to select a trip according to the criteria that matter to you. This is an exciting opportunity for students interested in spending an extended time in Israel.

Bronfman Youth Fellowships

ADDRESS: http://www.bronfman.org

DESCRIPTION: Bronfman Fellowships are offered to students entering twelfth grade. This site provides information, an application, an alumni questionnaire, and pictures from the previous summer's trip.

Jerusalem Fellowships

ADDRESS: http://www.jerusalemfellowships.org

DESCRIPTION: Aimed at young adults ages 18 to 29, these fellowships from Aish HaTorah fund a variety of study and travel programs in Israel. Details about the programs and application process are provided.

Touro College in Israel

ADDRESS: http://touro.ac.il

DESCRIPTION: At this writing, the site was under construction.

Visiting Israel Students Association

ADDRESS: http://www.visaisraelprograms.org

DESCRIPTION: "V*I*S*A* is a nonprofit organization dedicated to providing young Jews visiting Israel with the opportunity to learn and experience the beauty and relevance of Judaism and modern day Israel." Its site provides information about a variety of university- and yeshiva-based programs, an alumni questionnaire, a bulletin board, and details about an essay contest to win a free trip.

Volunteers for Israel

ADDRESS: http://members.aol.com/vol4israel/

DESCRIPTION: Similar to the Peace Corps, this program allows anyone from age 16 and up to spend time living and working alongside Israelis, at sites such as an IDF army base, a hospital, an archaeological excavation, or botanical gardens. At this site you'll learn about the various programs and their price, why you might want to volunteer, and what to expect. There is also regional contact information provided.

WUJS: World Union of Jewish Students

ADDRESS: http://www.wujs-arad.org/

DESCRIPTION: WUJS (World Union of Jewish Students) Institute offers young Jewish graduates and professionals (21–35) from all over the world study and travel opportunities in Israel. From this site you can learn about the program based in Arad, costs and scholarships, and employment opportunities in Israel. An FAQ and contact information for offices and representatives worldwide are provided. Links to other relevant sites are available as well.

ISRAELI CULTURE

Israeli Culture

ADDRESS: http://israeliculture.miningco.com/

DESCRIPTION: Created and maintained by About.com, this comprehensive site written by Ellis Shuman provides links to topics about Israeli film, art, music, and literature and a calendar of cultural events, as well as current news stories, updates on the peace process, and a guide to Israeli Web sites. You can also subscribe to an e-mail newsletter.

Rakia

ADDRESS: http://www.rakia.com

DESCRIPTION: This extensive, searchable site provides an annotated list by category of Israel's cultural institutions and an overview of 13 areas of artistic endeavor. Links to some relevant sites are also available. This is a rich resource for cultural information.

American-Israel Cultural Foundation

ADDRESS: http://aicf.webnet.org

DESCRIPTION: Find out about the history and calendar of events in music, dance, film, art, and drama supported by this foundation, which is dedicated to promoting Israeli arts and artists. Details on the foundation's scholarship and membership benefits are also outlined.

Axioma

ADDRESS: http://www.axioma.co.il

DESCRIPTION: A Hebrew journal about Israeli cultural events that covers film, music, television, theater, literature, the plastic arts, and special exhibits. Sections about the international cultural scene and gossip are also included. The entire site is searchable. The English version of the journal has some news articles and reviews and is also searchable.

Israelisms

ADDRESS: http://israelisms.simplenet.com

DESCRIPTION: An English-language humor magazine about life in Israel.

ISRAELI BUSINESS

Business Portal

ADDRESS: http://www.bizportal.co.il

DESCRIPTION: In a Yahoo-style display, this searchable site in Hebrew only provides access to Israeli and worldwide market information and indices, news, and statistics. Of particular note is the searchable Hebrew/English dictionary of business terms. This is an excellent starting point for those who read Hebrew and are interested in the Israeli market.

Matimop: Israel Industry Center for Research and Development

ADDRESS: http://www.matimop.org.il/

DESCRIPTION: "MATIMOP's activities are focused on promoting the development of advanced technologies in Israel and on creating fruitful partnerships through industrial cooperation, joint ventures and contract R&D." Its home page describes research and development opportunities in Israel and current projects and partners. You can also register online for contacts.

Yazam

ADDRESS: http://www.yazam.com

DESCRIPTION: This home page of an Israeli-based venture capital company highlights Internet startups. Its site provides a discussion lounge; an opportunity to submit a business plan; a selection of resources for entrepreneurs, including a glossary, reading list, and government assistance information; and a list of job prospects worldwide. You can subscribe to receive an e-mail newsletter.

DOING BUSINESS IN ISRAEL

Association of America-Israel Chambers of Commerce

ADDRESS: http://www.israeltrade.org

DESCRIPTION: "The Association of America-Israel Chambers of Commerce (AAICC) unites sixteen economic development organizations whose mission is to promote and facilitate bilateral trade and investment between the U.S. and Israel." Its home page lists member organizations, provides a calendar of events and contact information, and describes the benefits of membership. Of particular note is the section on Israeli Trade Information that provides links to relevant sites in the areas of contacts and trade assistance, publications, research, technology, and universities. This is an excellent starting point for information about doing business in Israel.

Duns 100

ADDRESS: http://duns100.dundb.co.il/index.html

DESCRIPTION: Compiled by Dun and Bradstreet, this list of the top 100 Israeli companies is arranged by sector and provides a profile and ranking for the company, along with information on top management. This English-language guide is part of a larger Hebrew site at http://www.dundb.co.il/ that provides a Dun's Guide to 15,000 Israeli companies and a comprehensive list of resources about doing business in Israel. This is an excellent starting point for information about top Israeli companies.

Infomedia

ADDRESS: http://www.infomedia.co.il/

DESCRIPTION: Search 11,000 businesses in Israel by company, product, text, or category at this site. The database contains information such as company profiles, description of products, and financial data. Israeli companies are invited to submit their data for free. This is an excellent directory of Israeli businesses.

Israel Export Institute

ADDRESS: http://www.export.gov.il

DESCRIPTION: "The Israel Export Institute provides a contact point between Israeli businesses and the international community. The Israel Export Institute site contains information about programs initiated by the institute, export–import–trade transactions and a directory of Israeli exporters and manufacturers." The site is available in English and Hebrew and provides an overview of the Israeli economy and its industries. The searchable site has a directory of Israeli exporters, an electronic matching service, trade leads, Israel industry exhibitions, publications, links to fellow organizations, forums and seminars, and Israel's Internet resources. You can also sign up to receive e-mail newsletters about the economy and updates in the areas of plastics, metals, and the environment.

Israeli Trade and Investment

ADDRESS: http://www.israeltrade.com

DESCRIPTION: Home page of the New England-Israel Chamber of Commerce, this site is most notable for its extensive list of U.S.-Israel business resources. These resources are divided into categories, including Contacts and Trade Assistance, Researching Potential Partners, Research Centers, Venture Capital, the Impact of the Peace Process, Economics, and an Online Library. The group's events and job opportunities are also listed. The entire site is searchable.

Association of Craft and Industry in Israel

ADDRESS: http://www.aci.org.il/

DESCRIPTION: Established more than 80 years ago, the association represents 45,000 small and medium-sized enterprises in the industrial and service sectors that generate 28 percent of Israel's gross national product. Material provided in English is a basic overview of the association and its sectors. The more extensive Hebrew material includes news, a description of member benefits, access to regional offices, a list of members and contact information, and links to similar organizations.

Australia-Israel Chamber of Commerce

ADDRESS: http://www.aicc.org.au

DESCRIPTION: This site provides news, a calendar of events, membership information, and contact information for Australians and Israelis looking to do business together.

Federation of Israeli Chambers of Commerce

ADDRESS: http://www.chamber.org.il

DESCRIPTION: This is the home page of one of Israel's largest business organizations. Its English-language section provides information about the group, has a database of Israeli trade representatives worldwide, and will have a database of members. It also offers the full text of the group's publication *Tradeline*. The Hebrew section provides sector reports, an online catalog of publications, and business advice.

FIDEL: France-Israel Developement of Economic Links

ADDRESS: http://www.france-israel.org

DESCRIPTION: The French-language site of this organization, devoted to linking businesses in France and Israel, outlines the history of group, its goals and activities, and provides contact information.

Israel Business and Fine Art Information Center

ADDRESS: http://aai.business.israel.net

DESCRIPTION: This site provides links to Internet site builders and to Brokers and Internet Traders, a procurement and marketing firm that performs traditional commodity trading and international commerce based on sources and distribution over the Internet.

Israel Trade Fairs and Convention Center

ADDRESS: http://www.israel-trade-fairs.com

DESCRIPTION: This site, in English and Hebrew, offers comprehensive information on current and past trade shows that have exhibited at the Exhibition Gardens in Tel Aviv. Information about the exhibit hall, including dimensions of rooms and a map, is provided. There is also a browsable schedule of events for the year.

Kenes: Convention Planners

ADDRESS: http://www.kenes.com

DESCRIPTION: The home page of this organizer of business conventions in Israel has a browsable list of all conventions from 1999 to 2002. News about the group and contact information are also provided, and the entire site is searchable.

Trendlines

ADDRESS: http://www.trendlines.net

DESCRIPTION: Trendlines provides international marketing services for Israeli businesses. Its "Window to Israel" section offers business news and links to many resources of interest to those doing business in the country.

ISRAELI BANKS

Bank HaPoalim

ADDRESS: http://www2.bankhapoalim.co.il/national/index.html

DESCRIPTION: This is the English-language site of the bank, which also has a version in Russian and a more extensive site in Hebrew. In addition to an overview of the bank and full-text copies of its financial reports, the site has information about trade and treasury services; details on international investing for individuals, including how to get a mortgage as a nonresident; tourist services; and a section on what's new. There is an overview of the Israeli economy, but as of this writing it had not been updated since 1998.

Bank Leumi

ADDRESS: http://www.bankleumi.com

DESCRIPTION: The English version of this site provides quick economic data along with more in-depth reviews of the capital markets, foreign currencies, the Euro, and the general economy. Information on services to individual and corporate customers and locations of branches worldwide is available. Press releases from the bank and its financial statements are also provided. You can also sign up to do banking online. The Hebrew site at http://www.bankleumi.co.il provides expanded versions of each of these sections in a searchable format.

Bank of Israel

ADDRESS: http://www.bankisrael.gov.il

DESCRIPTION: The Bank of Israel is the official bank of the state and sets foreign exchange rates and other financial indices. This site in Hebrew and English describes the work of the bank and its structure; lists the exchange rates for a variety of currencies; provides full-text access to its press releases, publications, and news items; and offers contact information for key personnel. Details of monetary auctions and the history of Israeli currency are provided. Of particular note is the searchable database of currency values that allows you to fix the value of the shekel at a particular moment in time.

Bank of Jerusalem

ADDRESS: http://www.bankjerusalem.co.il

DESCRIPTION: The English-language section of this Web site focuses on foreign investment, including details about rental properties. The Hebrew section describes the other services of the bank, including securities' investments and mortgages and contact information for its branches.

Bank Tefahot

ADDRESS: http://www.tefahot.co.il

DESCRIPTION: This mortgage bank's site is in Hebrew only. It provides information about the bank and its branches and services and the community programs it sponsors. Details about the *kupat gemel,* as well as mortgages, are here, and you can request applications and meetings online.

First International Bank of Israel

ADDRESS: http://www.fibi.co.il/

DESCRIPTION: This bank is part of the Safra Group, and its home page is available in English and Hebrew. It provides a complete financial report on the bank, contact information on its officials and branches, and a company profile. There are reviews of foreign currency, the economy, and the capital markets.

Israel Discount Bank

ADDRESS: http://www.israel-discount-bank.co.il and http://www.discountbank.net/ for Hebrew

DESCRIPTION: Available in six languages, this site provides details about the bank and its branches worldwide. It describes how to establish an account; advantages for foreign residents; exchanges and other services it offers, including investments, real estate loans, trust funds, and investment counseling. The full text of its Trends magazine is available and provides a current economic update. Of special note is the bank's art gallery, which provides an online exhibit of works from major Israeli artists.

Israel General Bank

ADDRESS: http://www.igb.co.il/bankhtml/index.html

DESCRIPTION: Now owned by the South African firm Investec, this bank is moving heavily into the online banking area. Its site in Hebrew and English outlines its services in the areas of private banking, corporate banking, and investment funds. Its section on Market Information provides a mortgage calculator and information on various indices and exchange rates.

Mercantile Discount Bank

ADDRESS: http://www.mercantile.co.il

DESCRIPTION: This site in English, Hebrew, and Arabic describes the services of the bank, including portfolio management and direct banking, along with the history of its relationship with the Israeli-Arab community. More specifics of the bank's offerings are provided in the Hebrew sections, including details on accounts for youth, telebanking, and financial services.

Mizrahi Bank

ADDRESS: http://www.mizrahi.co.il/html/home.htm

DESCRIPTION: The Hebrew site of this bank details its services to the individual, corporate, and young adult customer. The English site provides information about the bank's services to foreign customers and details on the securities' market.

Postal Bank Authority

ADDRESS: http://www.postalbank.co.il

DESCRIPTION: This Hebrew and English site describes the services of this bank and its branches, through which you can obtain international money orders and negotiate international monetary transfers. Foreign currency can be exchanged commission-free, and Israelis can purchase traveler's checks at the bank for free. Services for corporate customers are outlined in the Hebrew section of the site.

ISRAELI COMPANIES

Gifts to or from Israel

ADDRESS: http://www.order-click.co.il

DESCRIPTION: "Send flowers and gift certificates to your loved ones in Israel. Order Israeli music CDs, beautiful Judaica artifacts or the best learn-Hebrew CD." The site will also tailor an Israeli travel package for you and supply you with free updates by e-mail.

Israel Direct

ADDRESS: http://www.israeldirect.co.il

DESCRIPTION: A site from which to order gifts from Israel that include Judaica, music, food, and gift items.

Israeli Army Uniforms

ADDRESS: http://www.imp.co.il

DESCRIPTION: From this online catalog you can order Israeli military uniforms, combat gear, T-shirts, and insignias. The site has a link to its sister catalog, which sells nonmilitary T-shirts.

Israeli Cell Phones

ADDRESS: Pelephone—http://www.pelephone.co.il; and Cellcom—http://www.cellcom.co.il

DESCRIPTION: Each of these Hebrew-language sites details the benefits of its service and offers information of interest to those who wish to use their cell phones abroad.

Israeli Wishes

ADDRESS: http://www.israeliwishes.com

DESCRIPTION: This searchable site allows you to order online many Israeli specialties in the area of food, spices, books, music, videos, and gift certificates. The site has also begun a free singles service for Israeli singles and Jews in the United States. Of particular note is the online Hebrew library, that allows people to register for a small fee and borrow Hebrew-language books online.

Netcar

ADDRESS: http://www.netcar.co.il

DESCRIPTION: This Hebrew searchable database created by Roni Aharonowitz allows you to compare cars by make, model, price, reliability, comfort, driving ease, and rating. There is a guide to car buying, a guide to financing, a list of the top 10 cars in various categories, a section on car accidents, and a Hebrew/Hebrew dictionary of auto terms. You can chat in the discussion group, search its archives, and look at pictures of all the cars described. If you're looking to buy or lease a car in Israel and you can read Hebrew, this is a must-see site.

Neto Hi-Tech

ADDRESS: http://www.neto.co.il/

DESCRIPTION: This Yahoo-style directory provides an annotated listing of Israeli high-tech companies in 16 major categories. A job opportunity database searchable by category, location, and experience level is available. Links to news, stock quotes, updates, and e-mail newsletter registration form are also featured. There is a Hebrew version of the site at http://www.netohitech.co.il/.

SaleStorm

ADDRESS: http://www.salestorm.co.il

DESCRIPTION: This Hebrew-language site describes itself as "Israel's largest online classified auction" and provides an extensive FAQ for new participants.

Shekem

ADDRESS: http://www.shekem-electric.co.il

DESCRIPTION: Comparison shop for all types of electrical appliances at this searchable Hebrew-language site. You can also personalize the site to search for items of interest.

ISRAELI BUSINESS PUBLICATIONS

Analyst OnLine

ADDRESS: http://www.analystonline.co.il

DESCRIPTION: This Hebrew site allows you to analyze and track the Israeli economy through financial news, detailed information about companies and mutual funds you can search for by name or ticker symbol, financial indices, and market news. You can also personalize the page to retrieve updates and quotes on companies of interest. The entire site and its archives are searchable. This is a valuable resource for Hebrew speakers.

Globes Arena

ADDRESS: http://www.globes.co.il

DESCRIPTION: *Globes* is the main English-language business publication in Israel. Its extensive Web site offers new headlines for Israel and the world; a daily review of the stock market, including current quotations and news; price indices; the Tel Aviv Stock Exchange futures market overview; and the S&P Israel. There is a special section on high tech, with focuses on weekly startups and a startup guide. The features area provides press cuttings, real estate news, an overview of the Israeli economy, and the ability to search the archives. There is an equally extensive site in Hebrew.

Israel Internet

ADDRESS: http://israel.internet.com

DESCRIPTION: Part of Internet.com, this online magazine follows business and computer stories in Israel. There is a browsable archive of stories dating back to 1999, and the entire site is searchable. A link to The "List's" Israeli list of Internet service providers is also available. This site provides an excellent industry overview.

Israel Investor

ADDRESS: http://www.israelinvestor.com

DESCRIPTION: The goal of this online magazine-style investment site is to provide information to the English reading public about the broad range of Israeli companies available for investment. The site offers feature articles, market alerts, an IPO watch, trader talk, and a variety of forums. You can sign up for free and create a personalized portfolio, search for financial information and profiles on Israeli companies, and check the Israeli and financial resources listed. An archive of past issues searchable by seven different criteria is also available. This is an excellent starting point for anyone looking to invest in Israeli stocks.

Israel High-Tech & Investment Report

ADDRESS: http://www.ishitech.co.il

DESCRIPTION: This site presents a selection of articles from this newsletter covering the high-tech industry from the perspective of the investor. Archives of previous issues dating back to 1997 are available in Adobe Acrobat format. Stock quotes, news, and charts for all Israeli companies trading in the United States are also available, as is the newsletter's high tech portfolio model of stock picks. The site is beginning to provide a free job listing area.

Shai Maritime Magazine

ADDRESS: http://www.shipping.co.il/

DESCRIPTION: Published every two weeks, this magazine provides a comprehensive guide to the Israeli and international shipping and air-transport market. On its home page you can find shipping and flight schedules. While the print journal is in Hebrew, the home page is in English.

Simplex

ADDRESS: http://www.simplex.co.il

DESCRIPTION: Written by Dr. S. Goldman, this is an independent investment newsletter that offers several articles a month to online viewers. More in-depth versions are available by subscription.

Status

ADDRESS: http://status.co.il

DESCRIPTION: A full-text Hebrew management magazine.

ISRAELI STOCK EXCHANGE INFORMATION

Tel-Aviv Stock Exchange

ADDRESS: http://www.tase.co.il/

DESCRIPTION: This English-language site provides information about the exchange, its member banks and brokerage firms, its publications list, and the full text of its press releases dating back to 1996. The vast majority of the site focuses on the daily activity of the market and offers annual tables and a list of the monthly main indicators. It provides links to the pages of listed companies, members, data vendors, and institutions. You can also search for quotes by company or ticker symbol, and the entire site is searchable.

ISRAELI LAW

MishpatNet

ADDRESS: http://mishpat.net

DESCRIPTION: Arranged in a Yahoo-style format, this directory offers a structured subject approach to Israeli law in 16 major categories. The site provides access to a bookstore, a discussion group, and an online newsletter to which you can subscribe. The entire site is searchable.

Israeli Law Firms

ADDRESS: http://www.hg.org/firms-israel.html

DESCRIPTION: Part of the Hieros Gamos site, this home page provides a hypertext list of Israeli legal firms that have chosen to take advantage of the free listing.

Israeli Court System

ADDRESS: http://www.court-info.co.il/

DESCRIPTION: This site in Hebrew, English, and Russian describes the workings of the court system, with a special section on small claims court. As of this writing, the English and Russian sections do not seem to be functioning.

Permut & Folman Law Offices

ADDRESS: http://www.permlaw.com

DESCRIPTION: The searchable home page of this Israeli law firm is most notable for its online law library and extensive set of links to Israeli and American legal sites.

ISRAELI NEWS

Haifa & Northern Israel Journalists Association

ADDRESS: http://www.haifapress.org.il

DESCRIPTION: This English, Hebrew, and Arabic trade organization site provides an extensive selection of Israeli media sites on the Web, including online newspapers, RealAudio radio newscasts and RealVideo television news programs and updates, in-depth news analysis from major information services, and photojournalism exhibits. The categorized list is an excellent starting point for resources covering Israeli news stories. There is a foreign correspondents' guide, a press conference guide, association information, and a hypertext list of members as well.

Israel Line

ADDRESS: http://www.israelemb.org/boston/news.htm

DESCRIPTION: "Israel Line is a daily summary of major news items taken directly from the Israeli media." It is prepared for publication by a variety of consulates and embassies.

Israeli News Now

ADDRESS: http://www.israelinewsnow.com

DESCRIPTION: This is a convenient selection of headlines about Israel and the Middle East from a variety of newspaper and radio/TV resources, which is updated every 15 minutes.

Isranews

ADDRESS: http://isranews.com/

DESCRIPTION: Offered in English, Spanish, French, Hebrew, and Portuguese, this well-designed site offers links to leading Israeli stories from Israel Wire, BBC, Middle East Newsline, Arutz 7, Globes Arena, and the *Jerusalem Post*. Comparable links to major resources in the areas of world news, business, the Jewish press, intelligence briefs, the Internet, science and technology, and sports are also provided. You can check the weather, your stocks, Shabbat candle lighting, and your Hotmail e-mail account as well. This is an excellent and comprehensive starting point for news resources representing a variety of opinions.

Ariga

ADDRESS: http://www.ariga.co.il

DESCRIPTION: Ariga, meaning, "to weave," is owned and operated by Robert Rosenberg, a veteran journalist and writer based in Israel. "It is essentially organized into three sections—Business, which as of January 1 leads to Koldoon.com, the world's fastest growing database of startup technology companies and their investors. The other two sections at Ariga are Peace and Pleasure." The Pleasure section is essentially a magazine focusing on the arts and books. Of particular note, too, is the Yiddish glossary of phrases translated and transliterated into English and the extensive list of Israeli, Arab, and international peace links. The entire site is searchable.

Gamla: Politics, News and Views

ADDRESS: http://www.gamla.org.il/english/

DESCRIPTION: Named after the fortress that withstood Roman attack, this Hebrew and English site presents news and opinions "with the goal to explain and organize activity stressing the dire importance of Judea, Samaria, Gaza and the Golan Heights to the security of the State of Israel." The site is searchable and has browsable archives dating back to 1997.

Golan Heights Information Server

ADDRESS: http://www.golan.org.il/

DESCRIPTION: Hebrew, English, and Russian updates on the struggle to retain the Golan Heights. Of particular note are the links to Golan Heights related sites and the extensive hypertext directory of settlements on the Golan.

Haaretz

ADDRESS: http://www.haaretz.co.il

DESCRIPTION: *Haaretz* is the premier Hebrew-language newspaper of Israel. This site provides articles on news, business, sports, political opinion, culture, book reviews, real estate, health, classified ads, and computers. Archives are available for a fee, but the entire site is searchable. The daily edition can be downloaded for reading on a PalmPilot. An English version of the paper is also available here.

Hadashot

ADDRESS: http://www.hadashot.com

DESCRIPTION: Full-text Hebrew daily covering world and Israeli news, culture, sports, and the economy. An archive of past issues is available.

IMRA: Independent Media Review and Analysis

ADDRESS: http://join.virtual.co.il/cgi-win/imra.exe

DESCRIPTION: "Founded in 1992, by Drs. Aaron and Joseph Lerner, IMRA, Independent Media Review and Analysis provides ongoing analysis of developments in Arab–Israeli relations. IMRA's material includes unedited long-form interviews of all parties in the Arab–Israeli conflict covering the hardest of questions while allowing ample opportunity for the interviewees to make clear the logic of their positions, something frequently lost in tightly edited reports." Its searchable archives date back to 1996 and you can receive updates by e-mail.

Israel and the UN

ADDRESS: http://www.Israel-UN.org

DESCRIPTION: This site provides access to the latest news from Israel and its position at the United Nations, facts about Israel, the peace process, human rights, disarmament, international cooperation, and economic and social affairs.

Israel en Espanol

ADDRESS: http://www.ilespnl.com/

DESCRIPTION: This Web site comes from the Aurora Editorial Group, one of the largest Jewish editorial groups in the Spanish-speaking world nowadays. The site provides news about Israel and the Jewish world in Spanish, along with feature articles and opinion pieces in the areas of finance, Israeli–Latin American relations, and sports. There are columns on the weekly Torah reading, the weather, and foreign exchange rates, as well as information on subscribing to the print edition. Links to relevant Spanish-language sites are also available. If you are looking for Israeli news in Spanish, this is an excellent place to start.

Israel Resource Review

ADDRESS: http://www.israelvisit.co.il/BehindTheNews

DESCRIPTION: Edited by David Bedein, this site offers full-text articles, selected from different journalists who are registered with the Bet Agron

International Press Center in Jerusalem or with the Gaza Media Center under the jurisdiction of the Palestine Authority, that do not usually appear in standard news sources. Searchable and browsable archives dating back to 1997 are also available.

Israel Wire News Service

ADDRESS: http://www.israelwire.com

DESCRIPTION: Provided by Virtual Jerusalem, this daily newswire provides full-text news articles, letters, and a searchable archive dating back to 1995. There is also a focus section on stories from the past year.

Jerusalem Online Observer

ADDRESS: http://www.actcom.co.il/jeronline/

DESCRIPTION: This site, which describes itself as "Israel's first Internet news magazine," provides news from the country, the community, the worlds of art and business, and a calendar of events. As of this writing, it was undergoing a facelift.

Jerusalem Post

ADDRESS: http://www.jpost.co.il

DESCRIPTION: The main English-language newspaper of Israel provides full-text articles in news, business, real estate, opinion and feature columns, sports, the arts, books, tourism, computers, and health. Archives going back one year are available and searchable for free, but articles retrieved cost $1.95 to read.

Maariv

ADDRESS: http://www.maariv.co.il

DESCRIPTION: *Maariv* is one of the leading Hebrew-language newspapers of Israel. This site provides articles on news, business, sports, political opinion, culture, book reviews, real estate, health, classified ads, and computers. There are numerous magazine supplements available, including a section for children.

Online Israeli News Sources

ADDRESS: http://www.iguide.co.il/english/1.html

DESCRIPTION: This Hebrew and English directory offers links to resources covering general Israeli news, economic and financial stories, the weather, sports, lottery results, and even a section on Israeli speed traps.

Politics Now

ADDRESS: http://www.politicsnow.co.il/

DESCRIPTION: This full-text Hebrew site surveys the political arena in Israel. Of particular note is the lexicon, which provides an overview of each party's political philosophy. The extensive and well-indexed list of Israeli political sites, and election statistics. There is an archive of material and a discussion forum as well.

Tzemach News (formerly FYI)

ADDRESS: http://www.tzemach.org/fyi/

DESCRIPTION: The purpose of this news service is to feature articles and news items that are generally ignored by other Israeli news sources. Of particular interest is the section on this day in Jewish history. A newsletter is published on a weekly basis and is free via e-mail.

What's New in Israel

ADDRESS: http://new.co.il

DESCRIPTION: If you read Hebrew and want to know what's new in the world or in finance, sports, leisure, film, computers, art, and television or read feature articles in these areas, this is an excellent source of information.

ISRAELI POLITICAL PARTIES

Chadash

ADDRESS: http://www.hadash.org.il

DESCRIPTION: The home of the Israeli Communist Party, this English and Hebrew site describes the platform of the party, its activities, its branches, and its role in the Knesset.

Haichud Haleumi

ADDRESS: http://www.haichud-haleumi.org.il

DESCRIPTION: This Hebrew-language site outlines the current condition of the party and provides material to support its belief that the Golan Heights should remain part of Israel.

Labor Party

ADDRESS: http://www.aavoda.co.il

DESCRIPTION: This is the home page of the main political party in Israel. Its Hebrew site describes the party's platform, its current position, and its Knesset members and has a special section about former prime ministers Ehud Barak and Yitzchak Rabin. There is also information about activities for young people and a discussion forum.

Likud

ADDRESS: http://www.likud.org.il

DESCRIPTION: The Hebrew-language site describes the party's ideologies and affiliates and offers a set of links to similar sites.

Likud in Holland

ADDRESS: http://www.nedernet.nl/~likoed/index.html

DESCRIPTION: This site in English and Dutch offers a series of press releases from a variety of sources designed to support Likud's position with regard to the peace process.

Meretz

ADDRESS: http://www.meretz.org.il

DESCRIPTION: This Hebrew, English, and Russian site of the centrist Israel Democratic Party offers news, press releases, and accomplishments of the party. It outlines the party's platform, provides links to its members in the Knesset, and has a public forum for discussion.

Shinui

ADDRESS: http://www.shinui.org.il

DESCRIPTION: This Hebrew and English home page of the party devoted to freedom from religious coercion details the party's platform and history and the work of its members in the Knesset. The Hebrew portion of the page provides full-text access to the party newsletter archives dating back to 1999.

ISRAELI REAL ESTATE

HomeNet

ADDRESS: http://www.homenet.co.il/

DESCRIPTION: This online monthly Hebrew magazine reviews the entire real estate market, including sections on building projects, comments by all types of experts in the field, and articles on everything from gardening to construction materials. Of particular note is the searchable price list, with comparison prices for apartments for rent or sale, commercial properties, land, office space, renovations, plumbing, and electrical work.

Internadlan Comprehensive Israel Real Estate Index

ADDRESS: http://www.zf.co.il/nadlan

DESCRIPTION: An online directory of brokers, builders, mortgage banks, lawyers, commercial properties, land, and rentals, all of which are searchable by area of the country. Information about real estate taxes and currency regulations are provided, along with a list of relevant links. You can also sign up for a free e-mail newsletter. This is an excellent starting point for Israeli real estate research.

Israeli Real Estate Database

ADDRESS: http://www.nadlanet.co.il

DESCRIPTION: An English and Hebrew directory of companies, residential projects, and commercial building. A weekly special is also listed. The Hebrew listings are more extensive, with categories including foreign real estate; a searchable database of sales and rentals; general information about the industry, including a dictionary of terms; and vacation properties. The Hebrew section is definitely a must see for those comfortable reading the language.

Teleview

ADDRESS: http://www.teleview.co.il

DESCRIPTION: This Hebrew-language site offers a database of commercial and residential properties for sale or rent and raw land, searchable by number of rooms, price, and location. There are also annotated lists of construction companies, real estate agents, mortgage resources, home insurance companies, and home improvement companies, with contact information. If you read Hebrew, this is an excellent resource.

Andromeda Hill

ADDRESS: http://www.andromeda.co.il

DESCRIPTION: Holiday apartments for rent and sale in this project overlooking old Jaffa's port are described at this site. There are also floor plans of residential apartments that are for sale, along with a description of the health club and other facilities.

Anglo Saxon Real Estate

ADDRESS: http://www.anglo-saxon.co.il

DESCRIPTION: This English and Hebrew site is the home page of the largest English-language real estate company in Israel. Information on the company and its branches, homes for sale or rent, and new projects, all arranged by area of the country, is provided. There are also a Tips and Terms section and details on how to buy, sell, or rent a home, as well as international links to relevant sites. An online newsletter is currently available, and a real estate guide is planned.

Capital Property Consultants

ADDRESS: http://property.co.il

DESCRIPTION: "Capital is a specialist real estate company providing expertise and 20 years of experience in the central neighborhoods of Jerusalem." Its searchable site provides sections on properties for sale, currency, lawyers, brokers and estate agents, costs, survey, taxation, rentals, and mortgages. Of particular note are the maps of neighborhoods in central Jerusalem, marking schools and synagogues.

Dennis Barak Real Estate

ADDRESS: http://www.dennisbarak.co.il

DESCRIPTION: From this English and Hebrew site you can find commercial and residential real estate offerings in Shikun Dan and Ramat Hasharon.

Engel Construction

ADDRESS: http://www.engel.co.il

DESCRIPTION: This Hebrew and English site profiles the company, which specializes in residential construction, and describes its projects.

Isranadlan

ADDRESS: http://www.isranadlan.com

DESCRIPTION: This site, in English and Spanish, describes the services of this company in the areas of assessment of property inheritances, vacation rentals, and real estate management. The site also provides a price listing for most areas of the country for purchases and rentals.

Mishab

ADDRESS: http://www.mishab.co.il

DESCRIPTION: Available in English and Hebrew, this site describes the projects of this construction company specializing in projects for the religious community.

Net Real Estate

ADDRESS: http://www.netrealestate.net/

DESCRIPTION: This site provides details about the company's services in the areas of sales, vacation and short-term rentals, long-term rentals, property management, and land sales and purchases. Of particular note is the information provided about neighborhoods in which the company has offerings.

Project Eden

ADDRESS: http://www.jelco.co.il

DESCRIPTION: This site in four languages describes a building project southwest of Jerusalem specifically aimed at Diaspora Jews. Details of the project plan, along with a map, FAQ, and contact information, are available.

Shikun Ovdim

ADDRESS: http://www.shikun-ovdim.co.il/

DESCRIPTION: The largely Hebrew site of this major construction company provides a database of the company's apartments searchable by size and location and also includes a mortgage calculator.

ISRAELI TOURIST INFORMATION

Discover Israel Inside Travel Guide

ADDRESS: http://www.ddtravel-acc.com and http://www.israel-travel.net/

DESCRIPTION: You can locate all types of tourist information from this directory that addresses car rentals, cities, educational institutions, entertainment, travel insurance, flights, hotels, travel tips, attractions, maps, guide books, tours, visas, and the weather. Free quotes for hotel stays and tours are available, along with listings of other free services provided to tourists. This is a comprehensive, well-designed site that provides an abundance of information for the tourist to Israel.

Go Israel

ADDRESS: http://www.goisrael.com

DESCRIPTION: Created by the Ministry of Tourism in North America, this site offers sections for tourists, travel agents, and tour and group organizers. For tourists, there is basic information about the country, Israel by regions, and all aspects of the country including events, holidays, and news. Of particular note is the list of U.S.-based travel agents who have completed a certification course as Israeli travel specialists. There are also listings for cruise lines, hotel representatives, car rentals, public transportation, and airlines. The index offers access to 10,000 tourism resources. You may order a tourist kit from the ministry. Travel agents are also provided with information on the ministry's travel agent courses, conventions, and fact file. In addition, there is a list of wholesalers and tour operators.

Israel Tourism Guide

ADDRESS: http://www.index.co.il/tourism/

DESCRIPTION: Provides access to 10,000 entries about touring the country, including hotels, vacation villages, attractions, recreation, restaurants, and entertainment. The site is arranged by area of the country.

Bazak's TravelNet

ADDRESS: http://www.travelnet.co.il/

DESCRIPTION: Created by a major publisher of Israeli travel guides, this site in English, Hebrew, and German offers information on the country and its communities, religions, archaeology, cuisine, wine, restaurants, and accommodations. There are sections describing each major city, along with maps and suggested travel routes by bus and by foot. There are also separate sections aimed at Christian travelers, as well as one on Spain and one on Jordan.

Botanical Gardens in Jerusalem

ADDRESS: http://www.botanic.co.il/

DESCRIPTION: This English and Hebrew site provides an online tour of this botanical gardens on the grounds of the Hebrew University, which provides examples of the world's flora arranged by geographic area. The Hebrew portion of the site also describes the courses, research, and educational programs of the gardens. There is a planned searchable database in Hebrew of plant life as well.

Culinaris

ADDRESS: http://www.culinaris.co.il/

DESCRIPTION: This database of restaurants allows you to browse by region of the country and then by style of cuisine. There is a listing of basic contact information about the restaurants but no indication of their *kashrut*.

Gems in Israel

ADDRESS: http://www.GemsinIsrael.com

DESCRIPTION: This online magazine highlights places of interest both for first-time visitors to Israel and for those who have traveled there previously. Its full-text articles describe major attractions and little-known side sites that complement them. You may receive the magazine by e-mail and also browse through issues back to 1999. This is a well-written and informative resource.

Hello Israel

ADDRESS: http://www.helloisrael.net

DESCRIPTION: The online version of a weekly guide to country-wide events that is distributed in Israel hotels. This site highlights attractions, news, shopping, and dining that would be of interest to tourists. You can print out discount coupons and city maps as well.

Info-Net

ADDRESS: http://www.info-net.co.il

DESCRIPTION: This Hebrew and English site describes itself as "the Israeli guide of tourism and entertainment." It offers a database of tours and recreational activities searchable by location and subject. You can also participate in an art auction, join chat sessions, and check the classifieds. As of this writing, this new site seemed to have little content.

Israel Tourist Information

ADDRESS: http://israel-tourist-information.com

DESCRIPTION: Subtitled "Your Alternative Travel Guide to Tourism in Israel," this site offers information about tourist attractions, particularly in Jerusalem and the Dead Sea areas, along with other basic touring details. One handy item is the list of cybercafes in Jerusalem.

Israel's National Parks

ADDRESS: http://parks.org.il

DESCRIPTION: This is the official site of the Israel Nature and National Parks Protection Agency. Its searchable Hebrew and English site provides an attractive way to find information about the parks and reserves, touring routes, special events, and conservation activities. You may search the database by geographic area or keyword. This is an excellent resource for planning a trip around the natural wonders of the country.

Israeli Restaurant Guide

ADDRESS: http://www.rest.co.il/

DESCRIPTION: This searchable database in English and Hebrew allows you to look at restaurants by region, type of food, *kashrut,* and whether or not they deliver. Viewers can also add reviews.

Izrael

ADDRESS: http://www.izrael.co.il

DESCRIPTION: At this personal home page you can find links to car rentals, attractions, hotels, kibbutzim, bed and breakfast sites, cities, and travel agents, as well as listings for a variety of other home pages of interest to Israeli travelers.

Jerusalem Mosaic

ADDRESS: http://jeru.huji.ac.il

DESCRIPTION: This site provides access to the "new mosaic" that allows you to virtually travel the city through different time periods, meet the people, taste the food, enjoy the special costumes, and visit the sites. The "old mosaic" has maps, a chronology, and views of the city. There is also access to an exhibit of the Chagall windows at Hadassah Hospital. Even though this site has not been updated since 1998, it is still a useful resource.

Modern Places in Israel with Biblical Names

ADDRESS: http://members.aol.com/gnadenbund/israelplaces.html

DESCRIPTION: Created by a German Christian, this site, in English and German, is arranged by city name and quotes the portion of the Bible that mentions the city. Some tourist information is available as well.

Neot Kedumim

ADDRESS: http://www.neot-kedumim.org.il

DESCRIPTION: This English, Hebrew, and Russian site provides information about the 625 acres of land that recreate a biblical landscape. At the searchable site you can find details about the reserve's tours and trails, events, and newsletters. The Hebrew section also outlines educational programs for teachers.

@The Source

ADDRESS: http://www.israelinfoaccess.com/news

DESCRIPTION: This online magazine "addresses people who are interested in seeing and learning about Israel through its history, arts, and cultures." The Intimate Israel column highlights the lesser-known aspects of the country. There are also profiles of writers whose works are translated into English, details about learning experience tours, volunteer programs, and theme-based travel programs. You can receive a free copy of the magazine by e-mail.

Tourist Guide Magazine

ADDRESS: http://www.touristguide.co.il

DESCRIPTION: This Hebrew and English-language publication, which profiles the Israeli tourist industry, is aimed at business people affected by the industry, companies providing tourist services, and Israeli tourists traveling abroad. There is an online magazine, an archive of past articles, and an extensive English report on the history of Tel Aviv.

Yellow Pages for Tourists to Israel

ADDRESS: http://dapaz.yellowpages.co.il

DESCRIPTION: This site offers a Yahoo-like arrangement of services and business in Israel in both Hebrew and English. The site is searchable by subject, business, town, and area code. It also offers a chat forum, bulletin boards on a variety of topics, basic computer information, and access to searchable maps of the country. Of particular note is the access to telephone directories throughout the world, provided by the page. The site also allows searching for people by name in Hebrew and provides links to a large number of government sites and officials.

Israel Media

ADDRESS: http://www.israel-media.com

DESCRIPTION: Browsable directory of videos, music, and software focusing on Israel. Material may be ordered online.

ISRAELI ACCOMMODATIONS

Accommodation Search Engine for Israel

ADDRESS: http://ase.net/accom-bin/disp_country/ase/Asia/Israel

DESCRIPTION: You can search this site or click on its map to locate all types of accommodations with a variety of facilities and price ranges. The resulting search list describes the accommodation and offers comments about it. In many cases you can book online. This is an excellent starting point for exploring options in a wide variety of facilities.

Bed and Breakfast Accommodations in Jerusalem

ADDRESS: http://www.bnb.co.il/

DESCRIPTION: Supervised by "HAAJ"—the Home Accommodation Association of Jerusalem—this site allows you to reserve your holiday lodging directly from the owner. Types of accommodations provided include a studio, apartment or vacation suite, self-catering, bed and breakfast, or guesthouse style. The site offers access to owners' home pages, a list of the association's members, and relevant links.

Dan Hotels

ADDRESS: http://www.danhotels.co.il

DESCRIPTION: You can find out about this Israeli hotel chain, check for special packages and conference facilities, and book a reservation online at this site. Basic tourist information, including details about what to wear, tipping, the people of the country, the climate, geography, and the history of Israel, is also available.

Hei Hotels

ADDRESS: http://www.heihotels.com

DESCRIPTION: This site provides Information about staying at the Carmel Beach Hotel and Suites and the Nazareth Marriott.

Hotels and Resorts in Israel

ADDRESS: http://www.hotelstravel.com/israel.html

DESCRIPTION: A comprehensive, browsable, and searchable directory of hotels arranged by area of the country. The links take you to the home page of the hotel. There are also relevant links to attractions and online guidebooks available.

Israel Bed and Breakfasts

ADDRESS: http://www.ibbp.com/obb/israel.html

DESCRIPTION: At this guide to bed and breakfasts you can search for a suitable accommodation, look for specials, rate a B&B, visit the gift shop, and even look for inns for sale. There is general information about the country and its attractions as well.

Israel Hotel Association

ADDRESS: http://www.israelhotels.org.il

DESCRIPTION: This browsable, searchable directory provides access to descriptions of the facilities and rates of member hotels. The directory is arranged by city. There is a section on seasons that outlines the changes in rates based on time of year and a guest information section that provides guidelines about hotel policies.

Jerusalem Hotels

ADDRESS: http://www.jerusalem-hotels.co.il/

DESCRIPTION: This guide provides browsable access to hotels, apartment hotels, and hostels in the greater Jerusalem area. In many cases you can make reservations online. Special deals are also highlighted.

Kibbutz Hotels

ADDRESS: http://www.kibbutz.co.il/

DESCRIPTION: Click on this map for listings of kibbutz hotels throughout the country. You can also make reservations online.

Kibbutz Net

ADDRESS: http://www.kibbutznet.com

DESCRIPTION: Whether you are looking for a place to spend your vacation or searching for volunteer opportunities, this directory of kibbutzim is an excellent information resource. There is also a discussion forum and guestbook.

Lev Yerushalyim Suite Hotel

ADDRESS: http://sunap.com/lev-yerushalayim-hotel/

DESCRIPTION: Information is provided on renting or buying a one- or two-bedroom suite or penthouse at this apartment hotel in downtown Jerusalem.

Sheraton Hotels

ADDRESS: http://www.sheratonisrael.com

DESCRIPTION: In addition to basic information about hotel stays, this site provides information about bar mitzvah celebrations and tours, renewal of marriage vows ceremonies, and services for special needs children. You can also get a price quote online.

Tel Aviv Hotels

ADDRESS: http://www.telaviv-hotels.co.il/

DESCRIPTION: This guide provides browsable access to hotels, apartment hotels, and hostels in the greater Tel Aviv area. In many cases you can make reservations online. Special deals are also highlighted.

Ten Star Residential

ADDRESS: http://www.tenstarresidential.com

DESCRIPTION: This site in English and Spanish offers details about apartment hotels in Jerusalem.

Youth Hostels

ADDRESS: http://www.youth-hostels.org.il/Hostels/

DESCRIPTION: Through this clickable map of the country, you can find information about 31 youth hostels and make reservations online. Other tourist packages are also outlined.

ISRAELI CITIES

City Index

ADDRESS: http://www.cityindex.co.il/city_sys/index.asp

DESCRIPTION: This searchable Hebrew-language site indexes all the towns and cities in the country and provides basic information about them, including a map and links to relevant home pages. Without Hebrew-enabled Windows, the site is best used through the alphabetical list of cities that is offered. If you read Hebrew, this is an excellent directory for information, particularly for smaller locations.

Ashkelon

ADDRESS: http://www.ashkelon.muni.il

DESCRIPTION: This English and Hebrew site from the municipality describes the industry and tourism of the area.

Beit Shemesh

ADDRESS: http://www.shemesh.co.il/

DESCRIPTION: Aimed at residents and prospective settlers, this site offers details about the community, including a calendar of events, message board, mailing list, guestbook, parents resource center, information about volunteer groups, and live chat area. There is also a guide for newcomers to the country and a consumers' guide.

Best Jerusalem

ADDRESS: http://www.bestjerusalem.co.il

DESCRIPTION: This Hebrew and English site provides city news and details about entertainment, restaurants, fashion, cars, travel, sports, and shopping malls.

Eilat

ADDRESS: http://www.eilat.com/

DESCRIPTION: At this site you can check out the accommodations, attractions, tours, shopping, and entertainment offered by this southernmost city in the country.

Golan Heights Web Site

ADDRESS: http://www.golan.org.il/

DESCRIPTION: Hebrew, English, and Russian updates on the struggle to retain the Golan Heights. Of particular note are the links to Golan Heights-related sites and the extensive hypertext directory of settlements on the Golan.

Haifa

ADDRESS: http://www.haifa.gov.il

DESCRIPTION: Official site for the third largest city in the country, this Hebrew and English home page provides extensive information about the municipality and its educational institutions, cultural and business life, entertainment, tourism, and the environment. It also provides a set of relevant links, a photo gallery, and virtual postcards. In addition, you can e-mail a variety of city offices through the site. This is a well-designed and informative site that is an excellent starting point for researching a trip to Haifa.

Israel City Guide

ADDRESS: http://www.ddtravel-acc.com/cityguid.htm

DESCRIPTION: Part of the major "Discover Israel Inside" site, this page provides information about tourist attractions and accommodations in 16 cities throughout the country.

Jerusalem Website

ADDRESS: http://www.jerusalem.muni.il/

DESCRIPTION: This Hebrew, English, and Arabic site is the official home of the Jerusalem Municipality. There are sections on Jerusalem as the capital of Israel, with detailed information about its populations, a calendar of events, an Arts and Culture section, access to more than 100 sites of interest, virtual tours, tourist information and facilities, and descriptions of the economic and business bases of the city.

Karmiel

ADDRESS: http://webscope.com/karmiel/

DESCRIPTION: The home page of this town in the Galilee provides a map of the community and information about its cultural, educational, and religious institutions, and its entrepreneurial center and industrial park.

Kfar Ruppin

ADDRESS: http://www.kfar-ruppin.org.il

DESCRIPTION: Kfar Ruppin in the Jordan Valley is best known for its bird-watching center. Its Hebrew-language site describes the community, tours around the area, and its bird-watching programs.

Kiryat Tivon Unofficial Home Page

ADDRESS: http://www.tivon.israel.net/

DESCRIPTION: This site features maps, photos, and municipal information about this town located outside of Haifa. Access to relevant links is also provided.

Kotel Kam

ADDRESS: http://www.kotelkam.com/

DESCRIPTION: If you want to see the Western Wall in real time, click on this site. You can watch and hear what is happening at the Kotel, thanks to the camera that is trained on it all the time. At the Web site you can learn more about the history of the Kotel, sign the guestbook and read what others have written, send a prayer to be placed in the Kotel, take an online tour, and even put a picture of the Kotel on your desktop.

Ma'aleh Adumim

ADDRESS: http://www.jr.co.il/ma/

DESCRIPTION: Created by Jacob Richman, this well-organized home page provides bus schedules and information about the city council, climate, events, history, industries, location, projects, population, and tourist sites in this suburb of Jerusalem. There are pictures of the area and a directory as well.

Modiin

ADDRESS: http://www.modiin.co.il/

DESCRIPTION: This Hebrew and English site profiles the "city of the future" located halfway between Tel Aviv and Jerusalem. The English section describes the city, while the more extensive Hebrew site also provides maps and information on religious institutions, arts and culture, business opportunities, volunteer groups, services for children and young adults, and forums, a guestbook, and an e-mail listserv. The entire site is searchable in Hebrew.

Raanana in English

ADDRESS: http://www.raanana.muni.il

DESCRIPTION: This searchable site created by the municipality provides well-organized access to information about the educational, cultural, health, and religious facilities of this city near Tel Aviv. There are sections about services to senior citizens, young adults, and soldiers as well. A city map, list of local events, and details about the environment and business ventures and taxes are also available.

Rishon LeTzion

ADDRESS: http://www.rishon.co.il/

DESCRIPTION: This Hebrew-language site describes the history of the city, and its educational institutions, libraries, cultural centers, and sports facilities. There is a directory of phone numbers and local news as well.

Rosh Hanikra

ADDRESS: http://yaron.clever.net/nikra/nikra.htm

DESCRIPTION: Pictures and tourist information are provided about this Mediterranean coastal attraction in the northern part of Israel.

Safed

ADDRESS: http://www.safed.co.il

DESCRIPTION: This site in English, Russian, Hebrew, and Danish describes the history, tourist attractions, and accommodations of the city. A useful set of links to other sites about Safed is also provided.

Shaarei Shechem

ADDRESS: http://www.shechem.org/

DESCRIPTION: This mostly Hebrew site offers information for residents, news, maps and a virtual tour of the communities on the West Bank. Of particular note are the Torah search engines and the links to sources of information about the communities located in Shomron.

Tel Aviv City Connection

ADDRESS: http://tel-aviv.cc/

DESCRIPTION: This searchable site in English and Hebrew provides general information and city maps in a Yahoo-style presentation, as well as details about hotels, restaurants, transportation, entertainment, shopping, education, media and health facilities, sports, banks, and tourism in the largest city in the country. The site also outlines the 90-year history of the city and offers a free e-mail newsletter, photo gallery, and tip of the week. This is an excellent place to start researching a trip to Tel Aviv.

Yavne

ADDRESS: http://www.yavnet.co.il/

DESCRIPTION: This Hebrew-language home page has information about the educational, entertainment, and general facilities, as well as the history, *ulpan,* and community events of this town located in the southwestern part of the country. You can sign the guestbook as well.

ISRAELI TOURIST SERVICES

Weekends in Israel

ADDRESS: http://www.weekend.co.il

DESCRIPTION: This Hebrew and English searchable database offers information on travel throughout the country, including information about tours, tour guides, attractions, restaurants, museums, national parks, nightlife, and local events. There are relevant links and many maps. This is a comprehensive site with many resources, but the Hebrew version does not display well in non–Hebrew enabled Windows environments.

Bar and Bat Mitzvahs in Israel

ADDRESS: http://jem.ascender.com/iia/bar/

DESCRIPTION: This site describes the contents of the book *Bar and Bat Mitzvah in Israel: The Ultimate Family Sourcebook* by Judith Isaacson and Deborah Rosenbloom. It has many relevant links to sites about planning a bar/bat Mitzvah and about planning a trip to Israel.

Israel to Go

ADDRESS: http://www.israeltogo.com

DESCRIPTION: The searchable databases of this Queens, New York-based travel agency will help you find a flight, a rental car, and a hotel in Israel. Even if you don't use its services, you can glean comparative prices from searching its databases.

Israel Tour Guides Association

ADDRESS: http://www.israwebs.com

DESCRIPTION: From this English-language site you can choose a guide according to the languages he speaks. Appropriate contact information is provided.

Protexia Plus

ADDRESS: http://www.protexsiaplus.com

DESCRIPTION: Protexia Plus offers a variety of tourist services, including airport pickup, cell phone rental, short-term apartments, private tutoring, baby-sitting, tickets to local events, school registration, and help with customs.

ISRAELI TRANSPORTATION

Avis Rent a Car

ADDRESS: http://www.avis.co.il/

DESCRIPTION: Check out the locations, selection of cars, special offers, rates, and services at this site.

Budget Rent a Car

ADDRESS: http://www.budget.co.il/

DESCRIPTION: This English and Hebrew site allows you to check out the branch locations, selection of cars, special offers, rates, and services.

Eldan Rent a Car

ADDRESS: http://www.eldan.co.il/

DESCRIPTION: Information on this car rental company and its fleet, including branch locations and fees, is available at this site. You can make a booking online as well.

Sixt Israel Car Rental

ADDRESS: http://www.sixt.co.il/

DESCRIPTION: In addition to information about the locations, selection of cars, special offers, rates, and services of this company, there are also details about leasing programs, chauffeur service, and used cars available for sale.

Thrifty Car Rental

ADDRESS: http://www.thrifty-israel.com

DESCRIPTION: Check out the locations, selection of cars, rates, and services at this site. You can also get a rate quote, book a reservation, and use the Car Wizard to choose an appropriate vehicle.

Arkia

ADDRESS: http://www.arkia.co.il/

DESCRIPTION: Arkia is Israel's major internal airlines. Its home page provides company information, domestic schedule, and images of its planes. You can check out tours sponsored by the airlines and book a variety of tourist services online.

Ben Gurion Airport

ADDRESS: http://www.ben-gurion-airport.co.il

DESCRIPTION: This site, in Hebrew, English, and French, provides general information about Israel's international airport, including its shops and restaurants, pre-flight information, and parking and transportation into the country. You can also check arrivals and departures and search for timetable information by destination or airlines.

EL AL Israel Airlines

ADDRESS: http://www.elal.co.il/

DESCRIPTION: This English and Hebrew site provides flight information and details about services, the frequent flyer program, cargo deliveries, and worldwide routes. You can check arrivals and departures and schedules online, as well as book a flight. El Al tour packages are described, and there is information about the Laromme Hotels owned by the company.

Egged Buses

ADDRESS: http://www.egged.co.il

DESCRIPTION: This largely Hebrew site provides a searchable database, with pricing and schedules for all parts of the country.

Israel Railways

ADDRESS: http://www.israrail.org.il

DESCRIPTION: This Hebrew and English site provides information on both passenger and freight service, including schedules and rates. There is a clickable map showing the rail lines and stations and a searchable database of schedules.

JEWISH COMMUNITIES AROUND THE WORLD

Jewish Communties of the World

ADDRESS: http://www.wjc.org.il/communities/jewish_communities_of_the_world/index.html

DESCRIPTION: The information at this site is an abridged version of the print volume *Jewish Communities of the World*, published in 1998 by the World Jewish Congress and Lerner Publications Company and profiling Jewish life in 120 countries around the world. Arrangement is by region of the world, and there is an alphabetical index of countries. In addition to information about each community and its demography, history, religious and cultural life, sites of interest, educational institutions, and local contact information, the site provides charts and statistics about the state of world Jewry. There is also a link to a pen pal program and a guestbook. This is an excellent starting point to find a thumbnail sketch of Jewish communities worldwide.

Kulanu

ADDRESS: http://www.ubalt.edu/kulanu/index0.html

DESCRIPTION: Meaning "all of us," Kulanu is "dedicated to finding and assisting lost and dispersed remnants of the Jewish people." It provides links, arranged by country, to Jewish communities in small and often overlooked corners of the earth. There are also numerous links to relevant sites in a variety of Jewish topics. This is an excellent starting point for information on small Jewish communities.

Am Israel

ADDRESS: http://www.amyisrael.co.il

DESCRIPTION: Created by the Shema Yisrael network, this site provides information about Jewish communities by region and then by country. Rather than providing its own information, the directory offers a link to a local home page describing the various communities.

Jewish Network

ADDRESS: http://www.jewishnetwork.com

DESCRIPTION: This site allows organizations worldwide to list their events. It is arranged by region and then by country or state, with events color coded by type.

UNITED STATES

North American Jewish Data Bank

ADDRESS: http://www.jewishdatabank.com/index.html

DESCRIPTION: Established by the City University of New York's Center for Jewish Studies and United Jewish Communities, this database serves as a repository for computer-based population and survey data on Jewish communities in the United States and in Canada. It currently holds over 65 Jewish community studies, along with the National Jewish Population Surveys and Canadian censuses. Highlights of the 1970 and 1990 national studies are available here, as are the community studies. This is an excellent source for statistical information on the state of North American Jewry.

AtlantaChai

ADDRESS: http://www.atlchai.org/

DESCRIPTION: Created by two local students, this searchable site provides a directory of synagogues, schools, organizations, and local groups in the greater Atlanta area.

Baltimore

ADDRESS: http://www.jobol.com

DESCRIPTION: Aimed at the Orthodox Jewish community, this site provides news and a calendar of events, along with an interactive map of communities, *minyan* guide, and listings of synagogues, *shiurim*, restaurants, bakeries, butchers, caterers, supermarkets, bookstores, Judaica shops, schools, yeshivot, and other Jewish organizations. For people visiting the area, there is a list of hotels and places to stay for Shabbat.

Black Jews

ADDRESS: http://www.columbia.edu/~sbl7/

DESCRIPTION: Created by Rabbi Sholomo Ben Levy, this site describes the history of the Black Jewish community, its congregations, and its rabbinical alliance. It also includes an article on race in Judaism.

Boca Raton, Florida

ADDRESS: http://www.jewishboca.org and http://www.jewishsouthflorida.com

DESCRIPTION: Sponsored by the Jewish Federation of South Palm Beach, which services Greater Boca Raton, Del Ray Beach, and Highland Beach, this site describes the history of the Federation and its services, along with volunteer and philanthropic opportunities. There are directories of synagogues, community organizations, *kashrut* and Judaica, facts and figures about the community, and a map of the area.

Boston

ADDRESS: http://shamash.org/places/boston/index.html

DESCRIPTION: This guide to Jewish Boston includes a list of synagogues and Jewish community centers; resources for children, teenagers, and college students; Jewish learning opportunities; and information on arts, health, Israel, and social action programs.

Buffalo

ADDRESS: http://jbuff.com

DESCRIPTION: Links to book reviews, a community calendar, a hall of fame, recipes, a singles' board, television listings, and new library acquisitions are provided at this searchable site.

Chicago

ADDRESS: http://www.jewishchicago.com

DESCRIPTION: This site offers community news and a listing of events, along with directories of community resources, synagogues, Jewish organizations, educational institutions, kosher restaurants, and resources for singles. There are chat rooms, interactive forums, and message centers, as well as classified, real estate, and personal ads.

Cleveland

ADDRESS: http://www.jewishcleveland.org

DESCRIPTION: Sponsored by the Jewish Community Federation, this site offers information about the organization's services to all age groups, including those with special needs. The guide to Jewish Cleveland details the history of the community, its Jewish and local agencies, financial aid resources, synagogues, religious organizations and life-cycle needs, educational institutions, community services for all age groups, social services, *kashrut* information, libraries, museums, cultural institutions, and local and Jewish organizations. The guide is searchable and annotated.

Colorado Jewish Community Online

ADDRESS: http://www.jewishcolorado.org

DESCRIPTION: Presented by Allied Jewish Federation of Colorado, this searchable site provides a directory of Jewish schools, synagogues, organizations, and Israel programs. The site describes the services of the Federation and has a calendar of events, a chat room, a guest book, and links to relevant local and Jewish sites.

Dallas Virtual Jewish Community Center

ADDRESS: http://www.dvjc.org

DESCRIPTION: "The Dallas Virtual Jewish Community is a noncommercial community resource that promotes Jewish culture, education, and scholarship in greater Dallas." Its home page offers access to information about the organizations, synagogues, historical society, and schools of the community, along with details about programs for singles, young adults, and cultural activities. There is a calendar of community events, a guestbook, and a discussion forum, as well as links to a variety of Jewish sites.

Detroit

ADDRESS: http://www.metroguide.com/jewishweb/

DESCRIPTION: In addition to the Jewish Community Council's calendar of events, you can find information about local synagogues, schools, organizations, and businesses. The site also has discussion boards, personal ads, and links to relevant Jewish sites.

Florida

ADDRESS: http://jewishinflorida.com/

DESCRIPTION: This site describes the Jewish facilities in Florida with regard to synagogues, *mohelim, mikvaot,* schools, Judaica shops, restaurants and caterers, real estate, businesses, hotels, professional services, and retirement communities. Arrangement is by geographic area.

Florida

ADDRESS: http://www.jewishflorida.net

DESCRIPTION: This searchable database lists synagogues, agencies, events, schools, restaurants, food stores, Judaica stores, and groups for singles, youth, seniors, professionals, and bereavement throughout the state.

Florida Jewish

ADDRESS: http://www.floridajewish.com

DESCRIPTION: This site profiles the traditionally Jewish institutions of Florida. The highlight of the site is the Communities section, sorted by community, in which you can find synagogues, kosher restaurants, Federation agencies, day schools, and singles and social organizations. The Resources section lists Florida's Jewish publications, along with other Jewish sites.

Jewniverse

ADDRESS: http://www.jewniverse.com

DESCRIPTION: Covering Boston, New York, Los Angeles, and San Francisco, this searchable site offers classified ads for perusal. Topics covered include jobs, events, housing, book and restaurant reviews, resumes, and recipes.

Kansas City

ADDRESS: http://www.jewishkc.org/

DESCRIPTION: Sponsored by the Federation, this home page is part of the Jewish Community Information and Referral Service. It provides access to information about Jewish Kansas City, its synagogues, the federation, Jewish learning, news, service agencies, volunteer opportunities, and programs for seniors, young adults, and professionals. There are also "Ask the Rabbi," Arts and Entertainment, News, Life-Cycle Needs, and Israel sections. You can sign up to receive an online newsletter and also read the JCC's magazine online.

Knoxville

ADDRESS: http://www.jewishknoxville.org

DESCRIPTION: Sponsored by the Knoxville Jewish Federation, this site provides information about the organization, its history, and its services, as well as the local community center, synagogues, and organizations. There is a calendar of events along with a set of links to relevant local and Jewish sites.

LA Jewish Guide

ADDRESS: http://www.lajewishguide.com

DESCRIPTION: This site provides directories of schools, synagogues, restaurants, shopping and services, entertainment, travel, community services, jobs, and real estate, along with a calendar of events. It is also part of the Los Angeles Jewish Web Ring.

Long Island

ADDRESS: http://www.lijewishlinks.org

DESCRIPTION: Sponsored by the Suffolk Jewish Communal Council and the Conference of Jewish Organizations of Nassau County, this home page offers an extensive directory of Jewish organizations, schools, synagogues, cemeteries, community centers, Zionist groups, news sources, chaplains, social service groups, museums, *mikvaot,* and funeral homes. There is information about services for all age groups, as well as a community events calendar. Of particular note are the full-text pro-Israel guide and the collection of links to virtual tours of sites of Jewish interest.

Los Angeles

ADDRESS: http://www.lajewish.org

DESCRIPTION: Describing itself as "an online guide for observant visitors and residents," this site describes the neighborhoods, *mikvahs,* synagogues, and restaurants in the area. There is a listing of sites where one can participate in *daf yomi* studies, as well as links to relevant Jewish and local sites.

Machers of Brooklyn

ADDRESS: http://www.machers.com

DESCRIPTION: Through a series of drop-down menus, Machers provides access to a number of home pages of media, organizations, tours, food, travel, and music providers that advertise through its site. The focus of many of the groups is in Brooklyn. Of particular note are the directories for various parts of the United States, for federations, synagogues, senior living facilities, and regional news, which offer access to information of a broader nature.

Minnesota

ADDRESS: http://www.jewishminnesota.org/

DESCRIPTION: Covering St. Paul and Minneapolis, this searchable site provides access to information about local institutions such as synagogues, federations, education, Jewish agencies, local businesses and services, and local Jewish publications. There is a section describing programs aimed at all age groups, including new immigrants, people new to the area, and those looking to volunteer their services. The last section of the site covers online resources such as a community calendar, discussion forum, news, topics relating to Israel, and a link to online Jewish resources.

Northern New Jersey

ADDRESS: http://www.jewishbergen.org

DESCRIPTION: A service of the UJA Federation of Bergen County and North Hudson, this searchable site features information about the group, a community events calendar, local news, and volunteer opportunities. There are also two directories in the community guide, one arranged by services provided and the other arranged by type of service organization. The former details services offered to all age ranges, while the latter provides information about local Jewish schools, synagogues, organizations, kosher food providers, Israel programs, youth groups, and scholarships.

Philadelphia

ADDRESS: http://www.philly-direct.com/frum/

DESCRIPTION: Entitled "Orthodox Jewish Philadelphia," this site offers listings of neighborhoods, educational facilities, camps, synagogues, organizations, *kashrut* facilities, *eruvin*, *mikvaot*, and *mohelim*. There is a calendar, a list of classifieds, and merchandise for sale, along with a set of relevant links.

Portland, Oregon

ADDRESS: http://www.jewishportland.com

DESCRIPTION: This directory provides links to the home pages of various Jewish institutions, including synagogues, the Federation, community groups, and day schools.

San Antonio

ADDRESS: http://beth-elsa.org/jewsnsat.htm

DESCRIPTION: From Temple Beth El comes this directory of synagogues, organizations, *kashrut* facilities, and Jewish gift shops in the city.

San Diego

ADDRESS: http://www.sandiegojewish.org/

DESCRIPTION: This searchable site describes the Orthodox community in San Diego—its synagogues, schools, *mikvah*, organizations, and *kashrut* facilities. It also provides information on tourist attractions and accommodations. Of particular interest is the international database of yeshivot, searchable by numerous criteria.

San Francisco Bay Area

ADDRESS: http://www.jfed.org

DESCRIPTION: Sponsored by the Jewish Federation, FedNet services the Greater East Bay and Oakland areas. It provides information for individuals new to the area, listings of synagogues, institutions of Jewish learning, community events and services, and sections on Israel and art and culture. There are also links to the *Jewish Bulletin of Northern California*, a listing of volunteer opportunities, and other relevant sites of Jewish interest.

Seattle

ADDRESS: http://www.jewishinseattle.org

DESCRIPTION: Created by the Federation, this site provides a guide to Jewish Washington, including the synagogues, organizations, and *kashrut* facilities. Information about the Federation, its events, and services is also provided. There is a large section on education, with material on Israel programs, teacher resources, adult education, and the community Hebrew high school. The "getting connected" portion of the site is geared to newcomers to Seattle of various ages.

Silicon Valley

ADDRESS: http://www.jewish.org

DESCRIPTION: One of the first Jewish sites online, this home page was originally established by the Palo Alto Orthodox Minyan (now renamed "Emek Beracha"). It has joined with the Chabad of the South Bay to provide a resource center with information on kosher food, schools, synagogues, community services, Judaica shops, and *mikvaot* in the Bay Area. You will also find links to other select Jewish resources on the Web.

Southern Florida

ADDRESS: http://www.jewishsouthflorida.com

DESCRIPTION: Servicing Miami-Dade, Broward, and South Palm Beach counties, this site provides directories of synagogues, *mikvaot*, community organizations, kosher food providers, Judaica shops, and schools and educational institutions. A community events calendar and a business directory are also provided. In addition, there are lists of local attractions and travel and accommodations facilities.

Washington

ADDRESS: http://www.jirs.org/

DESCRIPTION: The Jewish Information and Referral Service is maintained by the Federation and features a browsable site, with resources searchable by keyword.

Washington D.C.

ADDRESS: http://www.jewishdc.org

DESCRIPTION: Focusing on the greater Washington area, including Virginia and Maryland, this site provides information about services in the areas of commerce and religious life of interest to Jewish residents. There are sections covering local news, community institutions, and educational facilities.

AUSTRALIA

Ozzies' Inter.net

ADDRESS: http://www.join.org.au/

DESCRIPTION: This magazine-style home page is the "electronic voice of Jewish Australia" and contains information about the community and its synagogues, educational institutions, libraries, youth movements, organizations, *kashrut* services, board of deputies, Federation, sports programs, and community council. You can read profiles of Jewish Australians and general articles of Jewish interest. In addition, the site sponsors two free e-mail discussion groups. Of particular note is the browsable, alphabetical listing of a large variety of Jewish institutions and services in Australia. This is an excellent starting point for surveying the Australian Jewish world.

WEJ: Jewish Australia on the WEB

ADDRESS: http://www.wej.com.au/

DESCRIPTION: This site provides details about the Jewish community and its businesses, events, synagogues, schools, and youth programs. Of particular note is the alphabetical index in the "World of WEJ" section.

CANADA

Calgary

ADDRESS: http://www.jewish-calgary.com

DESCRIPTION: Sponsored by the Calgary Jewish Community Council, this site provides a hypertext list of community agencies, including synagogues and schools, a calendar of events, an e-mail directory of key contact people, a list of hospitals and nursing homes, and links to other Jewish sites.

Montreal

ADDRESS: http://www.montreal-jewish.org/

DESCRIPTION: Created in 1996, this home page lists links to home pages of Jewish institutions in the city.

Toronto

ADDRESS: http://www.feduja.org/

DESCRIPTION: Created by the UJA Federation, this searchable site houses the home pages of many Toronto Jewish institutions, including schools, synagogues, libraries, community centers, and social service groups. In addition to details about the Federation and its activities, there are a community calendar and annotated links to relevant Jewish and local sites. Of particular note is the *kashrut* directory of the COR.

Vancouver

ADDRESS: http://www.jfgv.com

DESCRIPTION: Sponsored by the Federation, this site provides a hypertext listing of synagogues, centers, schools, camps, agencies, libraries, and activities for young adults and seniors. There is information about the Federation and its services, a community calendar, and Israel programs as well. A chat room and a set of links to other Jewish sites are also provided.

WESTERN EUROPE

European Council of Jewish Communities

ADDRESS: http://www.ecjc.org

DESCRIPTION: "The European Council of Jewish Communities (ECJC) is the networking agency of Jewish institutions and communities concerned with planning and coordinating action in the fields of social welfare, formal and informal Jewish education, leadership training and culture. Established in 1968, the ECJC comprises member communities and organizations in 37 countries." This site offers information about events and programs in the areas of education, social welfare, and culture taking place throughout Europe, as well as details on regional events and funding offerings. There is also an entire section on restitution for Holocaust survivors. Of particular note is the Links section, that provides a hypertext directory of Jewish sites by country throughout Europe. This is an excellent starting point for locating Jewish institutions in both Western and Eastern Europe.

Antwerp

ADDRESS: http://www.jewishantwerp.com

DESCRIPTION: This site provides access to the Jewish organizations that are online. It also lists the synagogues, Jewish schools, and community groups in the community, with basic contact information. Extensive details for tourists and practical travel information are also provided, including an interactive map, *kashrut* information, tourist attractions, and Jewish sites of interest. The site offers over 1,000 classified links of Belgian and Jewish interest.

Belgian Goedkosjer Jewish Consumers Defense Association

ADDRESS: http://www.goedkosjer.org

DESCRIPTION: Created by a group seeking lower kosher food prices, this site, in Dutch and English, provides access to news stories and a site called Jewish Antwerp.

British Jewish Network

ADDRESS: http://www.brijnet.org

DESCRIPTION: "Brijnet was formed in 1990 by Avrum Goodblat (founder of the Shamash service in the U.S.A.) and is the longest established Jewish Internet provider in the U.K." It hosts many organizations, including the Central Synagogue, United Synagogue, a number of book sellers, the Union of Jewish Students, the Agency for Jewish Education, Pikuah, the Anglo Israel Association, the London School of Jewish Studies, and others.

Everything Jewish in the UK

ADDRESS: http://www.jewish.co.uk/

DESCRIPTION: An extensive, magazine-style home page covering world Jewish news, Jewish holidays, and life-cycle and social events in the United Kingdom. There are a number of guides, including a synagogue directory, a travel guide to Israel, a Jewish film guide, and a glossary of Jewish terms. Of particular note is the extensive U.K. kosher guide, offering information on all types of *kashrut* issues; guides to Jewish life in North England, New Zealand, and Ireland; a people locator for finding lost friends; a large number of discussion boards; and personal, real estate, and classified ads. The entire site is searchable and you can sign up for an e-mail newsletter. If you are looking for anything related to Jewish life in the United Kingdom, this is an excellent starting point.

Jewishnet of the UK

ADDRESS: http://www.jewishnet.org.uk and http://www.SoJewish.com

DESCRIPTION: Designed as an online magazine, this British site provides news and feature articles on cooking, books, music, sports, and media, along with a desktop lawyer, business directory, member chat room, Agony Aunt, "ask the rabbi," and a directory of British synagogues. The site is searchable.

Newcastle and the North East Jewish Communities of England

ADDRESS: http://www.northeastjewish.org.uk

DESCRIPTION: Information on the Jewish communities in North East England and their educational, charitable, and social institutions, as well as youth groups, is available here.

Totally Jewish

ADDRESS: http://www.totallyjewish.com

DESCRIPTION: Designed as an online magazine, this British site provides news and feature articles on lifestyle, dating, the community, football, travel, food, health and beauty, weddings, parenting, bridge, business, personal ads, finance, jobs, and classifieds. There are a number of chat rooms, and the entire site is searchable.

U.K. Small Jewish Communities

ADDRESS: http://www.telecall.co.uk/~davar/uksmall.html

DESCRIPTION: Created and maintained by Tony Reese, this hypertext directory provides access to the home pages of small Jewish communities throughout the United Kingdom.

Communaute Online

ADDRESS: http://www.col.fr/

DESCRIPTION: This site houses the home pages of many associations and publications related to the Jewish community of France. There is an alphabetical listing of sites hosted here, as well as a number of discussion forums, personal announcements, and links to relevant international, French-language, and Jewish Web pages. Of particular note are the directories of synagogues and kosher restaurants, arranged by Parisian *arrondisements,* and the section on various communities throughout France.

French Language Jewish sites

ADDRESS: http://www.israelfr.com

DESCRIPTION: This site hosts the home pages of a variety of French-language Jewish sites worldwide. It also offers French-language discussion groups on Jewish topics and has sections for youth, Jewish culture, Israel, and public service announcements. You can receive a newsletter by e-mail and participate in an online poll.

French Speaking Israelis

ADDRESS: http://www.francophones.org.il

DESCRIPTION: Designed for French-speaking Israelis, this site offers access to a variety of services including French-Jewish ICQ chats, listings of French television shows in Israel, and job opportunities in French-language publications in Israel.

Judaica.net, premier annuaire du judaisme francophone

ADDRESS: http://www.judaica.net

DESCRIPTION: Arranged in a Yahoo-style format, this searchable French-language page offers annotated access to a variety of general and Jewish sites in 45 different subject areas.

JudeoWeb: Annuaire des Sites Juifs Francophones

ADDRESS: http://www.judeoweb.com/

DESCRIPTION: Arranged in a Yahoo-style format, this searchable French-language page serves as a directory for French Jewish sites in 19 subject areas.

Paris Kosher Restaurants

ADDRESS: http://www.geocities.com/NapaValley/2621/

DESCRIPTION: Created by David Cohen, this site in English and French provides a list of kosher restaurants arranged by *arrondisement* for Paris and by region of the country for the areas outside the capital. Basic contact information, type of cuisine, and rabbinical supervision are listed. There are also tips for the kosher visitor to France and a list of synagogues, Judaica shops, and *mohelim* in Paris.

TopJ

ADDRESS: http://www.topj.net

DESCRIPTION: This French-language site describes itself as a portal to the French-speaking Jewish community. In addition to the news, information about holidays, and feature articles focusing on France and Israel, the most notable features of this searchable site are the numerous directories it offers. There are listings for the top Jewish sites on the Internet, a yellow pages–style directory arranged by services, best sellers, most favored names, and community events nationwide.

Vie Juive

ADDRESS: http://www.viejuive.com/

DESCRIPTION: This searchable French site provides details about the life of the synagogue, including the Grand Rabbi and his teachings, the structure of the community, and a discussion group.

Berlin

ADDRESS: http://www.Jewish-Berlin-online.com

DESCRIPTION: Aimed at both residents and tourists, this searchable magazine-style site in English and German emphasizes the economic, political, cultural, and social aspects of life in the capital. It provides an extensive history of the Jews in Berlin, a calendar of events, a hall of fame, and a hypertext list of organizational addresses. The memorial section allows one to input the name of relatives or acquaintances who may have survived the Holocaust in Berlin.

Berlin

ADDRESS: http://www.hagalil.com/brd/berlin/enter.htm

DESCRIPTION: Presented in English and German, this site offers details about synagogues and services, *kashrut* facilities, Jewish groups, women's activities, Berlin rabbis, and the Jewish museum and library. Also provided are a history of the community and a number of city maps.

Germany

ADDRESS: http://www.talmud.de

DESCRIPTION: This English section of this site provides listings of *kashrut* facilities, Jewish communal organizations, and candle-lighting times for cities throughout Germany. The German portion has more extensive material, including a guide to Jewish life cycle, holidays, and religious practices.

Greek Jews

ADDRESS: http://www.greecetravel.com/jewishhistory/

DESCRIPTION: The basis for this site is a book by Nikos Stavrolakis, the founder and director of the Jewish Museum, on the history of Jews in Greece. The site is divided into time periods and provides access to artifacts from the Jewish Museum in Athens.

Organisation of Jewish Communities in the Netherlands

ADDRESS: http://www.nik.nl/

DESCRIPTION: In Dutch and English, this site describes the organization's history and work and provides Jewish religious articles and local news.

L'Isola della Rugiada Divina—Italian Jewish Network

ADDRESS: http://www.italya.net

DESCRIPTION: Articles in Italian about Jewish history and religion make up most of the offerings on this site.

Menorah-Ghesher Network Ebraico in Italian

ADDRESS: http://www.menorah.it

DESCRIPTION: This Italian-language site provides information about Jewish life in Italy and has articles on *kashrut*, Talmud, the weekly Torah reading, and other rabbinical topics. The section on Italia Ebraica lists synagogues, museums, organizations, and *kashrut* facilities throughout the country.

Morasha

ADDRESS: http://www.morasha.it

DESCRIPTION: This largely Italian site, designed in a magazine format, provides book reviews, a list of events, and sections on Jewish life cycle events, holidays, and *midrashim*, along with questions based on Rashi for each of the *parshiot*. There are links to a number of Italian Jewish organizations and publications as well. Of particular note are the sections in Italian and English on *kashrut* facilities and Jewish museums throughout the country.

Venice

ADDRESS: http://www.jewishvenice.org/

DESCRIPTION: Created by Chabad, this site profiles the work of Chabad in Venice and provides details about its restaurant and yeshiva. Of particular note is the tourist information offered, including a history and map of the ghetto, the Jewish museum and cemetery, a listing of hotels close to the ghetto, and details about tours.

Malta

ADDRESS: http://www.fred.net/malta/jewish.html

DESCRIPTION: Written by Lawrence Attard Bezzina, this is a narrative describing the Jewish community on this Mediterranean island.

Basel

ADDRESS: http://www.igb.ch/

DESCRIPTION: The English portion of this home page provides detailed information about *kashrut* facilities, the history of the community and its organizations, a searchable database of daily service times, and a set of links to relevant Swiss and Jewish sites. The German portion includes material about schools, youth groups, and cultural institutions such as the museum and library.

Helsinki, Finland

ADDRESS: http://www.helsinki.fi/~aschulma/srk/home.htm

DESCRIPTION: This site profiles the Jewish community and offers information about its history and its community organizations and structure. There is material of interest to visitors to the Jewish community and to Helsinki and Finland in general, as well as links to neighboring Jewish communities and other relevant Jewish Web sites. Most of the site is in English, with some information in Finnish.

Institutet for Judisk Kultur in Sweden

ADDRESS: http://www.ijk-s.se

DESCRIPTION: This Swedish-language home page profiles the activities and publications of this cultural organization and has a small amount of information in English about the first Jew to settle in Sweden. Links to other Jewish sites are provided as well.

Oslo

ADDRESS: http://www.dmt.oslo.no

DESCRIPTION: This bilingual site in Norwegian and English provides details about the Jewish community and its organizations, as well as information of interest to tourists. There is a calendar of events and a list of contact people within the community as well.

Scandanavia

ADDRESS: http://www.algonet.se/~hatikva/scandinavia/

DESCRIPTION: This portal provides a directory of links to Jewish communities of Norway, Sweden, Denmark, and Finland. It is an excellent starting point for sources related to this region of Europe.

Spanish Language Jewish Life

ADDRESS: http://www.hebreos.net

DESCRIPTION: Focusing on establishing communication among Spanish-speaking Jews, this searchable site hosts a number of chat rooms and areas where members may post personal pictures. You can subscribe to a Spanish newsletter about Judaism and look at the sections about holidays, recipes, and links to other Jewish and Israeli sites.

EASTERN EUROPE AND RUSSIA

Khazaria Information Center

ADDRESS: http://www.khazaria.com

DESCRIPTION: Subtitled "A Resource for Turkic and Jewish History in Russia and Ukraine," this is a comprehensive site for research in all aspects of this area of study. Kevin Brook, who maintains the site, has included a history of medieval Khazaria, maps, quotations, bibliographies, and links to research articles about the region. The center also publishes books on the region, that are described here along with information on how to order them. In addition, three mailing lists on the topics of Eastern European history and Khazar studies are available here. Of particular note is the extensive set of links to the Eastern European Jewish world, arranged by country. This is an excellent portal to the study of Eastern European Jewish history.

Dniepropetrovsk

ADDRESS: http://jew.dp.ua

DESCRIPTION: This searchable English and Russian site, based in the Ukraine, profiles the rabbi and the community; its history, cultural, religious, and educational programs; community publications; and ties with the international Jewish world.

Ukraine

ADDRESS: http://www.jfu.kiev.ua and http://www.public.ua.net/~jewish and http://www.jewish.kiev.ua

DESCRIPTION: Home page of the All Ukranian Jewish Congress, this site describes itself as "the largest Jewish organization in the Ukraine." It provides information about the group and the community and a directory of Jewish communities and contacts in the region.

Federation of Jewish Communities of the C.I.S.

ADDRESS: http://www.fjc.ru

DESCRIPTION: Available in English and Russian and arranged by country, "the Web site offers a comprehensive index of over 270 affiliated Jewish communities in the CIS, with conservative estimates of general population size and respective Jewish population size." In addition to information about each country and its Jewish life, there is a link to the

Rabbinical Alliance, the umbrella organization of rabbis in the CIS, as well as links to relevant Jewish sites dealing with the region.

Hungarian Jewish Website: Magyar Zsido Honlap

ADDRESS: http://www.interdnet.hu/zsido/

DESCRIPTION: In English and Hungarian, this site offers information about the history of the Jews in Hungary, Jewish life currently, the Holocaust in Carpatho-Ruthenia, synagogues in the country, the Jewish community school, and travel facilities. There is also a chat room, an auction site, and a guestbook, along with links to sites of Jewish interest and details about Jewish World War II assets.

Kishinev & Moldova

ADDRESS: http://www.kishinev.org

DESCRIPTION: Sponsored by the Friends of Kishinev Jewry in Brooklyn, this site highlights the work of the group in that region. It provides information on the history of the area and the current state of its educational and community institutions. News and events of the Friends group are also available.

Poland

ADDRESS: http://www.jewish.org.pl

DESCRIPTION: This well-designed portal in English and Polish offers news and information on associations, religious communities, educational institutions, and the Jewish press of Poland. There is a kid's club and material on Jewish holidays, along with an FAQ on Jewish life and links to relevant Jewish sites.

LATIN AMERICA

Brazilian Judaism

ADDRESS: http://www.judaismo.com.br/

DESCRIPTION: This Portuguese Web site serves as a portal to the Jewish community of Brazil. It provides a rated and annotated directory of Web sites for synagogues, institutions, schools, and clubs, as well as links to relevant media, food, shopping, humor, and personals listings. You can sign up for a listserv and search the site. This is an excellent portal for those who read Portuguese and want information on the Brazilian Jewish community.

Cuba

ADDRESS: http://jewishcuba.org

DESCRIPTION: More than 100 articles at this site detail the history of the community, its cultural and religious life, and its revival. There are listings of synagogues, events of Cuban Jewish interest, photographs, and information on arts and media. You can find out about traveling to Cuba and participating in the Cuba-American Jewish Mission.

Rishon: Argentine Jewry

ADDRESS: http://www.rishon.com.ar/rishon/default.htm

DESCRIPTION: Designed in a magazine-style format, this Spanish-language site serves as a portal for the Latin American Jewish community. There are news columns and features on art and culture, the Jewish community in Argentina, the economy, sports, politics, Israeli news, tourism, and a calendar of events. An archive of past issues is available. Of particular note is the section on Jewish communities of Latin America, offering thumbnail sketches of each group. This is an excellent portal for Spanish speakers looking for information on the Jewish communities of Latin America.

Shalom Online

ADDRESS: http://www.shalomonline.com

DESCRIPTION: This extensive Spanish-language portal provides daily news about Jews around the world and headlines from seven Latin American newspapers. Services to the community include free e-mail, clip art, chats, and a tourist guide to Latin America. Its Judaica section offers columns on Torah, the Holocaust, holidays, customs, Hebrew, the weekly *parsha*, and the Jewish calendar. If you read Spanish and are interested in Jewish life in Latin America, this is a good site to explore.

ASIA

Beijing

ADDRESS: http://www.istarnet.com/sinogogue

DESCRIPTION: From the Kehillat Beijing Synagogue comes this home page with information about the community and its history, events, and Shabbat and holiday services. You can sign up for Shabbat meals or to lead services and also print out the synagogue's address in Chinese. The links page offers additional details about Jewish resources in the city. You can sign the guest book and be placed on the synagogue's e-mailing list.

Bukhara

ADDRESS: http://www.getnet.com/~byblos/bukhara.htm

DESCRIPTION: Written by Donna Carr, this full-text research paper traces the history of the Jews of Bukhara and provides a bibliography as well.

Ethiopian Jewry

ADDRESS: http://www.circus.org/nacoej.htm

DESCRIPTION: In addition to news updates about the current situation in Ethiopia, this site provides background on Ethiopian Jewry, including its history, way of life, halachah and customs, its contact with world Jewry, and its mention in Jewish sources. The site also offers some basic Amharic, Ethiopian recipes, and a bibliography. You can read the quarterly newsletter, Lifeline, and check related Jewish and Ethiopian links.

Japan

ADDRESS: http://www.jewish.japan.co.jp

DESCRIPTION: From this home page you can find out about the community's Shabbat services and facilities for tourists, the religious school, and the social and cultural events in Jewish Tokyo.

Shanghai

ADDRESS: http://www.chinajewish.org

DESCRIPTION: This home page offers information about the community and its programs, activities, and library. There are a number of links aimed at tourists, including details on Shabbat services and meals and arranging for tours of Jewish Shanghai and the Ohel Rachel Synagogue. Of particular note are the links to Asian Jewish Web sites, arranged by geographic area.

Thailand

ADDRESS: http://www.jewishthailand.com

DESCRIPTION: This home page lists information of interest to tourists, including contact information for synagogues and kosher facilities.

JEWISH HOLIDAYS

VJHolidays

ADDRESS: http://www.virtualjerusalem.com/judasim/holidays

DESCRIPTION: Sponsored by Virtual Jerusalem, this comprehensive guide to the Jewish year features themes and customs of all major and minor festivals, along with suggested activities, kids' club, and educational guides. This is an excellent portal through which to begin the study of Jewish holidays.

Children's Jewish Holiday Sites

ADDRESS: http://members.tripod.com/~ProudMommy/holidays.html

DESCRIPTION: This site provides annotated lists of links to Jewish holiday sites appropriate for children. Links are arranged by holiday.

Everything Jewish

ADDRESS: http://www.everythingjewish.com/

DESCRIPTION: Arranged like a shopping mall, this site features Judaica for various holidays and life-cycle events, but each holiday section also has information on the origins, spiritual meaning, laws and customs, heroes and villains, and family fun activities. The site features an area on Jewish culture and art.

Gefilte Greetings

ADDRESS: http://www.gefiltegreetings.com

DESCRIPTION: Send a free holiday card from this site.

Holidays with a Twist

ADDRESS: http://www.wzo.org.il/encountr/holidays.htm

DESCRIPTION: Sponsored by the World Zionist Organization, this site offers access to articles about creative ways to celebrate the festivals of the year.

Jewish Holidays Magazine

ADDRESS: http://www.JewishHolidays.com

DESCRIPTION: Part of the Jewish Family series of online magazines, this periodical offers feature articles on holidays, life cycle events, blessings, and Shabbat. The entire site is searchable.

Kibbutz Holidays Institute

ADDRESS: http://www.chagim.org.il

DESCRIPTION: This Hebrew and English site houses the collection of secular liturgical materials for Jewish holidays, compiled by Aryeh Ben-Gurion, a founder of Kibbutz Beit Hashitta. The material is browsable by holiday and life-cycle event, and a list of the institute's publications is also available.

Ultimate Shabbat Site

ADDRESS: http://www.shabbos.org.il

DESCRIPTION: This site focuses on the creation of a traditional Shabbat. It includes sections on laws, songs, recipes, teachings about Shabbat, a step-by-step primer on how to create a Shabbat, audio and video classes, and candle-lighting times worldwide. Of particular note is the hospitality database, where you can locate Shabbat hospitality by city or country.

THE JEWISH LIFE CYCLE

Jewish Family

ADDRESS: http://www.mishpacha.org

DESCRIPTION: Sponsored by the Memorial Foundation for Jewish Culture, this site describes itself as a "virtual community" for Jewish families. You can discuss your Jewish family life with other parents and "Ask Judy" questions about Jewish life and practice. Of particular note is Mishpacha's Guide to Jewish Life, describing "how to understand Judaism as an adult and celebrate it as a family." There are articles in sections on Beliefs, Holidays, Jewish Practice, Community, the Life Cycle, and Parenting.

Jewish Life Cycle

ADDRESS: http://www.ahavat-israel.com/torat/lifecycle.html

DESCRIPTION: Part of the traditionally minded Ahavat Israel Web site, this page offers an extensive explanation of the laws and practices related to Jewish life-cycle commemorations, holidays, ritual objects, and concepts of *ahavat* Israel, *am* Israel, Torat Israel, and Eretz Israel.

Mazeltov.com

ADDRESS: http://Mazeltov.com

DESCRIPTION: From this site you can view personal ads, announcements, and classifieds by zip code, as well as search a business directory for *simcha*-related services.

SimchaGuide.com

ADDRESS: http://www.simchaguide.com

DESCRIPTION: This online resource will help you plan a Jewish celebration. It offers browsable listings for businesses in the areas of halls, photography, music, invitations, catering, make-up, decorations, bridal apparel, wedding bands, *ketubot*, accommodations, and gifts from companies that have signed up to be listed at this site. Information on how to become listed with the site is also provided.

BIRTH

Jewish Infertility

ADDRESS: http://www.atime.org/

DESCRIPTION: "A.T.I.M.E., an acronym for A Torah Infertility Medium of Exchange, is a nonprofit organization devoted to the support of infertile couples." Its Web site describes the group's services, which include an online newsletter, events, message boards, a reading list, and a set of relevant links to medical and Jewish sites.

Torah View

ADDRESS: http://www.torahview.com/

DESCRIPTION: The home page of Los Angeles-based *mohel* Rabbi Yehuda Lebovics, this home page describes the *bris* and the role of the *mohel,* provides an FAQ about circumcision, and gives a *bris* preparation checklist. You can also e-mail the *mohel* with questions about names.

BAR/BAT MITZVAH

Bar and Bat Mitzvahs in Israel

ADDRESS: http://jem.ascender.com/iia/bar/

DESCRIPTION: This home page was designed to accompany the print title *Bar and Bat Mitzvah in Israel: The Ultimate Family Sourcebook,* written by Judith Isaacson and Deborah Rosenbloom. The page lists Internet links to bar/bat mitzvah-planning sites and to sites for planning a trip to Israel. You can also check the book's table of contents and read reviews and comments by readers.

Cybarmitzvah

ADDRESS: http://www.cybarmitzvah.com

DESCRIPTION: For a fee this site will provide an online photo and video album space for bar/bat mitzvot.

MARRIAGE

Jewish Marriage Encounter

ADDRESS: http://www1.ridgecrest.ca.us/~debbie/JME/

DESCRIPTION: Although this home page has not been updated since 1998, it describes the Jewish Marriage Encounter program.

Ketubah Workshop

ADDRESS: http://www.ketubahworkshop.com/

DESCRIPTION: Based in Toronto and operated by Ted Labow, this site describes the history of the *ketubah*, discusses some of the variant texts, and provides a gallery of samples from which one can order a customized *ketubah*.

Prenuptial Agreement

ADDRESS: http://208.150.6.17/organizations/oc/prenup/default.htm

DESCRIPTION: This site is designed as a complement to the print volume entitled *The Prenuptial Agreement: Halakhic, Legal,and Pastoral Considerations*, edited by Rabbi Kenneth Auman and Rabbi Basil Herring. It offers a large amount of full text from the book detailing the reasoning behind the need for a prenuptial agreement to obviate the problem of *agunot*.

Wedding Resources

ADDRESS: http://www.mazornet.com/jewishcl/weddingr.htm

DESCRIPTION: Part of the Jewish Celebrations site, this home page offers resources in a large number of areas, including benchers, florists, make-up artists, banquet halls, groom's attire, musicians, bridal attire, party favors, bridesmaid dresses, invitations, photographers, *chuppot*, jewelry, thank-you notes, DJ services, *ketubot*, videographers, family's attire, kosher caterers, wedding gifts, guest accommodations, transportation, and honeymoons.

DIVORCE

Domestic Abuse and the Agunah Problem

ADDRESS: http://users.aol.com/agunah/index.htm

DESCRIPTION: Maintained by social worker Mark Cwik, this page provides articles on domestic abuse, Jewish abuse, and the *agunah* problem; halachah, documents, and responsa on Jewish family law; a bibliography of articles and books on these topics; a directory of resources for victims of Jewish domestic abuse, including shelters and contact persons; resources for *agunot*, including agencies and contact persons; personal stories; and links to other relevant sites.

Jewish Divorce

ADDRESS: http://www.kayama.org

DESCRIPTION: "Kayama is a nonprofit organization that provides information and assistance for obtaining a Jewish divorce." Its Web site describes what a *get* is, explains why one should obtain a Jewish divorce, and has an FAQ about the topic. The entire site is searchable.

Mevo Satum

ADDRESS: http://www.agunot.org

DESCRIPTION: The English and Hebrew home page of this Jerusalem-based organization devoted to the plight of *agunot* describes the mission, activities, and volunteer opportunities of the group and offers suggestions and a reading list for *agunot*. There are personal stories and information about the organization's book *Mevo Satum*.

DEATH

International Jewish Burial Society

ADDRESS: http://www.shemayisrael.co.il/burial/index.htm

DESCRIPTION: This site provides a comprehensive overview of the laws and customs of mourning from a traditional Jewish perspective. Topics covered include attitudes and behavior at a funeral, Jewish attitudes toward cremation, visiting the sick, confession, autopsy, and immortality of the soul. There are details about preparing the body for burial, shipping a body overseas, and comforting mourners. You can also e-mail a rabbi with questions about a Jewish burial.

Izkor

ADDRESS: http://www.izkor.gov.il

DESCRIPTION: This Hebrew-language home page serves as a memorial site for Israeli soldiers who have fallen in war. The site is searchable by name, place, and date of death. A copy of the prayer for fallen soldiers is available, along with information on Yom HaZikaron, the Israel Memorial Day.

Jewish Book of Life

ADDRESS: http://www.jewishbookoflife.com/

DESCRIPTION: This site allows you to create a family tree as a memorial. Its Book of Life is keyword searchable and sample inscriptions are provided. You can find information on Jewish mourning rituals and prayers as well.

Jewish Memorials

ADDRESS: http://www.jewishmemorial.com

DESCRIPTION: Tributes to loved ones can be left at this site. A browsable, alphabetical list of tributes is available, along with biographies of famous Jews and a set of Jewish links.

JEWISH TEXTS

Hypertext Versions of Jewish Classical Texts

ADDRESS: http://www1.snunit.k12.il/kodesh/kodesh.html

DESCRIPTION: This extensive and well-designed site offers hypertext versions of the major Jewish classical texts, including the *Tanach*, the Mishnah, *Tosefta*, the Babylonian and Jerusalem Talmuds, and the Rambam's *Mishneh Torah*. Each section is both browsable and searchable. For Hebrew speakers, this is an excellent portal to the study of classical Jewish texts.

Navigating the Bible

ADDRESS: http://bible.ort.org

DESCRIPTION: Originally conceived as a means by which a Jewish boy or girl could study and learn to recite his or her bar or bat mitzvah portion of the Torah, this site provides a searchable, interlinear translation and transliteration of the Pentateuch and *Haftarot*. Each page shows two versions of the Hebrew text: a notated version with vowels, punctuation, and musical notation; and an unnotated one, as it appears in the Torah scroll. An English translation and transliteration are also included, and audio files demonstrate the chanting of every verse. Other resources include a biblical atlas, glossary, and genealogy, along with *divrei* Torah and a searchable calendar that helps students locate their Torah portion and *Haftorah*. This is an excellent starting point for anyone interested in how the Torah is read in synagogues.

Web Shas

ADDRESS: http://www.aishdas.org/webshas/index.shtml

DESCRIPTION: Created by Mordechai Torczyner, Web Shas is an innovative subject guide to the Talmud. As of this writing, it has indexed 1,623 *amudim* of Talmud. You can access material by major categories; by, the alphabetical, browsable index; or through the search engine. A list of *amudim* that have been indexed is also available. This is an excellent starting point for anyone looking for primary source material from the Talmud on a given subject.

Dictionary of Sex in the Bible

ADDRESS: http://www.hobrad.com/and.htm

DESCRIPTION: A full-text reference book about gender and sexual issues in the Bible alphabetically arranged.

Insights into Pirkei Avot

ADDRESS: http://www.geocities.com/Athens/Oracle/4581/Avot_gen.html

DESCRIPTION: This personal home page contains texts and commentary on the section of the Talmud called "Ethics of the Fathers."

Mishnah

ADDRESS: http://chaver.com/

DESCRIPTION: Created by Moshe Kline, "this is the home site of a new edition of the Mishnah, Hamishnah C'Darchah. All six orders of the Mishnah are now freely available here in Hebrew (iso-8859-8-I) HTML. They are best viewed with Microsoft Internet Explorer 5. There is also a collection of articles, both in Hebrew and in English, which deal with 'woven texts' in general, and specifically, the Mishnah. All of seder zrayim and half of seder nzikin are color coded. The Color Code is accessed through the index page of the Mishnah text. It is possible to use these chapters as a first introduction to Hamishnah C'Darchah, by examining the divisions made in the chapters, together with the linguistic parallels indicated by the colors."

Mishneh Torah

ADDRESS: http://www.mechon-mamre.org

DESCRIPTION: You can download the text of the *Mishneh Torah* here in English or Hebrew. The site also houses a very extensive "Torah 101" site within a site that provides an overview of Judaism, with links to the *Mishneh Torah*.

Online Jewish Library

ADDRESS: http://hobbes.jct.ac.il/efi/torah.html

DESCRIPTION: This home page provides a set of links arranged by Jewish text to sites on the Internet that house the text and/or commentary on it. Included are *Tanach*, Talmud, halachic works, studies in mysticism and philosophy, prayer, and life-cycle events.

Rambam Resources

ADDRESS: http://www.panix.com/~jjbaker/rambam.html

DESCRIPTION: Created by Jonathan Baker, this site offers Immanuel O'Levy's translation of the first book of Maimonides' *Mishneh Torah,* his listing of the 613 commandments from *Sefer HaMitzvot,* a biography of the Rambam, and other resources about the medieval Jewish philosopher.

JUDAISM

Jew FAQ

ADDRESS: http://www.jewfaq.org

DESCRIPTION: Created by Tracey Rich, this searchable site "is an online encyclopedia of Judaism, covering Jewish beliefs, people, places, things, language, scripture, holidays, practices, and customs." Ms. Rich, who describes herself as an observant Jew, has written articles in sections on ideas, people, places, things, words, deeds, times, and life cycle. She provides links to reference resources and other relevant Jewish sites. Each of her articles is rated for beginner, intermediate, or advanced students. This is a rich resource for anyone looking for an explanation of Jewish principles and practices.

Judaism 101

ADDRESS: http://www.judaism101.org

DESCRIPTION: Sponsored by the Union of Orthodox Jewish Congregations of America, this site describes itself as "a comprehensive information base of basic Jewish terms, concepts, and practices that everyone, no matter their nationality, faith or personal creed, will find helpful, informative, and spiritually uplifting." There are articles on Jewish philosophy and belief, Shabbat, the holidays, and the weekly Torah reading, along with a glossary and e-mail access to the "Vebbe Rebbe," who will answer questions. The site also serves as a portal to the group's *kashrut* services, member synagogues worldwide, and organizational projects. A section on prayer is available with text and audio versions of *yizkor, Kaddish,* and prayers for the Israeli Defense Forces. You can also place a prayer in the Wailing Wall from this site.

Judaism from the Mining Company

ADDRESS: http://judaism.miningco.com

DESCRIPTION: This directory of links from About.com offers easy access to a wide range of resources about Judaism, arranged in 32 major categories. The site includes forums, a chat room, a newsletter, and links to related subject guides prepared by About.com. For those seeking a general introduction to topics about Jewish life and religion, this is an excellent portal.

Virtual Synagogue Tour

ADDRESS: http://ezra.mts.jhu.edu/~rabbiars/synagogue/index.html

DESCRIPTION: Created by Rabbi Amy Scheinerman, this site is part of a larger page on resources for Jewish family life and education. The virtual tour highlights the who's who and what's what of the synagogue, while describing the books, service, structure, and history of the synagogue. You can see the Torah scroll and its ornaments and learn how to have an *aliyah*. There is also a photo gallery of *bimas* and arks and a glossary of terms. This is a well-designed and engaging Web site that serves as a good introduction to the synagogue.

Columbia University's Jewish Studies Resources

ADDRESS: http://www.columbia.edu/cu/libraries/indiv/area/MiddleEast/Judaism.html

DESCRIPTION: Created by Columbia University librarian Frank Unlandherm, this site is intended as a starting point for scholarly research in Jewish studies. Links are provided in numerous areas, including Judaism.

Eruv

ADDRESS: http://www.eruv.net

DESCRIPTION: The home page of Manuel Herz and Eyal Weizman of Germany, this site provides access to a description of what an *eruv* is and the religious rationale for it.

Institute for Science and Halacha

ADDRESS: http://www.machon-science-halacha.org.il

DESCRIPTION: Based in Jerusalem, this institute deals with halachic solutions to technological issues. Its Web site describes its areas of research and educational facilities, along with a list of publications, an online order form, and a glossary of terms.

Jewish Law

ADDRESS: http://www.jlaw.com

DESCRIPTION: Jewish Law is sponsored by the Orthodox Union and is edited by Ira Kasdan, with assistance from Nathan Diament. Its goal is to examine halachah, Jewish issues, and secular law through articles, case summaries, commentary, law review articles, and legal briefs.

There are sections on halachic forms, law and policy, statutes, and press releases, as well as a law student's question and answer line, a legal dictionary, and news announcements. You can also listen to lectures through the Jewish Law Audio link. The entire site is searchable.

Jewish Topics

ADDRESS: http://www.jewishtopics.com/

DESCRIPTION: This directory of quotations provides a look at Jewish topics through the prism of the classic Jewish texts and is arranged into 30 different areas.

Judaism in the Workplace

ADDRESS: http://www.darchenoam.org/ethics/pe_home.htm

DESCRIPTION: Hosted by Darche Noam, this site seeks to apply the teachings of Jewish law and ethics to professional life. The page's contents include sections on competition, the professional world, philanthropy, strikes and unions, downsizing, accident prevention, gossip, and copyright issues. You can post a question, listen to lectures, and check the list of links to other relevant Jewish sites. A well-designed site that offers a great deal of timely material.

Judaism Reading List

ADDRESS: http://shamash.org/lists/scj-faq/HTML/rl/tra-index.html

DESCRIPTION: Part of the reading lists compiled by the newsgroup soc.culture.jewish, this list of books covers traditional liturgy, philosophy, ethics, responsa literature, prayer, the household, the life cycle, and holidays.

Midrash Ben Ish Hai

ADDRESS: http://www.midrash.org

DESCRIPTION: Named after a work by Hakham Yoseph Hayyim of Babylon, this site is devoted to the preservation of the Sephardic approach to Judaism. There is a section on laws and customs pertaining to the holidays and news about the organization, and its events, audio and video works, and *refuah* project. You can join the e-mail list and read the newsletter online. Back issues are also available.

Mikva Outreach International

ADDRESS: http://www.mikva-tikva.org

DESCRIPTION: This is the home page of an organization devoted to educating the Jewish community about the role of *mikvah* in Jewish life. The site describes the educational activities, outreach programs, lectures provided by the group and has a section in English, French, and Hebrew designed to dispel myths about *mikvah*. A bibliography of books on the topic is provided as well.

Shatnez Information Page

ADDRESS: http://www.geocities.com/ResearchTriangle/Thinktank/6997

DESCRIPTION: Published by the Kehilla Shatnez Testing Service in Los Angeles, this page provides an FAQ describing the *shatnez* prohibition of mixing linen and wool and also lists manufacturers that use this combination in their clothing.

Spanish Language Introduction to Judaism

ADDRESS: http://www.judaicasite.com

DESCRIPTION: From Argentina, this home page offers extensive information in Spanish on all aspects of Jewish life, including the mitzvot, holidays, Jewish symbols, family life, Hebrew, the weekly Torah portion, ritual objects, and life cycle events. Also provided are an "ask the rabbi" section and a children's area.

Virtual Judaism

ADDRESS: http://www.virtualjudaism.com/

DESCRIPTION: Describing itself as "a Jewish Supersite for close encounters of the virtual kind, where the People of the Book become the People of the Byte," this site has three main sections—a virtual art gallery, educational activities for teaching the Bible, and a bookstore affiliated with Amazon.com.

Virtual Tour of the Second Temple

ADDRESS: http://moshiach.com/mikdosh/

DESCRIPTION: Click on this bird's eye view of the Second Temple and you will see a close-up of one of 26 areas of the sanctuary, together with a description.

SCRIBAL ARTS

Jerusalem Scribe

ADDRESS: http://jscribe.simplenet.com/

DESCRIPTION: Although this is a commercial site looking to sell Judaica written by a scribe, the company provides information on the physical characteristics of Torah scrolls, *megillot, mezuzot,* and *tefillin.*

Mezuzah Doctor

ADDRESS: http://www.mezuzahdoctor.com

DESCRIPTION: While this is a commercial site for a scribe, the Web page offers information about *mezuzot, tefillin,* Torah scrolls, and *megillot.*

Sefer Torah Recycling Network

ADDRESS: http://www.i2.i-2000.com/~strnetmb/storah.html

DESCRIPTION: Created by Moshe Burt, this site describes a project to repair Torah scrolls no longer needed by American congregations and send them to small synagogues in Israel. The site outlines the needs in a variety of communities throughout Israel.

Sofer Stam

ADDRESS: http://thesoferstam.com/

DESCRIPTION: Although this is a commercial site advertising the work of a scribe, there is information on *mezuzot, tefillin,* Torah scrolls, and *megillot,* as well as an "ask the *sofer*" section.

Stam On Line

ADDRESS: http://www.geocities.com/Heartland/4792/

DESCRIPTION: The home page of a *sofer,* describing the intricacies of producing *tefillin, mezuzot, sifrei* Torah, and *ketubot.*

PRAYER AND GLOSSARIES

Learners' Minyan

ADDRESS: http://members.aol.com/judaism/lm

DESCRIPTION: Created by Jordan Lee Wagner, this site is designed as "a friendly place to learn about Jewish synagogue ritual, the prayer book, and related traditions." It includes a transliterated *siddur*, a collection of brain teasers, questions and answers based on the author's book *The Synagogue Survival Kit*, and links to relevant Jewish sites.

Glossary of Jewish Terms

ADDRESS: http://philo.ucdavis.edu/~bruce/RST23/gloss.html

DESCRIPTION: Prepared initially by Robert A. Kraft of the University of Pennsylvania, this glossary is part of Bruce Rosenstock's syllabus for his course on Introduction to Judaism taught at the University of California at Davis. The glossary is alphabetical, includes cross-references, and indicates the origin of the word.

THE ORTHODOX MOVEMENT

Union of Orthodox Jewish Congregations

ADDRESS: http://www.ou.org

DESCRIPTION: Designed in a magazine style, this home page of the umbrella organization of American Orthodox synagogues provides access to the projects and services of the group. You can access information about Shabbat, Jewish holidays, and basic Jewish beliefs and retrieve a list of synagogues worldwide. The site also serves as a gateway to Yerushalayim.Net, a project designed to create the largest Torah server on the Internet, with dozens of e-mail lists, thousands of pages of text, and hundreds of hours of audio and video. Of particular note is the extensive *kashrut* section, featuring a kosher primer, the group's Passover directory, and a list of restaurants in Manhattan and Brooklyn certified kosher by the organization. The entire site is searchable, and there are numerous indices for browsing.

National Council of Young Israel

ADDRESS: http://www.youngisrael.org

DESCRIPTION: Coordinating 150 Orthodox congregations in the United States and Canada and 50 in Israel, this group provides information about its constituent synagogues and support services offered to them, including youth activities, rabbinic training and placement, a women's league, a speaker's bureau, and a number of publications and *divrei* Torah. The searchable site also has a *daf yomi* section and a listing of events.

THE CHASIDIC MOVEMENT

Chabad

ADDRESS: http://www.chabad.org

DESCRIPTION: This is the official host of the worldwide Chabad-Lubavitch Movement and, in keeping with the outreach philosophy of the group, is provided in several languages. Its searchable, magazine-style site offers a rich variety of material in the areas of *divrei* Torah, the Messiah, a children's section, the life and teachings of the Rebbe, Jewish women, holiday guides, Jewish teachings about non-Jews, science and religion, and the Hebrew alphabet. The site offers a bibliography, a glossary, a Hebrew/English calendar, and a list of the positive and negative commandments. An extensive list of sites created by Chabad communities worldwide is provided, offering access to items such as full-textbooks from the Lubavitch Library.

Breslov Chasidim

ADDRESS: http://www.breslov.org

DESCRIPTION: This page presents a thumbnail biography of Rebbe Nachman of Breslov; a thumbnail biography of Reb Noson, the recorder of the teachings of Rebbe Nachman; and a brief introduction to the Breslov Research Institute and the teachings of Rebbe Nachman.

Chabad Web Ring

ADDRESS: http://www.geocities.com/Colosseum/Loge/7744/

DESCRIPTION: Created by Moshe Raichman, this Web ring will help you locate sites that have some Chabad content.

Chassidism Reading List

ADDRESS: http://shamash.org/lists/scj-faq/HTML/rl/joc-index.html

DESCRIPTION: Part of the reading lists compiled by the newsgroup soc.culture.jewish, this list of books covers historical Chasidism and the approaches of Lubavitch, Satmar, Breslov, and other groups.

Haredim

ADDRESS: http://www.manof.org.il

DESCRIPTION: This Hebrew and English site, created by an Israeli public relations firm, seeks to answer "Nine Questions People Ask about *Haredim*." The more extensive Hebrew section of the site includes discussions of religion and science, a demographic profile of the community, the depiction of the community in the news, and a collection of relevant Jewish links and news items.

Hasidic Culture and Customs

ADDRESS: http://www.pinenet.com/~rooster/hasid1.html

DESCRIPTION: Written by Yonassan Gershom, this three-part FAQ covers the origins, customs, denominations, and beliefs of Hasidism.

Hasidic Stories

ADDRESS: http://www.hasidic.storypower.com/

DESCRIPTION: Created by Doug Lipman, this site gathers together hasidic stories and arranges them into major categories, including stories of the Baal Shem Tov, stories of the early Rebbes, and stories of our times. Articles about the stories are also available and detail the sources and background of the tales, the theories behind the art of storytelling, themes, teachings, and how to tell the stories. The Resources section offers a bibliography, discography, and a list of storytellers who perform hasidic stories. Readers are encouraged to contribute stories to the database.

Internet Guide to Chabad Literature

ADDRESS: http://www.kesser.org

DESCRIPTION: Created by Yechezkal-Shimon Gutfreund, this site provides an annotated list of Web resources divided into sections on multimedia, learning centers, hypertext library, and other Chabad sites.

Modzitz Chasidim

ADDRESS: http://www.modzitz.org

DESCRIPTION: This home page features a history of this hasidic dynasty best known for its music and is available in English and Hebrew. Along with sample music files, there are also a browsable directory of *divrei* Torah for Shabbat and holidays, a guest book, and links to relevant Jewish sites.

THE CONSERVATIVE MOVEMENT

United Synagogue for Conservative Judaism

ADDRESS: http://www.uscj.org

DESCRIPTION: The home page of this umbrella organization of Conservative synagogues describes the history of the group and provides access to its constituent congregations, Solomon Schechter day schools, USY youth programs, Koach college programs, and individual regions. You can read selected articles from Review magazine, browse the publications catalog, join several online listservs, and check out the Israel Center. A set of Conservative-related links is available, and the entire site is searchable.

Conservative Center in Israel

ADDRESS: http://www.uscj.org.il

DESCRIPTION: This home page for the Center for Conservative Judaism in Israel describes the group's programs and activities, such as Project Oded, youth activities, a new educational center, continuing education courses, university-age projects, the yeshiva, summer and one-year high school programs, synagogue tours, and bar/bat mitzvah services.

Conservative Judaism Reading List

ADDRESS: http://shamash.org/lists/scj-faq/HTML/rl/jcu-index.html

DESCRIPTION: Part of the reading list series compiled by the soc.culture.jewish newsgroup, this list of books covers Conservative beliefs, practices, history, and liturgy.

Masorti Movement

ADDRESS: http://www.masorti.org.il

DESCRIPTION: Describing the Conservative movement in Israel, this home page has sections about the group's new *siddur*, its views, *yemai iyun*, projects and institutions, such as Midershet and Noam; responsa literature; and congregations. In addition, it contains material on the holidays, news about the movement, and links to relevant Jewish sites.

Practical Halacha for Conservative Jews

ADDRESS: http://www.personnelselection.com/halacha.htm

DESCRIPTION: Created by Joel Wiesen, this site describes a booklet he developed outlining practical halachah from a Conservative viewpoint. The booklet can be downloaded for free and is in Adobe Acrobat format.

THE REFORM MOVEMENT

Reform Judaism

ADDRESS: http://www.rj.org

DESCRIPTION: Created by the United American Hebrew Congregations, the association of Reform synagogues in the United States, this site describes the teachings of the Reform movement and offers links to its member groups, its publications and policies, its study and education programs, and details about its services. There is a self-guided tour of Reform Web sites and an "ask the rabbi" section as well. Of particular note are the searchable indices and directories that offer access to divrei Torah, the archives of *Reform Judaism* magazine, the index of Reform responsa, and the UAHC Jewish Education curriculum bank and religious school job bank.

Bluethread

ADDRESS: http://www.exo.net/bluethread

DESCRIPTION: Designed by Rosemarie Falanga and Cy Silver, this site invites participants to explore Torah study in the light of the Reform movement. The home page includes *divrei* Torah, a glossary, a bibliography, a set of references for "the amateur Torah scholar," an overview of Reform beliefs, and a guide to choosing a *Chumash*.

Click on Judaism

ADDRESS: http://www.clickonjudaism.org

DESCRIPTION: "The purpose of click onJudaism is to provide doorways into Judaism for Jews in their 20s and 30s, as well as those considering Judaism." Its major sections cover Judaism in the modern world, social action, searching for God, searching for community, and Jewish practices. The search page also includes a browsable index of topics arranged by section.

Reclaiming Judaism as a Spiritual Practice

ADDRESS: http://www.rebgoldie.com

DESCRIPTION: Created by Rabbi Goldie Milgram of the Academy for Jewish Religion, this site provides an exploration of Shabbat, Torah, prayer, holidays, *klal Yisrael*, mitzvot, life-cycle events, and sacred language from a liberal viewpoint. There are also articles on mysticism, meditation, ritual, and social action, as well as stories, bibliographies, and a schedule of retreats and classes.

Reform Judaism in the UK

ADDRESS: http://www.refsyn.org.uk/

DESCRIPTION: This site describes the programs and institutions affiliated with the Reform movement in the U.K., as well as its publications and news articles about the group. There are searchable discussion forums, links to member synagogues, and a directory of relevant Jewish sites arranged in 17 categories.

Reform Judaism Reading List

ADDRESS: http://shamash.org/lists/scj-faq/HTML/rl/jlu-index.html

DESCRIPTION: Part of the reading lists compiled by the newsgroup soc.culture.jewish, this list of books covers Reform beliefs, rituals and practice, liturgy, responsa, and history, as well as the Reform rabbinate.

THE RECONSTRUCTIONIST MOVEMENT

Jewish Reconstructionist Federation

ADDRESS: http://www.jrf.org/

DESCRIPTION: The home page of the umbrella organization of Reconstructionist synagogues describes the beliefs of the group and provides access to news and events, *divrei* Torah, discussion groups, and educational programs sponsored by the organization. There is a directory of member congregations and a set of relevant links as well. Selected articles from *Reconstructionism Today* are also available.

Reconstructionist Reading List

ADDRESS: http://shamash.org/lists/scj-faq/HTML/rl/jrc-index.html

DESCRIPTION: Part of the reading lists compiled by the newsgroup soc.culture.jewish, this list of books covers the philosophy of the movement, Reconstructionist education, and liturgy.

THE MESSIAH

Moshiach Network

ADDRESS: http://www.moshiach.net/

DESCRIPTION: Weekly audio classes sponsored by Chabad, describing the group's view of the Messiah.

Moshiach Online

ADDRESS: http://www.moshiachonline.com

DESCRIPTION: A searchable site from Chabad that deals with the Messiah in Jewish tradition. The site is divided into six sections on everything you wanted to know about the Messiah, weekly *divrei* Torah, audio lectures, questions and answers, and a study center. There is also a link to the group's virtual tour of the Second Temple.

MYSTICISM AND KABBALAH

Colin's Kabbalah Links

ADDRESS: http://www.digital-brilliance.com/kab/link.htm

DESCRIPTION: This annotated set of links, created by Colin Law on Kabbalah, is divided into sections on hermetic Kabbalah and hermetica, Jewish Kabbalah and Judaism, the history of Kabbalah, mystical Kabbalah, general occult links, and miscellaneous topics. The site is an excellent starting point for material on the topic.

Kavannah: Jewish Spirituality Links

ADDRESS: http://kavannah.org/links.html

DESCRIPTION: Created by Michael Sidlofsky, this annotated set of Jewish spirituality links is divided into sections on Internet mailing lists, Web sites on Kabbalah, Hasidism, and Jewish Renewal; teachers; institutes and retreat centers; general Jewish resources; and resources for other spiritual paths. This is a well-organized site for beginning research in the area of Jewish spirituality.

Essential Kabbalah

ADDRESS: http://www.digiserve.com/mystic/Jewish/Matt

DESCRIPTION: This site is part of a larger section on mysticism created by Deb Platt. This section contains quotations from the book *The Essential Kabbalah,* an anthology of kabbalistic writings that have been translated and edited by Daniel C. Matt.

Kabbalah, Mysticism, and Messianism Reading List

ADDRESS: http://shamash.org/lists/scj-faq/HTML/rl/mys-index.html

DESCRIPTION: Part of the reading lists compiled by the newsgroup soc.culture.jewish, this is a list of books covering academic treatments of Kabbalah, religious treatments of Kabbalah, spirituality, the Messiah, and hasidic approaches to spirituality.

JEWISH OUTREACH

Conversion to Judaism

ADDRESS: http://www.convert.org

DESCRIPTION: Created originally by Dr. Lawrence J. Epstein, this site provides a variety of information of interest to potential converts, including topics about the beliefs of Judaism, the conversion process, social and psychological issues involved in conversion, a list of books and videos, and access to rabbis who are willing to help converts. This is an excellent starting point for those considering conversion.

Intermarriage and Conversion Reading List

ADDRESS: http://shamash.org/lists/scj-faq/HTML/rl/int-index.html

DESCRIPTION: Part of the reading lists compiled by the newsgroup soc.culture.jewish, this list of books covers topics in intermarriage and conversion from perspectives of before and after marriage.

Jewish America

ADDRESS: http://www.jewishamerica.com

DESCRIPTION: This traditional site provides links to comparable Web sites in the areas of Jewish history, Judaism and culture, forums, Torah and thought, and Jewish continuity. You can subscribe to an online newsletter and sign the guest book.

Jewish Outreach Institute

ADDRESS: http://www.joi.org

DESCRIPTION: One of the oldest outreach sites on the Web, this home page offers bulletin boards for discussions; a list of outreach programs; information about pertinent surveys, books, and publications; a bibliography; a section on holidays; and links to other relevant sites.

Jewish Professionals Institute

ADDRESS: http://www.jpi.org/

DESCRIPTION: Operating primarily in the New York metropolitan area, this group offers free lunch hour classes, public lectures, and workshops aimed at professional Jews who have never had the opportunity to study Jewish topics. The site outlines offerings in 20 different formats, including courses in Hebrew, Israel summer programs, telephone outreach, home hospitality, and a tape and book library.

Melitz

ADDRESS: http://www.melitz.org.il/

DESCRIPTION: Melitz is an Israeli-based organization offering informal education programs dedicated to Jewish unity, continuity, partnership, and a democratic Israel. Its home page describes the organization, its monthly activities, programs, and resources and offers a chat room.

National Jewish Outreach Program

ADDRESS: http://www.njop.org/

DESCRIPTION: Founded by Rabbi Ephraim Buchwald, this group "reaches out to unaffiliated Jews by offering them positive, joyous, Jewish educational opportunities and experiences." Its home page describes its programs for Shabbat and learning Hebrew, offers an online bookstore with materials selected by the staff that can be purchased through Barnes and Noble, and provides a set of links to other Jewish sites.

Outreach Judaism

ADDRESS: http://www.outreachjudaism.org/

DESCRIPTION: The goal of this group is to respond to issues raised by missionaries and cults by exploring Judaism in contradistinction to Christianity. The site provides answers to frequently posed challenges made by missionaries to Jews and offers a number of videos for sale. You can also send a question to Rabbi Tovia Singer, the owner of the site.

THE K-12 SCHOOL COMMUNITY

K-12 ORGANIZATIONS

JESNA: Jewish Education Service of North America

ADDRESS: http://www.jesna.org

DESCRIPTION: This home page describes the activities, services, and events sponsored by this umbrella group of Jewish educational organizations. There are sections devoted to Canadian materials and to those working with special needs students. Access to the organization's publications in full text or abstracts is also provided. Of particular note are the databanks of resources for community center programs and for both formal and informal educational settings. The entire site is searchable. This is an excellent starting point for educational program ideas at any age level.

Snunit Educational Information System

ADDRESS: http://www.snunit.k12.il

DESCRIPTION: Created by the Israeli Ministry of Education, this searchable site, mostly in Hebrew, offers a portal to a vast array of educational material arranged in a Yahoo-style format. Its categories include news, enrichment activities, journals in full text, virtual museums, educational utilities, and access to other educational servers. The site also hosts a teacher's room and chat rooms and offers lists of recommended sites. The portal acts as a gateway to the special projects hosted by Snunit, including Galim for elementary school students, Shireshet devoted to Israeli and Hebrew poets, and Navat, which catalogs high-quality educational sites in English and Hebrew. In the English section of the site, a set of links to educational material in English, as well as resources for finding keypals and a bulletin board, are available. For those who read Hebrew, this is an outstanding resource for all areas of education.

Agency for Jewish Education

ADDRESS: http://www.brijnet.org/aje

DESCRIPTION: Part of the United Synagogue Council of Great Britain, the agency provides services in the areas of teacher training, curriculum design, family education, resource production, school development, statutory and voluntary inspections, and informal education, all of which are described here. The site has an online catalog of publications arranged by subject and information about the agency's resource center as well.

Agency for Jewish Education of Metropolitan Detroit

ADDRESS: http://www.ajedetroit.org

DESCRIPTION: This home page describes the services of the agency in the areas of adult learning, interfaith programs, family activities, programs for teens and for special education, as well as programs for schools. The agency is also starting an online curriculum bank. Of particular note is the Michigan Jewish Online Education area, with study materials, a teacher's guide, discussion area, and description of ritual objects aimed at bar/bat mitzvah students.

Amal Net

ADDRESS: http://www.amalnet.k12.il

DESCRIPTION: "Amal 1 is a network of educational institutions, engaged in the advancement of comprehensive and technological education for youth and adults." Its Hebrew and English home page describes its educational programs and its locations. Of particular note are its links to educational material about computers, Israel, education, society, technology, economics, humanities, sciences, language and literature, and health.

Associated Talmud Torahs

ADDRESS: http://www.att.org/

DESCRIPTION: Supervising more than 30 regional yeshivot in the greater Chicago area, this group offers continuing education courses for teachers, programs for special needs children, summer programs for students, and a *kollel*, all of which are described here. Of particular note are the Jewish educational software reviews that are provided in a browsable, alphabetical listing, as well as by subject and vendor.

Board of Jewish Education in Washington, D.C.

ADDRESS: http://www.bjedc.org

DESCRIPTION: This home page describes services offered by the board for schools and in the area of Jewish family life. It also describes the library and teacher center, as well as the publications and volunteer opportunities the board offers. The entire site is searchable.

Board of Jewish Education of Chicago

ADDRESS: http://www.bjechicago.org

DESCRIPTION: Divided into sections for early childhood, community connections, a learning center, and an area for teachers, this home page also describes the history, events, and offerings of this central educational organization in Chicago. Of particular note is the lesson library, searchable by subject and grade level.

Board of Jewish Education of Greater New York

ADDRESS: http://www.bjeny.org

DESCRIPTION: This searchable home page describes the organization and services of the board and provides access to its calendar of events and classes. You can use the online order form to purchase the center's publications, which are described in detail. Of particular note are the holiday lesson plans and curricula in Adobe Acrobat format that may be downloaded. Also of note is the set of links to Jewish and educational sites, including a private school locator.

Board of Jewish Education of San Francisco

ADDRESS: http://www.bjesf.org

DESCRIPTION: This searchable home page offers information about community-wide events and the community library, as well as programs for schools, students with special needs, family education, Israel study, and financial aid opportunities. Of particular note is the Battat Resource Center, providing online lessons, a catalog of print and audio-visual materials, and links to Jewish educational resources on the Internet.

Bureau of Jewish Education of Greater Los Angeles

ADDRESS: http://www.bjela.org

DESCRIPTION: This home page provides information about the educational services, youth programs, events, and committees of this umbrella organization for formal and informal Jewish education, along with a staff directory and database of schools searchable by type, ideology, region, and zip code.

CAJE: Coalition for the Advancement of Jewish Education

ADDRESS: http://www.caje.org

DESCRIPTION: This home page of the largest Jewish educators' organization in North America provides information on the group's events and access to a number of online newsletters. Of particular note are the curriculum bank that allows members to download curricula from a searchable database and a job bank posted for everyone.

Center for Jewish Education of Greater Baltimore

ADDRESS: http://www.cjebaltimore.org

DESCRIPTION: This home page has sections for parents, teachers, students, and principals and offers access to information about the programs, events, and resources of the center. Through the Resources section you can find a directory of affiliated schools.

Centre for Jewish Education in Great Britain

ADDRESS: http://www.knowledge.co.uk/cje/

DESCRIPTION: "The Centre for Jewish Education provides educational services for the Reform Synagogues of Great Britain, the Union of Liberal and Progressive Synagogues and the Leo Baeck College." The home page offers information on events, publications, courses, resources, news, and a directory of member groups. There are also links to related sites.

Jewish Education Council of Montreal

ADDRESS: http://www.total.net/~jecerc/about.html

DESCRIPTION: This site describes the services offered by the council for system-wide planning, day schools, supplementary schools, day-care centers, and adult and family education. There is information on professional development, the resource center and library, audio visual services, curriculum development, Yiddish committee, and the council's publications as well.

Lookstein Centre for Education

ADDRESS: http://www.biu.ac.il/JH/lookstein/index.html

DESCRIPTION: Housed at Bar Ilan University in Israel, this center describes itself as "a virtual resource center for Jewish education." Its home page offers announcements and a description of the center's programs and access to an interactive educator's forum with searchable archives. Of particular note is the resource library, that provides online access to materials by author, subject, level, and language.

Melton Centre for Jewish Education in the Diaspora

ADDRESS: http://sites.huji.ac.il/melton/

DESCRIPTION: This home page is divided into five sections—senior educators, an adult mini-school, the educator training institute, the pedagogic center and library, and senior educators from the former Soviet Union—and describes the offerings of the center in each area. Of particular note are the center's online catalog, that can be searched, as well as the listings of materials for teachers, librarians, academics, and researchers.

National Association of Temple Educators

ADDRESS: http://www.rj.org/nate/

DESCRIPTION: This home page describes the services to congregations and members offered by this group promoting Jewish education in the Reform community. The site hosts an e-mail newsletter to which you can subscribe as well.

Pirchei Shoshanim

ADDRESS: http://www.pirchei.co.il

DESCRIPTION: "The Pirchei Shoshanim societies were children's groups founded sometime in the late 1700s or early 1800s in Eastern Europe. Upon enrollment in the Pirchei Shoshanim, the parents would donate charity for the purchase of Jewish books in honor of the newborn 'Pirchei' as the child was referred to. The child's name was put inside the front cover of the book." This educational site from Lakewood, New Jersey, is devoted to the teaching of "*midos tovos, yiras shamayim,* and *ahavas hatorah.*" It has sections on learning programs, issues in Torah education, special education, the Chinuch Atzmi educational system, pen pals, computers, and a rebbe's corner with articles on the art of teaching. Of particular note are the pictorial series sections, offering full-text versions of eight of the group's print publications, including Pirkei Avot, Bircat HaMazon, and Shmirat HaLashon, among others.

K–12 INSTRUCTIONAL MATERIALS

Akhlah

ADDRESS: http://www.akhlah.com

DESCRIPTION: Subtitled "The Jewish Children's Network," this traditional site has sections on the weekly *parsha,* Israel, the alphabet, a Hebrew phrase of the day, Torah heroes, Jewish holidays, and coloring pages.

Arachim

ADDRESS: http://www.arachim.ac.il/

DESCRIPTION: Created by Dr. Yehudah Eisenberg of Michlala, this searchable Hebrew-language site provides several hundred pages of instructional material in 25 subject areas, including Bible, Israel, the Holocaust, prayer, holidays, Jewish philosophy, and Talmud. An alphabetical listing of resources is also provided. This is a huge repository of material that should be very helpful to anyone teaching Jewish studies.

Jewish Student Online Research Center

ADDRESS: http://www.us-israel.org/jsource/

DESCRIPTION: This project of the American-Israel Cooperative Enterprise provides encyclopedia-like articles on Jewish topics arranged in more than 35 subject areas. Articles are succinct and authoritative and often include bibliographies. There are also links to sections describing the economic relationship between Israel and various U.S. states and links to the full text of the agency's publications, as well as a Virtual Israel Experience tour. This is a well-designed, comprehensive site that serves as an online Jewish encyclopedia. It should be a first stop for students researching any Jewish topic.

Navat Educational Library from Snunit

ADDRESS: http://navat.snunit.k12.il/

DESCRIPTION: Designed by the Israeli Ministry of Education, Navat is a searchable, annotated directory of educational Web sites arranged in a Yahoo-style format. Of particular interest to the Jewish educator is the section on Israel and Jewish studies. Sites are rated according to grade level, suitability for instructional use, and form. If you read Hebrew, this is an excellent starting point for locating instructional Jewish sites.

Nurit Reshef

ADDRESS: http://www.ualberta.ca/~yreshef/nuritmenu.htm

DESCRIPTION: Nurit Reshef, the Curriculum Coordinator for the Talmud Torah School of Edmonton, Canada, provides an extensive collection of Jewish educational programs she has created. Her menu includes games and activities for Shabbat, the holidays, Zionism, Hebrew, Israel, and Bible study. Mrs. Reshef makes very creative use of the Web as a Jewish educational tool. Her site should be visited by anyone involved in Jewish education.

IdeaNet

ADDRESS: http://www.jewishyouth.com

DESCRIPTION: "Published, edited, and moderated by Avi Frier, IdeaNet is the e-mail service that enables you to network and share ideas with fellow Jewish Youth Professionals worldwide." Back issues are available in browsable format. In addition, there is a compendium of contributed ideas arranged by topic that can be purchased. A job bank for those seeking employment or employees and an extensive set of Jewish links are also provided.

Jewish Activities for Parents and Children

ADDRESS: http://www.JewishHome.com

DESCRIPTION: Part of the Jewish Family and Life magazine series, this online periodical has feature articles of interest to parents and children. Included are columns on arts and crafts, education, books, food, reflections, discussions, gardening, health, and holidays. A bibliography is also available.

Jewish Learning Group

ADDRESS: http://www.jewishlearninggroup.com/

DESCRIPTION: This online catalog features educational materials for home and school created by Chabad. Materials may be ordered online.

Learning Plant

ADDRESS: http://www.learningplant.com

DESCRIPTION: Searchable, online catalog of instructional materials for use in Jewish schools. Orders may be placed online.

Torah Tots

ADDRESS: http://www.torahtots.com

DESCRIPTION: Aimed at younger children, this site offers material on the weekly Torah reading and holidays, along with music clips, a guest book, and a gift shop.

ZigZag

ADDRESS: http://www.zigzagworld.com/

DESCRIPTION: This company produces a number of computerized instructional games for teaching Hebrew and Jewish topics. Many of its Java-based demo pages can be used for classroom instruction.

K-12 DISCUSSION GROUPS

Jewish Home Educator's Network

ADDRESS: http://snj.com/jhen

DESCRIPTION: This site is home to a quarterly newsletter about Jewish home schooling. It includes an FAQ on the topic and some links to other home schooling sites.

KASHRUT AND FOOD

Kosher Info

ADDRESS: http://www.kosherinfo.com/

DESCRIPTION: A service of Kashrus Magazine, this site provides information for the kosher consumer and the kosher trade. Included are articles from the magazine, pages by the various *kashrus* agencies listing their certified products and establishments, and opportunities to browse and purchase kosher books, tapes, guides and magazines. Kosher travel and dining information are planned. You can sign up for an e-mail newsletter as well.

KosherQuest

ADDRESS: http://www.kosherquest.org/

DESCRIPTION: Created by the Kosher Information Bureau and supervised by Rabbi Eliezer Eidlitz, this home page provides access to a database of certified foods; the table of contents of the group's magazine, Kosher Conscience; Passover information; recipes; updates and alerts; tourist information; general *kashrut* articles; and a directory of *kashrut* symbols.

All Kosher Index

ADDRESS: http://www.kosher.co.il

DESCRIPTION: Created by the United Kashrut Authority in Israel, this searchable site is available in English, Hebrew, French, and German. It features a worldwide database of kosher restaurants, companies, and factories, indexing 10,000 manufacturers and over 100,000 products. You can also read the group's magazine, The Kosher Times, and Archey Kashrut, an industry journal edited by Rabbi Akiva Katz. Searchable databases of *mikvaot* and *kashrut* authorities worldwide are also available.

LAWS OF KASHRUT

How Do I Know It's Kosher?

ADDRESS: http://www.ou.org/kosher/primer.html

DESCRIPTION: Created by the Union of Orthodox Jewish Congregations, one of the largest certifiers of kosher food in the United States, this page offers a detailed explanation of many of the laws surrounding kosher food.

Kosher Dietary Laws

ADDRESS: http://www.jewfaq.org/kashrut.htm

DESCRIPTION: This hypertext article, aimed at intermediate learners, describes many aspects of the laws relating to kosher food, including why *kashrut* is observed, laws relating to kosher meat, utensils, grape products, and *kashrut* certification.

KASHRUT SUPERVISION

All-Kosher Index

ADDRESS: http://www.kosher.co.il/

DESCRIPTION: Maintained by the United Kashrut Authority in Israel, this home page describes itself as "the largest database available, indexing nearly 10,000 manufacturers and over 100,000 products." The site, which is searchable in Hebrew, English, German, and French, provides directories of restaurants, *mikvaot*, and *kashrut* authorities worldwide. Access to the group's Hebrew-language magazine, The Kosher Times, is also provided. This is a large database whose worldwide perspective and resource list make it a valuable starting point for kashrut research.

American Asian Kashrus Services

ADDRESS: http://www.kashrus.org/

DESCRIPTION: Operating under the auspices of the London Beth Din and the Court of the Chief Rabbi, this is the home page of a firm specializing in providing kosher supervision of manufacturing facilities throughout Asia and America. The Kosher Living section provides an excellent introduction to questions about *kashrut* and links to other relevant *kashrut* sites. Of particular note are the sections on living kosher in Asia, Asian Jewish information, and kosher Asian food. The first and second of these offers extensive details for travelers to Asia who keep kosher. The section on kosher Asian food features recipes arranged by geographic area. This is a comprehensive site whose focus on Asia is of particular note.

OU Kashrut Department

ADDRESS: http://www.ou.org/kosher/

DESCRIPTION: Divided into sections for the commercial world and the consumer, this home page of the Union of Orthodox Jewish Congregations, the largest *kashrut* authority in the United States, has sections on newly certified products, *kashrut* alerts, a kosher question and answer section, and a *daf hakashrut* newsletter aimed at those who certify foods as kosher. You can receive e-mail updates, ask a rabbi a *kashrut* question, and look at the Manhattan and Brooklyn restaurant directory. Of particular note is the kosher primer, designed to help people understand the laws of *kashrut*, as well as the Kosher for Passover food directory.

Kashrut Division of the London Beth Din

ADDRESS: http://www.kosher.org.uk/

DESCRIPTION: This is the home page of the largest European *kashrut* certifier. It offers a list of bakeries, caterers, delis, fish shops, food manufacturers, hotels, and restaurants that it oversees, as well as details on purchasing the agency's book entitled *The Really Jewish Food Guide*. You can join an e-mail list for updates as well.

Kof-K Kosher Supervision

ADDRESS: http://www.kof-k.com

DESCRIPTION: The home page of this *kashrut* certifier based in Teaneck, New Jersey, provides a browsable list of its products, a hypertext list of the companies it serves, articles on *kashrut* and the kosher food industry, alerts, recipes, a list of restaurants the group certifies arranged by type of restaurant, and a list of restaurants in New York City that are kosher for Passover.

Koshernews

ADDRESS: http://www.koshernews.com

DESCRIPTION: Produced by Rabbi Yaakov Spivak of United Kosher Supervision in Monsey, New York, this home page has sections on industry news, kosher alert updates, recipes, and new products. Of particular note is the section on halachah that describes many of the intricacies of kosher laws.

OK Kashrus

ADDRESS: http://www.ok.org/

DESCRIPTION: This searchable site is the home page of the Organized Kashrus Laboratories of Brooklyn. The site features a kosher food guide divided into sections for the commercial user and the consumer, *kashrut* alerts, and new certifications, as well as a guide for Passover. Access is provided to the full text of the group's magazine, *The Jewish Homemaker,* and archives dating back to 1996 are available.

Star K Kosher Supervision

ADDRESS: http://www.star-k.org

DESCRIPTION: The home page of this *kashrut* certifier, based in Baltimore, provides news and alerts and product, restaurant, and company lists through an alphabetical subject directory. Its Passover section features articles on the holiday and a product directory arranged by food type. Of particular note are the FAQ about *kashrut* questions and the section on KitchenAid Sabbath mode appliances.

KASHRUT FOOD SUPPLIERS

Empire Kosher Meats

ADDRESS: http://www.empirekosher.com/ and http://www.empirenational.com

DESCRIPTION: Arranged in a magazine-style format, this page describes what makes a chicken kosher, provides a virtual tour of an Empire plant, and gives a listing by state of distributors. Of particular note are the recipes arranged alphabetically, with indications of those appropriate for Passover.

Kashrut.Com

ADDRESS: http://www.kashrut.com/

DESCRIPTION: Developed and maintained by Arlene J. Mathes-Scharf, this site describes itself as "The Premier Kosher Information Source on the Internet." Its goal is to provide up-to-date information on kosher products and the kosher food industry. The site has sections on Passover, consumer issues, commercial issues, travel, feature articles, recipes, and *kashrut* alerts. You can sign up for an e-mail list as well.

Kosher Bison

ADDRESS: http://www.kosherbison.com

DESCRIPTION: Learn how to buy and cook bison from this home page. Purchases can be made online by individuals or institutions, and recipes are provided.

Kosher Channel One

ADDRESS: http://www.kosherchannel1.com/ and http://www.kosherfest.com/

DESCRIPTION: This site, aimed at the kosher food industry, provides trade information about exhibits mounted by Integrated Marketing Communications, the sponsor of Kosherfest and the Kosher Food Ingredient Show. The home page offers news updates, a list of exhibitors, and access to the Kosher Today newsletter and its archives. Of particular note is the searchable database of products and manufacturers, the history of *kashrut* in the United States, and a browsable directory of USDA International Food Reports, arranged by country of origin. If you work in the kosher industry, this is an excellent portal.

Kosher Cheese

ADDRESS: http://www.koshercheese.com/

DESCRIPTION: In addition to the free coupons offered here, this site provides access to pictures of the products of two major cheese producers, Miller and HaOlam.

Kosher Club

ADDRESS: http://www.kosherclub.com

DESCRIPTION: This online kosher supermarket, based in California, offers items for sale under RCC supervision in the categories of meat and poultry, dairy and fish, groceries, baked goods, organic food, wine, and sugar and lactose-free foods. Items ordered are shipped Federal Express. There is an "ask the rabbi" section.

Kosher Finder

ADDRESS: http://www.kosherfinder.com

DESCRIPTION: This searchable magazine-style page features two databases, one for restaurants worldwide and the other for kosher food. In addition, the site hosts many articles of a general Jewish nature. You can read bulletin boards and sign up for a newsletter as well.

Kosher for Passover

ADDRESS: http://www.kosher4passover.com

DESCRIPTION: Arranged in a Yahoo-style directory format, this site provides links to online resources in the areas of shopping, recipes, *Haggadot*, vacations, study sites, selling *chametz*, kashering your home, kids' activities, greeting cards, guides, clip art, songs, explanations, humor, and counting the *omer*. This is a well-organized and comprehensive site for researching the holiday.

Kosher Grocer

ADDRESS: http://www.koshergrocer.com/ and http://www.koshermall.com

DESCRIPTION: Shop online for kosher food and have it delivered to your house with this service that offers items in the categories of groceries, deli, meat, baked goods, vitamins, sweets, venison, wines and spirits, pizza, prepared meals, gift baskets, holiday items, specialty items, cards and art, and services. The certifying *kashrut* authority for each item is indicated. You can personalize a shopping cart for yourself so you can automatically log on the next time you return. The entire site of this Lakewood, New Jersey–based operation is searchable as well.

Kosher Nosh Homepage

ADDRESS: http://www.koshernosh.com/

DESCRIPTION: Specializing in deli, smoked fish, and appetizing selections, this is the home page of an actual store in Bergen County, New Jersey, under the supervision of Rabbi Isaiah Hertzberg, that will ship requested items overnight by Federal Express. The searchable site offers coupons, catering information, links to Jewish sites, and an extensive Yiddish dictionary. There is also an e-mail list you can subscribe to.

Kosher Supermarket

ADDRESS: http://www.koshersupermarket.com

DESCRIPTION: Shop online at the world's largest kosher supermarket and in many cases get same day delivery. You can choose from over 4,000 products, including groceries, dairy products, candy, baked goods, fish, frozen foods, meat, poultry, deli, gift items, and Passover and holiday foods. The site is searchable and browsable by category.

Kosher Vitamins

ADDRESS: http://www.koshervitamins.com and http://koshervitaminshoppe.com

DESCRIPTION: An online store that allows you to purchase kosher vitamins. This searchable site allows you to browse by category or brand and sells vitamins, herbal supplements, personal care items, herbal teas and throat drops, books, and juicers. There is also an encyclopedia of vitamins, describing their nutritional benefit, and a question and answer section on nutrition.

Kosher Zone

ADDRESS: http://www.kosherzone.com/

DESCRIPTION: This site provides information of interest to travelers in the United States through a clickable map, resulting in a list by geographic area of *kashrut* facilities. There are also sections on inspirational and hasidic tales, Shabbat and holidays, recipes, and links to the Jewish "link of the week."

Kosherline

ADDRESS: http://www.kosherline.com

DESCRIPTION: This Chabad-sponsored site provides a searchable directory of kosher restaurants throughout the United States. You can search by geographic area; milk, meat, or vegetarian food; price range; and cuisine style.

Manischewitz Foods

ADDRESS: http://www.manischewitz.com/

DESCRIPTION: This site traces the history of this kosher food company; lists its products and new items; provides a holiday calendar, greeting cards, and recipes; and allows you to locate a distributor near you. You can search for items for a specific diet and check the FAQ for *kashrut* and company questions.

Rokeach Food Distributors

ADDRESS: http://www.rokeach.com/

DESCRIPTION: This site traces the history of this kosher food company, lists its products and new items, provides access to customer service, and allows you to shop online or locate a distributor near you.

KOSHER RECIPES

Jewish-Food Recipe Archives

ADDRESS: http://www.chebucto.ns.ca/~ab522/jewishfood.html

DESCRIPTION: This site offers over 300 links to recipes and information about Jewish cooking arranged into categories, including appetizers, side dishes, Jewish specialties, main courses, desserts, dairy recipes, foreign dishes, holiday specialties, and Passover foods. The entire site is searchable by recipe, ingredient, or submitter. This is a rich database for researching Jewish recipes.

Mimi's Cyber Kitchen

ADDRESS: http://www.cyber-kitchen.com/index/html/gp21.html

DESCRIPTION: Created by Mimi Hiller, this page provides an alphabetical, annotated, and rated list of kosher and Jewish food recipes online. This is an excellent starting point for exploring resources related to kosher food.

Rec.food.cuisine.jewish Archives

ADDRESS: http://www.cyber-kitchen.com/rfcj

DESCRIPTION: Taken from the newsgroup devoted to Jewish cooking, this keyword searchable collection of recipes is divided into 36 categories and includes a *kashrut* FAQ and a bibliography of 200 cookbooks. This is an excellent site for finding recipes and cookbooks.

Epicurious

ADDRESS: http://www.epicurious.com/e_eating/e06_jewish_cooking/main.html

DESCRIPTION: This site features more than 100 recipes for Rosh Hashanah, Yom Kippur, Chanukah, Passover, and Purim, along with recipes for classic Jewish dishes. It also offers access to recipes from the book *The Jewish Holiday Kitchen,* written by Joan Nathan, along with reviews of other Jewish cookbooks and sections on wine and beer. Be aware that the larger Epicurious site has recipes that are not kosher.

Jewish Cookbook Site

ADDRESS: http://www.xs4all.nl/~uris/

DESCRIPTION: Created by Jody Sluijter, this home page describes the largest private collection of Jewish cookbooks in the world, currently numbering more than 550. There is a browsable, alphabetical listing by title, as well as a list of relevant Jewish links. The site is available in English and Dutch.

Jewish Cuisine

ADDRESS: http://jewishcuisine.com

DESCRIPTION: Created by Gloria Kaunfer Greene, this home page features material from her book *The New Jewish Holiday Cookbook*. Sections include recipes, household hints, cooking tips, and holiday information, as well as reviews of the book and information about the author. There are links to relevant Jewish and cooking sites as well.

Kosher Express

ADDRESS: http://www.koshercooking.com/

DESCRIPTION: This site hosts recipes that have been submitted to it in the categories of holiday food and everyday food. The holiday sections for Passover, the High Holidays, and Chanukah include links to relevant sites. The everyday section is divided into breakfast, assorted dishes, meat and poultry, and desserts. There are also sample recipes from the authors of five kosher cookbooks, several feature articles on kosher cooking, and links to relevant Jewish and *kashrut* sites.

KOSHER RESTAURANTS

Kosher Delight

ADDRESS: http://www.kosherdelight.com/restaurants.htm

DESCRIPTION: This worldwide kosher database provides browsable access to restaurants, arranged by state and by country. The list has contact and basic information about each restaurant. Its scope makes it a good beginning site for finding kosher restaurants throughout the world.

Kosher Restaurant Database from Shamash

ADDRESS: http://shamash.org/kosher/krestquery.html

DESCRIPTION: This is the oldest and most extensive kosher restaurant database on the Internet. You can search by name, geographic area, and type of restaurant. Search results include notes submitted by database users, rabbinical supervision, price range, as well as standard contact information. This is the number one portal for worldwide kosher restaurant information.

Culinaris

ADDRESS: http://www.culinaris.co.il/

DESCRIPTION: Arranged by geographic region and city, this database provides a listing of restaurants throughout Israel, arranged by food type. The listing consists of the name of the restaurant and its telephone number, and there is no indication of the *kashrut* of the establishment.

Dining Kosher in New York City

ADDRESS: http://www.diningkosher.com/

DESCRIPTION: This page serves as a complement to the print volume *The Authoritative New York City Kosher Dining Guide* by Bela Flom. In addition to updates about restaurants, the site offers in-depth reviews, articles about kosher dining, a "restaurant of the month" section, and access to an online kosher bookstore and a bulletin board discussion group.

Dinner Site Israel

ADDRESS: http://www.dinnersite.co.il/israel.htm

DESCRIPTION: This is the largest collection of restaurant home pages for restaurants in Israel. Arrangement is by city and region of the country. You can then search by type of food and also specify its *kashrut*. Information provided includes price range, take-out services, basic contact information, and sometimes menus and photos. This is a good database to search when looking for an Israeli kosher restaurant.

Israeli Kosher Restaurants

ADDRESS: http://www.eluna.com

DESCRIPTION: Describing itself as the "best resource on kosher restaurants in Israel," this site provides a listing of restaurants by city. Information about the restaurants has been provided by the establishments themselves, many of who offer discount coupons to users of eLuna. Diners also have the opportunity to comment and write reviews on a restaurant. You can sort the resulting search list by food type and neighborhood and also choose only *glatt* or *mehadrin* restaurants. There is a good selection of annotated, relevant Jewish food sites, as well as sections on kosher travel and wine. This is an excellent site for researching kosher restaurants in Israel.

Israeli Restaurant Guide

ADDRESS: http://www.rest.co.il/

DESCRIPTION: This searchable database of Israeli restaurants is available in English and Hebrew and allows you to search by type of food and geographic region. You can also specify kosher restaurants and restaurants that deliver.

Kosher Link

ADDRESS: http://www.kosherlink.com/

DESCRIPTION: This site, which offers free Web hosting for New York City restaurants, provides a database searchable by type of food and neighborhood in New York City and Long Island. You can also view the restaurant's menu. As of this writing, there are 200 restaurants in the database. You can also view the list by alphabetical order.

Kosher Restaurants

ADDRESS: http://www.mazornet.com/jewishcl/kosherfd.htm

DESCRIPTION: Arranged by state and city, this is an alphabetical listing of restaurants that provides the name of the establishment and its telephone number. This is part of the Jewish Celebrations home page.

U.S.A. Kosher

ADDRESS: http://www.kosherzone.com/usakoshr/

DESCRIPTION: "This is much more than a list—it is the home pages of kosher restaurateurs and storeowners who want your business and are willing to offer you a complete look at their cuisines, menus, and merchandise. You will get the complete picture, including, in many instances, a map by which to find their establishments. Even their *mashgiach*'s name and phone number are readily available. Just point at your destination on the map."

KOSHER WINE

Kosher Wines on the Internet

ADDRESS: http://www.kosherwine.com/

DESCRIPTION: This online wine merchant, a division of Hungarian Kosher Foods in Skokie, Illinois, provides the largest kosher wine site on the Internet, with a database searchable by color, varietal, price, region, producer, and *mevushal*. You can also search by keyword and place an online order by the bottle or the case. There are links to the home pages of some kosher wine producers as well.

Abarbanel Wines

ADDRESS: http://www.kosher-wine.com

DESCRIPTION: This home page describes the history of this French company and of kosher wine and offers a browsable listing of products and retailers. News about the company, its awards, and *kashrut* certification is also available.

Carmel Wines

ADDRESS: http://www.carmelwines.co.il/

DESCRIPTION: This home page in English and Hebrew details the history, awards, products, *kashrut*, and news about the Carmel Mizrachi wines of Israel. Information on tours of the plant is also available.

Gan Eden Wines

ADDRESS: http://www.ganeden.com

DESCRIPTION: The home page of this California wine company offers a browsable listing of its products, along with a price list, reviews, awards list, and information about the winemaker, Craig Winchell. As of this writing, orders can be placed over the telephone or by e-mail, but online ordering is projected for the future.

Hagafen

ADDRESS: http://www.hagafen.com

DESCRIPTION: Based in California, this wine company's home page offers a newsletter, a list of products and awards, recipes, and online ordering.

Royal Kedem Wines

ADDRESS: http://kedemwines.com/

DESCRIPTION: The home page of this winery, operated in the United States by Baron Herzog, details the history of the company, describes what makes wine kosher, offers recipes, and provides access to a wine newsletter and its archives. You can search the database for wine by color and taste and also locate a local retailer by state. Wines may be ordered online as well.

Schapiro Wine Cellars

ADDRESS: http://www.schapiro-wine.com/

DESCRIPTION: This site allows online purchase of wines created by this New York City-based winery. Its inventory is searchable and browsable. There is a history of the company and the winery, as well as information on tours. The links section includes a walking tour of the Lower East Side of New York, a glossary of Hebrew and Yiddish terms, and Passover recipes.

LIBRARIES AND LIBRARIANS

BiblioMaven

ADDRESS: http://www.bibliomaven.com

DESCRIPTION: Created by Ethan Starr, this site is designed "to serve as a one-stop reference to the Web pages of research-level Judaica collections in libraries and archives." It is arranged by geographic region and covers the entire world. An excellent starting point.

Jewish Libraries

ADDRESS: http://www.angelfire.com/on2/smbergson/jlibraries.htm

DESCRIPTION: Librarian Steven M. Bergson has compiled this list of Judaica library Web sites worldwide. This is an excellent starting point for locating home pages of Jewish libraries anywhere.

Albert and Temmy Latner Jewish Public Library of Toronto

ADDRESS: http://webhome.idirect.com/~alephtav/index.htm

DESCRIPTION: Located in Toronto, the home page of this public library provides information about the collection, its history, and its staff. Other links lead you to a partial Canadian-Jewish e-mail directory; a list of Jewish books, newsgroups, and periodicals on the Internet; ready reference sites; some Canadian-Jewish sites; samples from the library's postcard collection; and a list of the latest acquisitions. Steven Bergson, the librarian who designed the page, has created a virtual Jewish library, staffed by a reference librarian with whom you can interact using a telnet connection or through a MOO.

American Jewish Archives

ADDRESS: http://huc.edu/aja/

DESCRIPTION: Located in Cincinnati, this archive "is committed to preserving a documentary heritage of the religious, organizational, economic, cultural, personal, social and family life of American Jewry." The Web site describes the holdings of the archive and provides a full-text inventory by subject and alphabetically. Cataloging for these materials is provided through RLIN, and the site includes a link to the search form. Full-text articles from the AJA Journal are also available, along with a newsletter, a description of the fellowship program, and links to relevant sites in American Jewish history. The entire site is searchable. Of particular note is the full text booklet entitled *Creating the Synagogue Archive.*

Bibliography of Guides and Directories in Israel

ADDRESS: http://iew3.technion.ac.il:8080/~kutten/aron5.shtml#g2

DESCRIPTION: Written by Aharon Kutten, this title is a print publication, currently in its fourth edition. The home page offers an alphabetical list of guides, a subject index, and similar arrangements for the supplement.

Bloom Southwest Jewish Archives

ADDRESS: http://dizzy.library.arizona.edu/images/swja/swjalist.html

DESCRIPTION: The home page for these archives, located at the University of Arizona, describes resources related to Southwest Jewish history and Crypto-Judaic studies. The site presents educational exhibits on area synagogues and Jews as pioneers. Between 1992 and 1995, the Archives distributed a quarterly newsletter, *Southwest Jewish History,* whose articles are available for you to read. References to the sources used in descriptive sections, a suggested readings list, and a page with links to selected Web sites are also available. Consult the Finding Aids for guides to where materials are housed within Special Collections.

Books for Jewish Children

ADDRESS: http://www.geocities.com/CollegePark/6174/jewish-children.htm

DESCRIPTION: This searchable list of books for children was compiled by Lori Sheiman, with an eye to providing "books that help children develop pride in being Jewish and learn about our history, customs, and what makes Judaism 'special.'" Categories covered include Bible Stories, Folk Tales, Introductory Hebrew, History and Historical Fiction, Jewish Life, Life Cycle, Holidays, Shabbat, Bar/Bat Mitzvah books (Fiction and Nonfiction), and General Fiction, Historical Fiction, the Holocaust, and Nonfiction for intermediate and teenage readers. The site is linked to Amazon.com.

Canadian Jewish Congress Archives

ADDRESS: http://www.cjc.ca/archives.htm

DESCRIPTION: This site from Montreal, in English and French, describes the work of the Congress and its history. There are links to each region's home pages and press releases. There is a link to the Ontario Jewish Archives with a description of its collections and contact information. Most of the site describes the archival holdings in the areas of genealogy, art, personal papers, organizational papers, and material chronicling the history of Canadian Jewry. You can browse the holdings alphabetically, search the staff directory for contacts, and check the publications list.

Central Zionist Archives

ADDRESS: http://wzo.org.il/cza

DESCRIPTION: This site, in English and Hebrew, describes the holdings of this library in Jerusalem devoted to the history of Zionism. There is a full-text guide to the collections and several online exhibits, as well as links to the papers of Max I. Bodenheimer.

Early Hebrew Printing

ADDRESS: http://www.uottawa.ca/~weinberg/hebraica.html

DESCRIPTION: Created by Michael Davidson, this page is "a virtual guide to the great Jewish libraries and rare book collections online housing Hebrew manuscripts, incunabula, and written antiquities." The guide is fully annotated and illustrated and serves as an excellent starting point for studies in the area.

Elazar Classification System for Judaica Libraries

ADDRESS: http://www.geocities.com/Athens/Acropolis/6527/index.html

DESCRIPTION: David Elazar has created a classification system for Judaica used in many libraries. The book's table of contents and excerpts from it are available here, along with ordering information. The home page includes links to relevant sites in general and Jewish librarianship, a questionnaire, a guest book, and a memorial page for David's brother Daniel, who also figured prominently in the world of Judaica librarianship.

Fortunoff Video Archive for Holocaust Testimonies

ADDRESS: http://www.library.yale.edu/testimonies/homepage.html

DESCRIPTION: Housed at Yale University, this archive contains more than 3,800 oral history testimonies by Holocaust survivors, comprising over 10,000 recorded hours of videotape. The archive's home page describes the work of the center and its educational programs and allows you to search the catalog.

Hebrew Cataloging

ADDRESS: http://infoshare1.princeton.edu/katmandu/hebrew/hebrewtoc2.html

DESCRIPTION: From Rachel Simon at Princeton University and Joan Biella at the Library of Congress comes this collection of cataloging tools, including sections on the Chapters of the Talmud, Cataloging Biblical Materials, Hebrew Abbreviations, Hebrew Transliteration Table, Hebrew Diacritics, and a Romanization FAQ.

Index to Jewish Periodicals

ADDRESS: http://www.jewishperiodicals.com

DESCRIPTION: This page describes this index to Jewish periodicals, that appears in print and CD-ROM format. In addition to ordering information, a list of serials that are indexed by the publication is provided.

Institute of Microfilmed Hebrew Manuscripts

ADDRESS: http://sites.huji.ac.il/jnul/imhm/imhm.htm

DESCRIPTION: Located in the Jewish National and University Library in Israel, "The Institute of Microfilmed Hebrew Manuscripts has undertaken the task of collecting microfilm copies of all Hebrew manuscripts extant in public and private collections. Over 60,000 reels, representing more than 90 percent of known Hebrew manuscripts, are available for the use of scholars and interested laymen." This Web page describes the history, publications, and catalogs of the institute, along with contact information for libraries that can provide photocopies of manuscripts.

Israel Center for Libraries

ADDRESS: http://www.icl.org.il

DESCRIPTION: "The Center for Libraries is a professional body that renders services in various areas for all libraries in Israel, with a special emphasis on public libraries." Its Hebrew and English home page describes the group's cataloging services, online courses, publications, and services for publishers. Links to the pages of various Israeli public libraries are also available.

Israel Society of Special Libraries and Information Centers

ADDRESS: http://www.asmi.org.il/

DESCRIPTION: The home page of this librarians' group describes its courses, awards, special interest groups, publications, and local activities. It provides access to the group's online newsletter, *Egeret,* and its listserv and posts employment opportunities. A set of links to library and information science Web sites is also provided.

Jewish Community Library in Los Angeles

ADDRESS: http://www.jclla.org

DESCRIPTION: This home page serves as a virtual Jewish public library. In addition to its searchable catalog, the site has sections devoted to library programs, book lists, lesson plans, Jewish music, and a video collection searchable alphabetically or by subject. The teachers' lounge hosts links to sites in general and Jewish education and educational Jewish software. Children can participate in an online summer reading program.

Jewish Theological Seminary Library

ADDRESS: http://www.jtsa.edu/library/

DESCRIPTION: This home page from one of the largest Judaica libraries in the world describes the collections and services of the library. You can search the catalog, view a list of CD-ROMs, view presentations from several exhibitions, and order material from the publications desk online.

Jewish Women's Archive

ADDRESS: http://www.jwa.org/main.htm

DESCRIPTION: "The mission of the Jewish Women's Archive is to uncover, chronicle and transmit the rich legacy of Jewish women and their contributions to our families and communities, to our people and our world." Its resource section features educational materials, a bat mitzvah guide, a speakers list, recommended reading, and links to relevant Web sites. The searchable virtual archive and exhibits areas present displays on Rebecca Gratz, Emma Lazarus, Molly Picon, Justine W. Polier, Hannah G. Solomon, and Lillian Wald.

Judaica Archival Project

ADDRESS: http://www.archival.org/

DESCRIPTION: Based in Jerusalem, the Judaica Archival Project is dedicated to preserving Sifrei Kodesh and has preserved over half a million pages from thousands of rare, out-of-print, and classic Hebrew works in Rabbinics. From this site you can browse its catalog in free text by title or subject area and order these titles in conventional and electronic facsimile editions. The site also describes the preservation process and includes a chronology of Hebrew printing.

Judaica on Microforms

ADDRESS: http://www.nross.com/judaica/judaica1.htm

DESCRIPTION: This home page from Norman Ross Publishing describes the Judaica microforms available for sale through the company. Included are historical newspapers from around the world, Judaica from Eastern Europe, and archives from major collections worldwide.

MALMAD

ADDRESS: http://libnet.ac.il/~libnet/malmad.htm

DESCRIPTION: This home page of the Israeli universities' library consortium devoted to digital materials describes the online databases available to the member libraries and serves as a portal to those databases for subscribing libraries. From this site you can also access a list of electronic journals in Israeli libraries, arranged by subject and alphabetically, and read the group's newsletter. A variety of other links allows you to search the union list of holdings and of serials and to search RAMBI, the database of journal articles in Judaica.

Moses Mendelssohn Center for European Jewish Studies

ADDRESS: http://www.uni-potsdam.de/u/mmz/000mmz.htm

DESCRIPTION: This German-language site describes the work of the center, including its publications, conferences, projects, and library. A list of relevant Jewish sites is also available.

NACO Hebraica Funnel

ADDRESS: http://www.library.brandeis.edu/judaica/rosal4.htm

DESCRIPTION: Subtitled "Hebraica Web Resources: Formats, Fonts and More," this home page provides access to cataloging resources, Hebrew fonts, and background papers on Hebrew scripts online that will be of use to Hebraica catalogers.

National Yiddish Book Center

ADDRESS: http://www.yiddishbookcenter.org

DESCRIPTION: Founded by Aaron Lansky and located in Amherst, Massachusetts, this center is "dedicated to rescuing unwanted and discarded Yiddish books and sharing the treasures they contain" with research libraries worldwide. Its home page describes the center, its programs, exhibits, and courses. There is an online virtual tour of the center, as well as details on how to donate books to the center and order sheet music from it. You can view the tables of contents and selected articles from the center's publication *Pakn Treger* and access its archives dating back to 1997.

On Time Subscription Service

ADDRESS: http://www.ontime.co.il/ontime.htm

DESCRIPTION: Allied with the EBSCO periodical subscription service, On Time offers a way for libraries to obtain any book or serial published in Israel. For Israeli companies and libraries, On Time offers subscription services for any publication or serial published worldwide. This Hebrew and English page describes the company's services.

Online Library for Hebrew Books in the U.S.

ADDRESS: http://www.IsraeliWishes.com/IW-Library.htm

DESCRIPTION: Part of the Israeli Wishes cybermall that offers all types of Israeli products, this is an online Hebrew subscription library that allows members to borrow Hebrew material for one month. A browsable catalog of original and translated material is provided, along with availability indications. All titles have a brief description, and readers may add reviews. This is an ingenious cybertwist on the traditional concept of a subscription library.

Philadelphia Jewish Archives Center

ADDRESS: http://www.libertynet.org/pjac/

DESCRIPTION: This site describes the collections and projects of the archives center. There is a section on genealogy and an online exhibit as well.

Princeton University Library—Jewish Studies Resources

ADDRESS: http://www.princeton.edu/~pressman/jewish.html

DESCRIPTION: This page is devoted to resources in Jewish studies and lists databases, libraries, archives, and research centers with relevant material. There are collections of links for subject sites in topics such as Jewish history and Bible, Israeli-based programs, and news sites and listservs. Information is available on displaying Hebrew online, and a listing of resources at Princeton is also provided.

Salomon Ludwig Steinheim Institute for German-Jewish History

ADDRESS: http://sti1.uni-duisburg.de/

DESCRIPTION: This site in German and English describes the goals, research projects, and Judaica library of the Institute. The more extensive German section of the site details more about the Gidal and Goldstein archives and the periodical and book holdings of the Judaica collection and offers an annotated list of relevant Jewish Web sites.

Shaar Zion/Beit Ariela

ADDRESS: http://www.tel-aviv.gov.il/Tel-Aviv/tarbut/ariela.htm

DESCRIPTION: This home page belonging to the Tel Aviv Public Library describes in Hebrew the programs, collections, and services of the library and its 25 branches. You can search the union catalog in English and Hebrew and view a list of CD-ROMs, bibliographies, and new and recommended books in Hebrew. Of particular note is the collection of Internet links to sites in English and Hebrew, arranged by subject area.

Taylor-Schechter Genizah Research Unit

ADDRESS: http://www.lib.cam.ac.uk/Taylor-Schechter/

DESCRIPTION: This Web site from Cambridge University describes the Genizah materials collection and the research unit's work. The collection is searchable online and there is a bibliography and online exhibit, as well as access to the unit's newsletter, *Genizah Fragments.*

Yeshiva University

ADDRESS: http://www.yu.edu/libraries/

DESCRIPTION: Through the school's online catalog, YULIS, you can search the university's holdings by author, title, subject, and keyword. Libraries supported include the Dr. Lillian and Dr. Rebecca Chutick Law Library, the D. Samuel Gottesman Library (Medicine/Psychology), Stern College's Hedi Steinberg Library, the Mendel Gottesman Library of Hebraica/Judaica, and Yeshiva College's Pollack Library—Landowne Bloom Collection. Information on the school's archives is also provided.

YIVO

ADDRESS: http://www.yivoinstitute.org/

DESCRIPTION: "Founded in 1925 in Vilna, Poland, as the Yiddish Scientific Institute and headquartered in New York since 1940, YIVO is devoted to the history, society, and culture of Ashkenazic Jewry and the influence of that culture as it has developed in the Americas. As the only pre-Holocaust scholarly institution to transfer its mission to the United States, YIVO is the preeminent center for the study of East European Jewry and Yiddish language, literature, and folklore." Its home page describes the YIVO Library and Archives, the world's largest collection of Yiddish books; its scholarly publications, conferences, cultural programs, lectures, exhibitions, and courses. Portions of the library's holdings in various subject areas are available in table format. This is a treasure trove of materials related to Yiddish and is an excellent starting point for any studies in this area.

MALLS

1-800-Judaism

ADDRESS: http://www.judaism.com/

DESCRIPTION: A browsable and searchable selection of books, software, music, children's items, ritual objects, and art.

Internet Jewish Store

ADDRESS: http://www.jewishstore.com

DESCRIPTION: A browsable catalog of general and Jewish merchandise that can be ordered online. This site also offers an affiliate program for fundraising.

Jewish Mall

ADDRESS: http://www.ipol.com/jmall/

DESCRIPTION: A searchable and browsable directory of items for sale in various categories, including art, books, food, gifts, jewelry, Judaica, music, and software.

Mitzvah Mall

ADDRESS: http://www.mitzvahmall.org

DESCRIPTION: Created by Chabad, "MitzvahMall is a nonprofit fundraising program for Jewish schools and organizations. There is no cost to the participating institutions or to our shoppers, and each participating organization receives a full 100 percent of the commissions generated by its supporters. The way it works is simple. Many online retailers pay commissions to sites that send them customers. (This is referred to as an 'affiliates' or 'associates' program.) MitzvahMall is an 'affiliate' of several hundred online merchants, whose links we have gathered together to create an online mall. The commissions that MitzvahMall thus earns are distributed to our participating institutions." The searchable site lists participants in 12 major categories, arranged on 3 virtual floors.

Net Judaica

ADDRESS: http://www.netjudaica.com/

DESCRIPTION: Searchable and browsable directory of items for sale in various categories, including art, books, food, gifts, jewelry, Judaica, music, software, videos, children's items, and household goods. An affiliate program for fund raising is available.

YidBid

ADDRESS: http://www.YidBid.com

DESCRIPTION: Online auction of all types of Judaica, featuring Chinese auctions and classified ads.

MAPS

Maps of the Middle East

ADDRESS: http://www.lib.utexas.edu/Libs/PCL/Map_collection/middle_east.html

DESCRIPTION: A browsable collection, arranged by country, of Middle Eastern maps from the Perry Castaneda Library Map Collection at the University of Texas at Austin. Most of the maps were created by the CIA and are available in a variety of sizes, all of which are marked.

Maps of Israel

ADDRESS: http://www.emap.co.il

DESCRIPTION: Similar to Mapquest, this site in English and Hebrew allows one to search in either language for a specific address, travel directions, or an area map of regions in Israel. You can choose to display banks, gas stations, hospitals, and one-way streets on the resulting maps. This is the best online map system for sites in Israel in both Hebrew and English.

Atlas Israel

ADDRESS: http://www.atlas-israel.co.il

DESCRIPTION: This is the Hebrew-language home page of a map company that develops software for providing online maps of Israel. Its software powers three map sites, access to which is provided here. Walla's maps offer location information, Rapid's maps allow the user to view a region, and Dapey Zahav's maps show routes. A list of the printed maps the company offers for sale is also provided. If you read Hebrew and can enable your computer to search with Hebrew fonts, this is an interesting site to explore.

THE MEDIA

CAMERA: The Committee for Accuracy in Middle East Reporting

ADDRESS: http://www.camera.org

DESCRIPTION: "The Committee for Accuracy in Middle East Reporting in America is a nondenominational, educational organization devoted to promoting accurate and balanced coverage of Israel and the Middle East. Members hold diverse political views but are united in opposing media bias and misinformation." The site's home page provides access to the group's media reports dating back to 1992, full-text publications, press releases, feature columns, and background articles that examine news stories in depth. There are sample articles from a wide variety of news resources, designed to demonstrate the bias of a given news resource toward Israel. You can also view columns by journalists.

MEMRI: Middle East Media and Research Institute

ADDRESS: http://www.memri.org

DESCRIPTION: MEMRI is "an independent, nonprofit organization providing translations of the Arab media and original analysis and research on developments in the Middle East." Its searchable home page offers access to the full text of the group's publications and to relevant links, including government agencies, publications, research institutes, and interest groups. A video library and archive section are planned. You can join the free listserv and find out about internship programs as well.

Harry Leichter's Jewish Publication's World

ADDRESS: http://www.haruth.com/HarryLeichtersJewishPublications.html

DESCRIPTION: An alphabetical collection of links to 96 Jewish publications worldwide in a variety of languages.

American Jewish Press Association

ADDRESS: http://www.ajpa.org/

DESCRIPTION: Information about the activities of this voluntary not-for-profit professional association for the English-language Jewish press in North America, representing more than 150 newspapers, magazines, individual journalists, and affiliated organizations throughout the United

States and Canada. The site features a browsable directory by state of members, a job bank for listing want ads and resumes, and a resource directory of relevant Jewish and general Internet sites.

Jewish Television Network

ADDRESS: http://www.jewishtvnetwork.com/

DESCRIPTION: JTN develops Jewish programming that is aired through public television stations throughout the United States. Its home page provides local schedules arranged by state, gives descriptions of programs by type, and provides a link to the store through which you can purchase videos and books.

Jewish Telegraphic Agency

ADDRESS: http://www.jta.org/

DESCRIPTION: The home page of this international news service provides full-text global stories of Jewish interest, as well as coverage of news in the Middle East, the United States, and around the world. There are feature columns and stories about American Jewry as well. A searchable archive dating back to 1996 is available, as well as information on a variety of products, including daily and weekly e-mail editions and a community news reporter. This is an excellent news resource for stories about Jewish issues worldwide.

JEWISH RADIO

Arutz 7

ADDRESS: http://www.a7.org/

DESCRIPTION: Broadcasting from a ship just outside Israeli territorial waters, Arutz Sheva provides "politically conservative programming with a traditional Jewish-Zionist orientation." Its home page provides a broadcast schedule, access to a variety of recorded shows in Hebrew and English, and musical selections. The newspaper section also offers daily news, articles from the Arab press, opinion pieces, and "good news." A browsable news archive dating back to 1999 is also available. The video section provides footage in Hebrew and English of recent news events and can be viewed with Real Player. For those interested in reportage from a conservative vantage point, Arutz 7 is an excellent starting point.

Radio Kol Chai 93FM

ADDRESS: http://kolchai.moreshet.co.il

DESCRIPTION: "Radio Kol-Hai offers a variety of programs of interest to the modern Orthodox and *haredi* public, among which are current events programs with sectorial appeal; Jewish thought; halachic *she'elot utshuvot, shiurim, chesed*; consumer and medical magazine formats; and youth programming ,which is very popular among *haredi* youth. The music that is mainly played on the station is a variety of hasidic music, from the old, well-known songs to the most modern ones. Passages of *hazanut*, Mediterranean music, modern songs, and classical music are also played." The home page describes each of the programs and offers a broadcast schedule. You need to have Windows Media Player installed to listen to the programs.

Shalom America

ADDRESS: http://shalom-am.com/

DESCRIPTION: Phil Fink's program is broadcast weekly on WELW 1330 AM in Cleveland Ohio from 7–9 A.M. EDT Sundays and daily Sunday through Friday on the World Wide Web. To listen to it or to the music samples he provides, you need Windows Media Player. You can also join a discussion list sponsored by Shalom America.

Cable to Jewish Life

ADDRESS: http://www.cablejew.org

DESCRIPTION: Sponsored by Chabad, this is the home of a Jewish television program hosted by Rabbi Yosef Katzman that airs over the National Jewish Television network. The home page provides a broadcast schedule and offers previous shows for sale on videotape. You can also watch videos online and sign up for a weekly newsletter.

Jewish Short Stories

ADDRESS: http://www.kcrw.org/b/jss.html

DESCRIPTION: National Public Radio presents a series of Jewish short stories read aloud that you can listen to with Real Player or order on cassette. The site presents 13 programs with 2 stories each.

Radiowest

ADDRESS: http://www.radiowest.co.il

DESCRIPTION: Israel's only all-English radio station. The station has been having a problem with its license and as of this writing has not yet resumed broadcasting.

Yiddish Voice

ADDRESS: http://www.yiddishvoice.com and http://www.yv.org and

DESCRIPTION: The home page of this Brookline, Massachusetts, Yiddish-language radio show, serving Boston's Yiddish-speaking community, also serves as an Internet resource for listeners outside its broadcast area. Program schedules are listed, along with news and access to other radio shows and Yiddish links on the Internet. You can listen to sample interviews and music with Real Player, read about recent programs, and purchase items from the station's gift shop. There's even a live interview with Sholom Aleichem available. This is a good collection of Yiddish-related materials.

HEBREW-LANGUAGE RADIO

Radio Israel

ADDRESS: http://www.radioisrael.com

DESCRIPTION: At this site from Sabra Net you will find a weekly Israeli show and live Israeli radio broadcasts directly from Israel, with an emphasis on Israeli music. The weekly show is a paid service and you need Real Player to listen to the four-hour program. The home page has a "what's new" section with free music samplings, as well as listings in Hebrew and English of the top 10 hits. There is also a chat room and a music store. Of particular note is the extensive set of links to sites for individual Israeli performers, Israeli music in general, and Israeli radio stations that broadcast over the Internet. This is an excellent starting site, particularly for Israeli music.

Amfm.co.il Net Radio—Israel's Radio Portal

ADDRESS: http://www.amfm.co.il/index2.asp

DESCRIPTION: This customizable Hebrew-language site allows you to choose the radio stations you want to see when the page opens. The database of worldwide stations is searchable by location, style of programming, and language and provides a short description of the type of programs offered. You can also join an online e-mail group and rate your stations of choice.

Israeli Music Online

ADDRESS: http://www.sabra.net/theisraelhour/

DESCRIPTION: "If you're in Central New Jersey, tune in to 'The Israel Hour' every Sunday at 1:00 P.M. E.S.T. on Rutgers University's WRSU Radio (88.7 FM)." If you live outside the Central New Jersey area, you can listen to the online broadcasts, that include news and Israeli music. The home page highlights new programs and provides a music news center, a list of the top 20 all-time hits, and coverage of the Eurovision contest. You can read the message board and subscribe to an online newsletter as well. Of particular note are the links that cover individual Israeli performers, Israeli music in general, Israeli news and media sites, and Israeli radio stations broadcasting on the Internet.

Israelive

ADDRESS: http://www.israelive.com/israelive.htm

DESCRIPTION: This home page, in English and Hebrew, offers live broadcasts of music, news, sports, and talk shows. Sample, prerecorded shows are free. Other broadcasts require a fee.

Kol Israel

ADDRESS: http://www.israelradio.org

DESCRIPTION: "This site is an independently produced guide to the Israel Broadcast Authority radio networks known in Hebrew as Kol Israel—the Voice of Israel." The site provides access to English news in Real Audio format and Hebrew news on Reshet Bet. There is information on Persian broadcasting, a phone-in show for Israelis abroad, and broadcasting schedules worldwide. In addition to links to various Kol Israel networks, a history of radio in Israel is also available. The official site of the Israel Broadcast Authority at http://www.iba.org.il was under construction as of this writing.

Radio 10

ADDRESS: http://www.radio10.co.il/

DESCRIPTION: Broadcast live from Jerusalem, this radio station features programs of religious interest and has some Internet programming in Real Player format.

Radio 99

ADDRESS: http://www.99fm.co.il/

DESCRIPTION: This Hebrew-language home page describes the music offerings of this station that is sponsored by Orange, an Israeli telecom company. The station's programs can be received on cell phones using the GSM protocol. You can listen to programs using Windows Media Player and there is a broadcast schedule, information on DJs, and news from the music world. You can also participate in the forum discussion.

Radio Emtza Haderech 90 FM

ADDRESS: http://www.90fm.co.il

DESCRIPTION: This is the home page of a radio station that services the regions from the Sharon Valley to the Carmel. There is a broadcast schedule and information on a course for radio announcers.

Radio Galei Zahal

ADDRESS: http://www.glz.co.il

DESCRIPTION: This is the searchable Hebrew-language home page of the Israeli Army's radio station, which features full-text articles in news, economics, sports, and culture, along with radio clips you can listen to with Microsoft Media Player.

Radio Haifa

ADDRESS: http://www.1075fm.co.il/

DESCRIPTION: As of this writing, the station was planning to resume live broadcasting soon.

Radio Hazak

ADDRESS: http://www.radiohazak.com/

DESCRIPTION: Created by Larry Yudelson, Radio Hazak provides news, reviews, message boards, and articles about Israeli music. Information is available by artist, and there is a set of links to additional details about each one. There are also polls and lists of best-selling titles and albums.

Reshet Bet

ADDRESS: http://bet.netvision.net.il/

DESCRIPTION: Reshet Bet is Israel Radio's news network. A two-hour weekly program called InterBet is broadcast over the Internet in Real

Player format. This home page provides a program schedule, as well as a broadcast schedule for Kol Israel.

Sunset Radio from Israel

ADDRESS: http://www.sunsetradio.com/nations/il/il01.html

DESCRIPTION: Sunset Radio offers access to eight Israeli radio stations and four Israeli newspapers.

Tel Aviv FM 102

ADDRESS: http://www.102fm.co.il

DESCRIPTION: Using Real Player, you can listen to the programs of this Tel Aviv radio station that include humor and music.

Voice of Peace

ADDRESS: http://www.thevoiceofpeace.co.il/

DESCRIPTION: The new site of the Voice of Peace radio station is under construction but has sections devoted to news, entertainment, what's hot, and links.

ISRAELI TELEVISION

Israeli TV Guide

ADDRESS: http://www2.iol.co.il/tv/index.stm

DESCRIPTION: Search this Hebrew-language database by channel, day, and time for television listings.

Channel 2

ADDRESS: http://www.channel2.co.il/

DESCRIPTION: Channel 2 broadcasts on both television and radio, and its home page provides program and schedule information for both media. There are sections for both young people and the public, as well as an area on ratings. The entire site is searchable.

Channel 3

ADDRESS: http://www.3tv.co.il/

DESCRIPTION: This Hebrew-language home page provides program listings, news about the channel, and discussion forums.

Channel 4

ADDRESS: http://www.4tv.co.il

DESCRIPTION: You can check the highlights of the week's broadcasts from this station, which features movie screenings.

Channel 5

ADDRESS: http://channel5.netvision.net.il/default1.asp

DESCRIPTION: Channel 5 is Israel's sports channel. Its searchable page in English and Hebrew provides information about soccer, football, and basketball teams in Israel, Europe, and the United States, as well as a variety of other sports. You can also participate in chat groups and online discussions.

Channel 6

ADDRESS: http://www.shesh.co.il

DESCRIPTION: Channel 6 is devoted to children's programs, and its Hebrew-language home page has information about its broadcasts, along with comics, games, and discussion areas.

Channel 8

ADDRESS: http://shmone.netvision.net.il

DESCRIPTION: Israel's science channel on television.

Israel Educational Television

ADDRESS: http://www.education.gov.il/ietv/

DESCRIPTION: This site provides a browsable directory arranged by subject of the courses offered through Israeli instructional television on channels 1, 2, and 23, along with a programming schedule.

MEDICINE

Israel Physician's Guide

ADDRESS: http://www.physician.co.il and http://www.doctor.co.il

DESCRIPTION: This database features a listing of Israeli doctors, searchable by specialty and location. It also offers browsable directories of Israeli medical organizations, hospitals and laboratories, Israeli drug and medical products, Israeli cosmetics, used medical equipment, and medical real estate. You can check out medical news, look at employment opportunities, purchase mailing lists, and join medical newsgroups. Of particular note is the section on worldwide medical links, that offers an extensive set of links arranged by medical specialty. This is an excellent starting point for anyone interested in medicine in Israel.

Medical Resources

ADDRESS: http://shamash.org/shuls/einstein/medlinks.html

DESCRIPTION: Last updated in 1998, this set of links created by Albert Einstein Medical School Synagogue provides a still-useful collection of access points for general Jewish medical sites, sites on medical ethics and halachah, Jewish genetic diseases, rehabilitation and treatment, and hospitals, medical schools, and research facilities.

Kupat Cholim Clalit

ADDRESS: http://www.klalit.co.il/ or http://www.clalit.co.il

DESCRIPTION: This searchable Hebrew and English site details the history and services of this Israeli health-care provider.

Kupat Cholim Meuhedet

ADDRESS: http://www.meuhedet.co.il

DESCRIPTION: This Hebrew-language site details the services offered by this Israeli health-care provider in areas ranging from dental care to old age homes. There is a selection of links to sites of general medical interest as well.

Maccabi Healthcare Services

ADDRESS: http://www.maccabi-health.co.il/

DESCRIPTION: This searchable Hebrew and English site details the history and services of this Israeli health-care provider. You can join discussion groups and check the suggested list of general medical sites as well.

American Physicians Fellowship for Medicine in Israel

ADDRESS: http://www.apfmed.org

DESCRIPTION: "The American Physicians Fellowship for Medicine in Israel is an organization of North American physicians and others dedicated to advancing the state of medical education, research, and care in Israel" by offering fellowships to Israeli medical students and by supporting projects between North America and Israel. Its home page describes the work of the group and offers access to a browsable archive of its newsletters dating back to 1996. You can subscribe to several listservs, join chat rooms and a discussion board, and read about medical meetings and news from Israel. Of particular note is the Chevra/SIG section, that includes a Jewish Medical History. A list of relevant Jewish and medical sites is also available.

Institute for Jewish Medical Ethics

ADDRESS: http://www.ijme.org

DESCRIPTION: The home page of this organization based in San Francisco provides information about the institute and past and upcoming conferences, along with a browsable archive of articles. You can send halachic questions to the institute, join a mailing list, access the speaker's bureau, and purchase books and audio and video products. There is a collection of links to related Jewish and medical sites as well.

Jerusalem Center for Research: Halachah and Medicine

ADDRESS: http://www.J-C-R.org

DESCRIPTION: "The Jerusalem Center for Research studies the halachic implications of modern medical developments and practice." Its home page describes the goals and activities of the center and lists the publications, lecture topics, and courses offered by it.

Jewish Health

ADDRESS: http://www.JewishHealth.com/

DESCRIPTION: Part of the Jewish Family and Life magazine series, this online journal offers several articles about health.

Magen David Adom

ADDRESS: http://www.mda.org.il/

DESCRIPTION: The Hebrew and English home page of this organization, the Israeli Red Cross, describes the work of the group and lists volunteer opportunities, courses, and relevant medical Internet sites.

Maytal: Israel Institute for Treatment and Study of Stress

ADDRESS: http://www.maytal.co.il/

DESCRIPTION: The Hebrew and English home page of this Israeli mental health group describes the work of the organization and offers a browsable archive of papers in English and Hebrew. There are also links to psychology sites on psychotherapy, trauma, and electronic journals and Israeli sites on the topic. You can participate in Maytal's poll and in online discussion groups as well.

Medsite

ADDRESS: http://www.medsite.co.il/

DESCRIPTION: Built with the cooperation of the Ministry of Health and the Ministry of Education, Medsite is a Hebrew-language medical portal that seeks to provide information to lay people about medical issues. Topics covered include dentistry, the economics of health, health care and the law, and medication. The drop-down menus do not seem to display properly without Hebrew-enabled Windows, but the site does offer a large amount of information for Hebrew speakers.

National Institute of Judaism and Medicine

ADDRESS: http://www.nijm.org

DESCRIPTION: The home page of this New York–based organization describes its mission, membership benefits, and conferences and provides access to conference tapes that can be purchased. An annotated list of relevant Jewish and medical Internet sites is also provided.

Thirteen Principles of Medical Ethics

ADDRESS: http://members.aol.com/Sauromalus/index.html

DESCRIPTION: Created by Dr. Jay B. Levine, this site lists 13 principles of medical practice, along with comments and proof texts from Jewish sources. There are also some links to sites about Judaism and vegetarianism.

HOSPITALS

Albert Einstein College of Medicine of Yeshiva University

ADDRESS: http://www.aecom.yu.edu

DESCRIPTION: The home page of this medical school in New York describes the educational programs, academic departments, research facilities, clinical programs, and affiliated institutions of the school. Of particular note is the access provided to online searching of the school's library, along with links to medical sites and other medical libraries.

Alyn Children's Hospital

ADDRESS: http://www.alyn.org/

DESCRIPTION: Based in Jerusalem, "Alyn is Israel's only orthopedic hospital and rehabilitation center for physically handicapped children." Its home page offers a virtual tour of the facility, describes its services and research projects, lists its support chapters worldwide, and allows you to sign up for its forum discussion.

Assaf Harofeh Medical Center

ADDRESS: http://www.doryanet.co.il/assaf/

DESCRIPTION: Affiliated with the Sackler Faculty of Medicine of Tel Aviv University, the home page of this hospital describes its services and offers access to a number of Israeli medical newsgroups.

Hadassah Medical Organization

ADDRESS: http://www.hadassah.org.il/

DESCRIPTION: This extensive, searchable English and Hebrew home page for the Jerusalem-based hospital lists the staff and services of all of the hospital's many departments. It also details upcoming conferences, what's new at Hadassah, employment opportunities, and patents open for licensing. You can find information about Hadassah's medical school, its outreach and community services, and its research and development projects. Of particular note is the extensive set of links to medical sites in Hebrew, Hadassah women, the Chagall Windows, and recommended medical sub-sites on Hadassah's server.

Laniado Hospital

ADDRESS: http://www.laniado.com/index.html

DESCRIPTION: The services and facilities of this Netanya-based hospital are described at this site, and you can view a video of the hospital with Real Player.

Rambam Medical Center

ADDRESS: http://www.rambam.org.il/

DESCRIPTION: The searchable English and Spanish home page of this Haifa-based hospital provides information about the facility, its departments and administration, its research and academics, and its postgraduate studies. You can take an online tour and check the e-mail staff directory.

Sackler Faculty of Medicine

ADDRESS: http://www.tau.ac.il/medicine/

DESCRIPTION: The home page of this medical school, part of Tel Aviv University, describes the schools, departments, services, teaching, education, and research conducted by the school. There is a personnel directory and a list of affiliated hospitals and institutes. Of particular note is the school's medical library, which can be searched online; an extensive set of medical links created by the university's library staff; listings of new additions to the library; and online access to databases, electronic journals, and books.

Shaare Zedek Medical Center

ADDRESS: http://www.szmc.org.il

DESCRIPTION: The searchable home page of this Jerusalem-based hospital offers information about the facility, its woman and infant center, nursing school, Ardon Tapestries, conferences, medical electives, news highlights, world offices, medical directors, and annual report. Its research section provides full-text articles on projects dating back to 1996, and its video library allows you to witness a live birth and heart surgery. You can take an online tour of the facility and sign up for an online newsletter. The center also sells Rosh Hashanah cards that can be purchased online. Of particular note is the medical ethics section, which describes the work of the Schlesinger Institute and provides access to the publications and responsa project sponsored by the institute. Another outstanding feature of the site is the access it provides to searching the hospital's medical library.

Soroka Medical Center

ADDRESS: http://soroka.bgu.ac.il/

DESCRIPTION: The English and Hebrew home page of this Beersheva-based hospital, affiliated with Ben Gurion University, describes the departments, services, and research conducted by the center. Of particular note is the drug database, searchable by generic and commercial name.

THE MIDDLE EAST

MERIA: Middle East Review of International Affairs

ADDRESS: http://www.biu.ac.il/SOC/besa/meria/index.html

DESCRIPTION: MERIA is a project edited and directed by Professor Barry Rubin at the Begin-Sadat Center for Strategic Studies. Its goal is to advance research on the Middle East and foster scholarly communication and cooperation. The site provides access to *MERIA Journal,* a quarterly academic publication, and *MERIA News,* a monthly newsletter. Back issues are archived on the home page and there is a subject index to them both. Of particular note are the full-text research guides on a number of Middle Eastern topics and an extensive database of U.S.-Middle East foreign policy dating back to 1980. In addition, the site lists the current contents of journals covering the region, dating back to 1998. This is an extensive and rich source of academic material about the Middle East.

Middle East Resources from Columbia University

ADDRESS: http://www.columbia.edu/cu/libraries/indiv/area/MiddleEast/

DESCRIPTION: Created by Columbia librarian Frank Unlandherm, this list of Internet resources covers bibliographies, biographies, libraries, resources by region and subject, and material on food, languages, literatures, minorities, music, political violence, religion, water, and women of the area. There are also links to directories, electronic publications, graphical resources, scholarly associations, publishers, and bookstores that deal in Middle East studies. This is an excellent starting point for Internet material on any Middle Eastern topic.

Middle East Newsline

ADDRESS: http://www.menewsline.com/

DESCRIPTION: Middle East Newsline is run by independent journalists and presents headlines from regional and international news sources.

MISSIONARIES

Jews for Judaism

ADDRESS: http://www.jewsforjudaism.org/

DESCRIPTION: This home page describes the services of the national and regional offices of this group that seeks to counter missionaries and cults. You can find out what's new, check out missionary alerts, participate in discussions, and sign up for an online newsletter. From the Services section you can check the speakers' bureau, find out about counseling, and order publications online. Of particular note is the Resource section, that provides an FAQ, reference area, personal stories, audio clips, and links to relevant sites. This is an excellent starting point for information on anti-missionary techniques and services.

Jerusalem Institute of Biblical Polemics

ADDRESS: http://www.jibp.israel.net

DESCRIPTION: The home page of this group devoted to refuting missionary teachings describes the group's activities and provides samples from its magazine, a catalog of its publications, and a "tract of the month," a full-text reproduction of a missionary tract.

Yad L'Achim

ADDRESS: http://www.yadlachim.org

DESCRIPTION: The Hebrew and English home page of this Israeli-based group describes how missionaries approach people and techniques for combating them. It offers several FAQs and details the activities of missionaries in Israel, the nature of their propaganda, and their approaches to Russian Jews and young adults.

MUSEUMS

MUSEUMS IN THE UNITED STATES

Jewish Museum in New York

ADDRESS: http://www.jewishmuseum.org

DESCRIPTION: This home page provides general information about the museum and its programs and describes the permanent exhibition, the Contemporary Artist Project, and special exhibitions. It also offers access to the museum shops, from which you can purchase items online. You can sign up for the museum's e-mail list as well.

National Museum of American Jewish History

ADDRESS: http://www.nmajh.org

DESCRIPTION: Based in Philadelphia, this museum's home page offers full online exhibits, along with information about the museum, a fun page for children, and a calendar of events. You can shop online from its store, sign up for an online newsletter, and explore the links in the areas of Jewish museums worldwide, news sites, history sites, Jewish cultural sites, and Philadelphia-area links. Of particular note is the searchable timeline that presents side-by-side Jewish, American, and worldwide events.

Florida Holocaust Museum

ADDRESS: http://www.flholocaustmuseum.org/

DESCRIPTION: From this home page you can find general information about the museum and its history, traveling exhibits, teaching materials, and events, as well as purchase items from its gift shop online.

Museum of the Southern Jewish Experience

ADDRESS: http://www.msje.org/

DESCRIPTION: From this home page you can find general information about the museum and its goals, current exhibit, and events, as well as purchase items from its gift shop online. You can also check out a number of tours of the Mississippi region sponsored by the museum.

Sanford L. Ziff Jewish Museum—Florida

ADDRESS: http://www.jewishmuseum.com/

DESCRIPTION: This museum, dedicated to the history of Jews in Florida, provides information about its programs and newest events. You can sign the guest book and purchase items online from the gift shop. The museum's online newsletter is posted, and archives dating back to 1998 are available. Of particular note is the searchable Mosaic Photo Collection of 650 photographs about Jewish life in Florida.

Judah L. Magnes Museum

ADDRESS: http://www.jfed.org/magnes/magnes.htm

DESCRIPTION: "The Magnes Museum in Berkeley, California, collects, preserves, and exhibits treasures of Jewish art, history, and culture from throughout the world." Its home page provides information about the permanent collections, special and traveling exhibits, the libraries and archives, poetry and video competitions, books and publications, education and docent programs, and the museum shop. There are links to the Commission for the Preservation of Pioneer Jewish Cemeteries and Landmarks and to the Jewish-American Hall of Fame as well.

Fenster Museum of Jewish Art

ADDRESS: http://www.jewishmuseum.net/

DESCRIPTION: Based in Tulsa, Oklahoma, this museum offers a rich variety of online exhibits divided into five categories: Archaeology, Ritual Objects, Life Cycle, Ethnology, and History. You will also find a complete list of illustrations with hyperlinks to both views and text. There is an extensive section on the Oklahoma Jewish Experience, that includes information on American Jewish immigration, Oklahoma memorabilia, and the Prairie Landsmen Project.

Jewish American Hall of Fame

ADDRESS: http://www.amuseum.org/jahf/

DESCRIPTION: Through this site you can take a virtual tour of American Jewish history via short entries on people, places, and events. There are entertaining quizzes as well, and you can nominate someone for induction into the hall of fame. You can also order the museum's medals online. This is an excellent starting point for information on American Jewish history.

Dennis & Phillip Ratner Museum

ADDRESS: http://www.ratnermuseum.com/

DESCRIPTION: The museum has been established with one purpose in mind: to foster love of the Hebrew Bible through the graphic arts. You can view works in progress and finished pieces in the areas of Genesis, Exodus, Song of Songs, Kabbalah, the Ratner Bible, and heroes and heroines and learn about museum programs at its home in Bethesda, Maryland.

United States Holocaust Memorial Museum

ADDRESS: http://www.ushmm.org

DESCRIPTION: This monumental and searchable site offers numerous online tours, along with information on the museum and its events, corporate partners, employment opportunities, internships, and volunteer positions. You can purchase a large variety of books, academic publications, music, and teaching materials through the museum shop online. Information on the work of the Center for Advanced Holocaust Studies and the Committee on Conscience is also provided, along with an international list of current activities regarding Holocaust-era assets. Of particular note are the collections, archives, and library, all of which are searchable online. In addition, the museum maintains a Registry of Jewish Holocaust Survivors. Also, there are extensive teaching materials in the Education section. This is a rich resource for materials relating to the Holocaust.

Skirball Museum

ADDRESS: http://www.skirball.org

DESCRIPTION: The home page of this Los Angeles museum provides information about its programs, events, and services, such as its speakers bureau, gift shop, and resource center.

MUSEUMS IN ISRAEL

Israel's Museums

ADDRESS: http://www.israelemb.org/miami/museums.htm

DESCRIPTION: This list of links offers access to a large number of Israeli-based museums.

Israel's Museums

ADDRESS: http://owl.education.gov.il/museums/

DESCRIPTION: This Hebrew-language site, created by the Ministry of Education, allows you to access Israeli museums by subject or location. Basic information about each museum is provided. For Hebrew speakers, this is an excellent starting point for locating less well-known museums in Israel.

Babylonian Jewry Heritage Center

ADDRESS: http://www.babylonjewry.org.il/

DESCRIPTION: In English and Hebrew the home page of this research center for Iraqi Jewry provides access to the group's news, events, publications, and research projects. You can access selected full-text articles from the museum's journal, *Nehardea,* dating back to 1981; sign the guest book; and participate in online chat rooms. Several sections of the site are of particular note. First, there is an online tour of the museum, which is located in Or Yehuda. You can also view a large number of artifacts from the museum's archives. Links to Iraqi, Sephardic, and relevant Jewish sites are also available. Finally, there is a set of articles about Iraqi Jewry in Los Angeles, New York, and the Far East. The entire site is searchable as well.

Beit HaTefutsot: Museum of the Jewish People

ADDRESS: http://www.bh.org.il

DESCRIPTION: The English and Hebrew home page of this museum located in northern Tel Aviv provides information on the permanent, special, and traveling exhibitions; genealogical materials; music collections, with selected clips for listening; a bibliography of the museum's video productions; and educational materials. You can also purchase items online from the museum's gift shop. Of particular note are the searchable databases of personal names and of Jewish communities, along with an extensive set of links to Internet sites related to Jewish Museums and Art Museums, Academic and Cultural Organizations, Libraries and Archives, Jewish Organizations, Jewish Communities on the Web, Jewish Press, Music, Genealogy, and the Holocaust.

Bloomfield Science Museum in Jerusalem

ADDRESS: http://www.mada.org.il

DESCRIPTION: In English and Hebrew this home page provides general information about the museum, its exhibitions, and its activities. The section on "The Young Scientist" includes areas on famous scientists and inventors, science news and innovations, science journals, and a browsable listing of science projects.

Dead Sea Scrolls

ADDRESS: http://sunsite.unc.edu/expo/deadsea.scrolls.exhibit/intro.html

DESCRIPTION: This online exhibit, originally mounted by the Library of Congress, is divided into five sections: an introduction, the Qumran Library, the Qumran Community, the scrolls today, and conclusions. There are also links to selected readings, resource materials for teachers, and a glossary, as well as the Project Judaica Foundation page, the sponsor of the exhibit.

House of Bible Museum

ADDRESS: http://inter-s.com/bible/museum.html

DESCRIPTION: Basic information about this Tel Aviv–based museum, originally the home of Meir Dizengoff, the first mayor of the city.

Hungarian Jewry Museum

ADDRESS: http://www.hungjewmus.org.il/

DESCRIPTION: This site, in English, Hebrew, and Hungarian, describes the memorial museum located in Safed and provides online access to its newsletter.

Israel Bible Museum

ADDRESS: http://www.israelbiblemuseum.com

DESCRIPTION: Based in Safed, this museum houses the work of Phillip Ratner. Samples of his work on biblical themes may be viewed on the Web site.

Israel Museum

ADDRESS: http://www.imj.org.il

DESCRIPTION: This searchable site offers information about the museum and its branches, programs, and departments. You can take a virtual online tour and see highlights of the museum's collections from the Shrine of the Book, the Art Wing, Archaeology, Judaica and Jewish Ethnography, the Art Garden, and the Youth Wing.

National Museum of Science in Haifa

ADDRESS: http://mustsee.org.il/

DESCRIPTION: This brief site in English and Hebrew provides an overview of the museum.

Old Courtyard in Kibbutz Ein Shemer

ADDRESS: http://www.courtyard.co.il

DESCRIPTION: This museum is a restoration of an early kibbutz settlement. Its home page in English and Hebrew provides information about the archaeology, history, and agricultural machinery of the kibbutz.

Reuben and Edith Hecht Museum

ADDRESS: http://research.haifa.ac.il/~hecht/

DESCRIPTION: Dedicated to the theme of "The People of Israel in Eretz Israel," this archaeological museum based at Haifa University also houses artwork with an emphasis on Impressionism and the Jewish School of Paris. Its home page offers an online tour of the museum and provides access to the permanent and temporary exhibits, with examples from each, along with samples of the artwork. You can check the museum's publications list and its newsletter.

Tower of David Museum

ADDRESS: http://jeru.huji.ac.il/info_museum.htm

DESCRIPTION: A one-page information site in English and Hebrew on this museum, located inside Jaffa Gate in the old city of Jerusalem.

Yad Vashem

ADDRESS: http://www.yad-vashem.org.il

DESCRIPTION: Israel's official memorial to the Holocaust offers information about the time period, an online exhibit, excerpts from the foundation's publications, details about its archives and library, and a section on educational materials. There is also an online magazine. Of particular note is the section on "the righteous among the nations," which includes biographies of those who have been honored by Yad Vashem as rescuers of Jews.

MUSEUMS IN OTHER PARTS OF THE WORLD

Austrian Jewish Museum

ADDRESS: http://www.oejudmus.or.at/oejudmus

DESCRIPTION: From this site, in German and English, you can find basic information about the museum and its permanent exhibits, as well as a history of the Jewish Quarter in Eisenstadt, where the museum is based. There is a list of publications, a guest book, and a set of relevant Internet links.

Berlin's Jewish Museum

ADDRESS: http://www.hagalil.com/juedisches-museum/

DESCRIPTION: With text in German and English, this home page offers information about the museum, along with some samples of its artifacts.

Jewish Heritage Centre of Western Canada

ADDRESS: http://www.jhcwc.mb.ca/

DESCRIPTION: This site provides details about the services and events of the center in Winnipeg, the museum it houses, information about genealogical resources it contains, and the work of the Jewish Historical Society of Western Canada. Of particular note is the Search section of the site, that lists all of the family names of genealogical resources housed at the center.

Jewish Moroccan Heritage

ADDRESS: http://www.users.skynet.be/JMH/

DESCRIPTION: In English and French, this site describes the holdings of the center's library and audio-visual collection. Of particular note is the link to the Jewish Moroccan Art Museum containing samples of the collection in the areas of ritual objects, the yearly and life cycles, popular traditions, crafts, clothing and jewelry, music and painting, and photographs, engravings, and postcards.

Jewish Museum in Prague

ADDRESS: http://www.jewishmuseum.cz/index.htm

DESCRIPTION: From this site in English and Czech, you can take a virtual tour of the museum, read its current newsletter and older issues dating back to 1996, and find general information about the museum and its programs.

Jewish Museum of Australia

ADDRESS: http://home.vicnet.net.au/~jmuseum

DESCRIPTION: Based in Melbourne, this museum home page describes the facility and its events, gift shop, educational programs, and past and permanent exhibits. An online exhibit entitled "Art and Remembrance" about the Holocaust is also available.

Jewish Museum of Belgium

ADDRESS: http://www.mjb-jmb.org/

DESCRIPTION: This site, in English, French, and Dutch, describes the exhibits, events, and acquisitions of this museum in Brussels. You can also check out genealogical resources, the gift shop, and a set of relevant links.

Jewish Museum of London

ADDRESS: http://www.ort.org/jewmusm/

DESCRIPTION: From this Web site you can find information about the museum and its exhibitions, events, traveling exhibits, educational programs, and publications. You can also visit the permanent online exhibit on Yiddish theater in London and check the set of relevant Internet links.

Mechelen Museum of Deportation and the Resistance

ADDRESS: http://www.cicb.be/shoah/welcome.html

DESCRIPTION: "The Shoah Museum in Belgium is established in a place with which it has historical connections: a wing of the former General Dossin de Saint-Georges barracks in Malines. This small Flemish town is located halfway between Brussels and Antwerp where most of the Jews in this country live." Its home page describes the creation and contents of the museum and offers access to the National Memorial Foundation of Jewish Martyrs in Belgium and the Association of Jewish Deportees in Belgium.

Memorial to the Unknown Jewish Martyr

ADDRESS: http://www.paris.org/Musees/Juif.Inconnu/

DESCRIPTION: This one-page Web site describes the memorial in Paris.

Museo Sefardi in the Transitio Synagogue of Toledo

ADDRESS: http://www.servicom.es/museosefardi/

DESCRIPTION: This home page in Spanish offers only information about the museum and a visitor's guide.

Rhodes Jewish Museum

ADDRESS: http://www.rhodesjewishmuseum.org/

DESCRIPTION: Take an online tour of the Juderia in Rhodes and learn about the traditions and foods of the community from this Web site. You can purchase items from the gift shop; look at the historical exhibition, that is located in the rooms formerly used as the women's prayer rooms at the "Kahal Shalom" synagogue; and check the list of relevant links. Of particular note is the list of over 1,100 tombstones found in the Jewish cemetery.

Sidney Jewish Museum

ADDRESS: http://www.sjm.com.au/

DESCRIPTION: The home page for this museum, housing two permanent exhibits devoted to the Holocaust and Australian Jewry, is currently under construction.

Irish-Jewish Museum

ADDRESS: http://www.eecs.tufts.edu/~zblocker/ijm/

DESCRIPTION: Written by Zachary Blocker, this site is a visitor's review of the museum in Dublin. The page provides official information, along with a written review and several pictures.

Venice Museum

ADDRESS: http://www.doge.it/ghetto/oggettin.htm

DESCRIPTION: Samples of five artifacts from this museum, based in one of the old synagogues of Venice.

ORGANIZATIONS

EDUCATIONAL GROUPS

92nd Street Y

ADDRESS: http://www.92ndsty.org

DESCRIPTION: From the home page of this New York City group you can learn about the adult and children's programs, summer camp, concerts, dance performances, health and sports facilities, Jewish programs, tours and travel, and singles events sponsored by the "Y." You can also check the de Hirsch residence facility to find a short-term stay option in New York.

Educational Alliance

ADDRESS: http://www.edalliance.org

DESCRIPTION: The searchable page of this New York–based group describes its Jewish community center, family, and camping services, as well as its treatment programs. Employment opportunities are listed as well.

National Foundation for Jewish Culture

ADDRESS: http://www.jewishculture.org

DESCRIPTION: This site details the goals of the group, its membership benefits, and its support for theater, film, museums, archives, libraries, and research projects. You can learn how to apply for a grant; check the group's newsletter, *CultureCurrents,* whose archives date back to 1998; and read selected articles from the foundation's magazine, *Jewish Culture News.*

Jewish Bible Association

ADDRESS: http://www.jewishbible.org/

DESCRIPTION: This organization's goal is to bring the *Tanach* to the people. Its home page offers access to several methods for achieving that goal. Of particular note is the searchable 24-year index *to The Jewish Bible Quarterly,* published by the association, and the extensive Bible quizzes offering sets of questions about each parsha.

POLITICAL GROUPS

AIPAC: American Israel Public Affairs Committee

ADDRESS: http://www.aipac.org

DESCRIPTION: "The American Israel Public Affairs Committee, America's Pro-Israel lobby, is the only American organization whose sole mission is to lobby Congress about legislation that strengthens the relationship between the United States and Israel." Its searchable site provides a large number of primary source documents on the U.S.-Israel relationship, the peace process, Iran and other threats, and the status of Jerusalem. There is a section devoted to programs for students, as well as a listing of events. You can read the full text of the current issue of *Near East Report* online, along with selected articles from back issues.

American Jewish Congress

ADDRESS: http://www.ajcongress.org

DESCRIPTION: This group's goal is to "protect fundamental constitutional freedoms and American democratic institutions, particularly the civil and religious rights and liberties of all Americans and the separation of church and state." Its home page describes the history of the organization and offers access to its press releases, regional offices, and policy stands on women's issues, health and bio-ethics, legal issues, and Israel and the Middle East.

Freeman Center for Strategic Studies

ADDRESS: http://freeman.io.com/ and http://www.freeman.org

DESCRIPTION: Based in Texas, this center "attempts to aid Israel in her quest to survive in a hostile world, commissions extensive research into the military and strategic issues related to the Arab–Israeli conflict and disseminates pertinent information to the Jewish community and worldwide." You can order publications online, read selected articles from *The Maccabean Online,* and search its archives back to 1995. There is a set of relevant Jewish and news links, including a section on Christian Zionism.

IRIS: Information Regarding Israel's Security

ADDRESS: http://www.netaxs.com/~iris/

DESCRIPTION: "Information Regarding Israel's Security (IRIS) is an independent organization dedicated to informing the public about the security needs of the State of Israel, especially vis-à-vis the current peace process." You can sign up for its online mailing list and search its archives back to 1994. Along with recent headlines, you can access terror charts, which unfortunately have not been updated since 1998; security maps; Israel size maps; documents on PLO background material; and PLO quote sheets.

Jerusalem Center for Public Affairs

ADDRESS: http://www.jcpa.org

DESCRIPTION: "JCPA is an independent, nonprofit institute for policy research and education serving Israel and the Jewish people." In addition to information about the group's mission, research projects, and annual report, the Web site offers access to a number of resources, including a browsable publications catalog, selections from the newsletters *Jerusalem Letter* and *Jerusalem Letter/Viewpoints*, and full-text articles from the entire run of the journal *Jewish Political Studies Review*, dating back to 1992.

Jewish Council for Public Affairs

ADDRESS: http://www.jewishpublicaffairs.org

DESCRIPTION: The Jewish Council for Public Affairs is devoted to "safeguarding the rights of Jews here, in Israel, and around the world and promoting a just American society." Its searchable home page describes the group's resolutions, agendas, and policies and provides legislative updates. It allows provides access to its newsletter, JCPA Insider, and archived articles dating back to 1999. A set of links to similar sites is also available.

Jewish Peace Fellowship

ADDRESS: http://www.jewishpeacefellowship.org

DESCRIPTION: This group is committed to nonviolence and supports conscientious objectors. Its home page offers news and events of the group and access to selected articles of its *Shalom Newsletter* dating back to 1996. A browsable catalog of publications is also available. You can find articles about the Middle East, conscientious objection, capital punishment, war and peace, the draft, and social justice, along with reading lists and links to similar sites.

Republican Jewish Coalition

ADDRESS: http://www.rjchq.org

DESCRIPTION: "The Republican Jewish Coalition, founded in 1985, is the sole voice of Jewish Republicans to Republican decision makers and the Jewish community, expressing our viewpoint on a wide variety of issues." Its searchable home page discusses its policy platform and provides access to its bulletin, local chapters, and activities. There are links to relevant Republican and Jewish sites as well.

United States Information Service in Israel

ADDRESS: http://www.usis-israel.org.il

DESCRIPTION: Published by the United States Embassy in Israel and housing material formerly in the hands of the U.S. Information Agency, this searchable site provides extensive information on cultural activities, educational programs, press resources, and the search for peace in the Middle East. There is a searchable digital library, access to all the departments of the American government, and sections on U.S. initiatives, policy, and current issues. Details on embassy information and activities are also provided. This site houses many primary source documents, along with Arabic and Russian bulletins that are updated daily, and a link to Russian-language documents.

Virtual Israel Political Action Committee

ADDRESS: http://www.vipac.org

DESCRIPTION: The goal of this virtual political group is "to petition the U.S. government for a policy that is more supportive of Israel's security, historical, and biblical claims in Judea, Samaria, Gaza, and the Golan Heights." You can sign up to receive the group's newsletter and check its archives. The site also provides a list of government e-mail addresses and links to relevant Web sites.

RELIGIOUS GROUPS

AishDas Society

ADDRESS: http://aishdas.org/

DESCRIPTION: "The AishDas Society is committed to the advancement of meaningful worship in the Orthodox Jewish community. We must weld the *aish*, the fire of faith, with the *das*, the dictates of halachah." The group's home page describes its projects and offers access to a number of sites it houses. You can purchase *Toras Aish divrei Torah* on

CD, download *Ashirah Lashem: A Siddur for Friday Night Davening,* and read *divrei* Torah from Rabbi Yosef Gavriel Bechhofer. The site provides searchable access to the archives of Avodah, a mailing list that focuses on Jewish thought, and the archives of *Aspaqlaria,* a collection of *divrei* Torah. Of particular note are the links to projects by Rabbi Mordechai Torczyner. HaMakor is a *mar'eh mikomos,* a set of references to traditional Jewish literature.

Board of Deputies of British Jews

ADDRESS: http://www.bod.org.uk/

DESCRIPTION: The Board of Deputies is "the elected, national representative body of the British Jewish community." Its home page describes the group's positions on community issues, intergroup relations, and international issues, along with details about its Jewish Way of Life Exhibition and Jewish London Experience tour. The site also provides links in six areas: Israel, Holocaust Era Assets, Education, Community, Media, and Synagogal Bodies.

Cantors Assembly

ADDRESS: http://www.cantors.org

DESCRIPTION: The home page of this professional organization of cantors from the Conservative Movement describes the group's work and convention and provides links to other Jewish music and Conservative Movement sites. You can also order liturgical music, educational materials, choral music, Yiddish books and music, and cassettes and videos from its online store.

Chief Rabbi of the United Kingdom

ADDRESS: http://www.chiefrabbi.org/

DESCRIPTION: This searchable home page of Rabbi Jonathan Sacks features his speeches in transcript form and Real Player audio and video format; an archive of press releases dating to 1999; a searchable archive of feature articles written by the Chief Rabbi; the group's newsletter, *Renewal;* the history of the institution itself; and personal information on the man who currently holds the title.

CLAL, the National Jewish Center for Learning and Leadership

ADDRESS: http://www.clal.org

DESCRIPTION: "The pillars of CLAL's philosophy are living pluralism, dynamic engagement with Jewish texts and with the experiences of the

Jewish people, and a commitment to the sacred unity of clal Yisrael, the Jewish people in its entirety." Its Web page provides access to news and press releases dating back to 1998 and highlights its programs for educational and community leaders and for policy development. You can also e-mail its faculty through the staff directory, order its publications online, and read and sign up for a weekly electronic newsletter.

Edah

ADDRESS: http://www.edah.org

DESCRIPTION: "The mission of Edah is to give voice to the ideology and values of modern Orthodoxy and to educate and empower the community to address its concerns." At this time the site is under construction.

Gesher Center

ADDRESS: http://www.gesher.co.il

DESCRIPTION: Gesher's mission is "to help foster better understanding between the religious and secular communities and to encourage Israeli Jews from across the religious spectrum to develop a deeper sense of Jewish identity." Its home page in English and Hebrew describes the group's projects, its database of Jewish educators, and its two hostels in Jerusalem and Safed. You can participate in polls on Israeli religious issues and read the results, sign up for a mailing list, and vote on the "who is a Jew" issue.

Hineni

ADDRESS: http://www.hineni.org/

DESCRIPTION: Founded by Rebbetzin Esther Jungreis and dedicated to Jewish renewal, this page describes the group's events, programs, and publications and provides a question and answer section.

Israel Religious Action Center

ADDRESS: http://www.irac.org

DESCRIPTION: This searchable site in Hebrew and English describes the work of this group, "the public and legal advocacy arm of the Israel Movement for Progressive Judaism." Of particular note are the full-text documents relating to a wide variety of personal issues impacted by Israeli law, including adoption, burial, conversion, freedom of worship, and *kashrut*.

Masorti Movement in Israel

ADDRESS: http://www.masorti.org

DESCRIPTION: Affiliated with the Conservative movement, the home page of this umbrella Israeli religious organization lists the member congregations and provides news and views about the group. You can read selections from its *siddur,* along with prayers it has created such as "The Driver's Prayer." *Divrei* Torah dating back to 1997 are available, and you can sign up to receive them weekly online. The group's views on a variety of religious topics, a table of contents for responsa literature written by the group's rabbinical leaders, and two online lists, Shofar and Kesher, you can sign up to join are also listed. In addition, the site offers access to the group's youth program, Noam, and its adult study program, Midershet Iyun. Finally, there is a set of links to other like-minded synagogues.

National Council of Young Israel

ADDRESS: http://www.youngisrael.org.il

DESCRIPTION: The searchable home page of this umbrella organization of Orthodox synagogues offers a list of constituent members and information about services offered to them, an events calendar, a speaker's bureau, youth activities, social action projects, the women's division, and *divrei* Torah. Links to similar pages are provided as well.

New York Board of Rabbis

ADDRESS: http://www.nybr.org

DESCRIPTION: Details on the history and services of this rabbinical group and access to its online bulletin. You can find out how to "ask the rabbi" through the Rav Line.

Orthodox Caucus

ADDRESS: http://www.orthodoxcaucus.org

DESCRIPTION: The goal of this group is "to address a variety of pressing issues and challenges facing Orthodoxy and the Jewish community, in the most practical and effective way possible." The page describes its projects, including a prenuptial agreement. Of particular note is the call for discussion on women and Orthodoxy.

Rabbinical Assembly

ADDRESS: http://www.rabassembly.org/

DESCRIPTION: The searchable home page of this professional organization of Conservative rabbis provides information about the group and links to other Conservative sites. You can read selected articles from the group's journal, *Conservative Judaism,* dating back to 1997. There is a reserved section for members as well.

Rabbinical Council of America

ADDRESS: http://www.rabbis.org

DESCRIPTION: The searchable home page of this professional organization of Orthodox rabbis provides information about the group and its publications. There is a reserved section for members as well.

Union for Traditional Judaism

ADDRESS: http://www.utj.org

DESCRIPTION: "The Union for Traditional Judaism is an organization of lay people, educators, talmudic scholars, cantors, and pulpit rabbis who are dedicated to the principles of Traditional Judaism." Its home page contains its Declaration of Principles and an FAQ and provides access to its publications, discussion lists, and programs such as the MTV Challenge. You can learn about the group's rabbinical *metivta* study program and read samples from two of its newsletters, *Hagahelet* and *Kosher Nexus,* as well as *divrei* Torah from Rabbi Mordechai Friedfertig.

Union of American Hebrew Congregations

ADDRESS: http://uahc.org

DESCRIPTION: The home page of the synagogue arm of Reform Judaism features sections on adult study, learning for children, Torah resources, publications, and information about Reform Judaism. You can find links to NFTY, the group's youth movement, along with its college, Israel, and camp programs. Services to congregations are detailed, along with links to Internet Reform resources, discussion groups, Jewish news sources and directories, study and music, and Torahnet.

Union of Orthodox Jewish Congregations of America

ADDRESS: http://www.ou.org

DESCRIPTION: Home to a large number of Orthodox sites, this searchable site features information about the group's programs, e-mail lists, events, jobs hotline, public affairs, and public relations. You can check links to indices of worldwide Orthodox synagogues, Torah education, Shabbat Learning Center, teachers, holidays, *kashrut*, and Yerushalayim.net. Publications and Torah tapes can be purchased online, and you can "e-mail G-d" by sending a message to be placed in the Western Wall. Access is provided to the group's youth movement, NCSY; the monthly publication *Jewish Action* and its archives; a Jewish I.Q. quiz; projects such as Pardes and Yachad; and women's study seminars.

United Synagogue of America

ADDRESS: http://www.uscj.org

DESCRIPTION: The home page of this umbrella organization of Conservative synagogues describes the history of the group and provides access to its constituent congregations, Solomon Schechter day schools, USY youth programs, Koach college programs, and individual regions. You can read selected articles from *Review* magazine, browse the publications catalog, join several online listservs, and check out the Israel Center. A set of Conservative-related links is available, and the entire site is searchable.

United Synagogue of Great Britain

ADDRESS: http://www.brijnet.org/us/

DESCRIPTION: This home page of the traditional congregations of Great Britain helps you locate member synagogues and allows you to read and sign up for the weekly newsletter, *Daf Hashavua*.

ZIONIST GROUPS

Jewish Agency

ADDRESS: http://www.jafi.org.il/

DESCRIPTION: The searchable, multilingual home page of the group whose mission is to rescue and settle Jews worldwide in Israel describes its work in six major categories: Coming Home, Discover, Together, Mission, Connecting, and Caring. Coming Home focuses on *aliyah*, Discover describes the group's educational programs online and offline, Together deals with issues of unity and pluralism, Mission describes the history and structure of the organization, Connecting focuses on relations with world Jewry, and Caring describes the group's rescue and resettlement programs. You can also access the listservs sponsored by the organization and its new search engine and portal called NU. This is an excellent site for information related to Zionist topics.

World Zionist Organization

ADDRESS: http://www.wzo.org.il

DESCRIPTION: Formerly known as the Student Department of the World Zionist Organization, this group seeks to foster the relationship between world Jewry and Israel and to facilitate *aliyah*. In addition to describing its recent activities, the site has sections on *aliyah*, Israel programs, and materials of interest to university students. The entire site is available in Spanish as well. Of particular note is the extensive set of links to *hadracha* and educational resources, Zionist youth movements, government Web sites, and Zionist resources. This is a rich resource for Zionist information and materials.

American Zionist Movement

ADDRESS: http://www.azm.org

DESCRIPTION: This movement's goal is "to involve more Jews in Zionism and to take an activist posture on the Jewish scene." Its home page describes its programs, lists its member organizations, and offers access to its regional offices and calendar. You can read essays on Zionism, browse the catalog of publications, and check the relevant set of links to Zionist sources.

Amit Women

ADDRESS: http://www.amitchildren.org

DESCRIPTION: AMIT "stands for "AMericans for Israel and Torah" and its goal is to "nurture and educate Israel's children to become self-reliant and self-respecting members of society so that they will be prepared to make a valuable contribution to Israel." Its home page provides a browsable directory of the schools it operates in Israel, arranged by city. You can read selected articles from its magazine, AMIT, and find out about past and current events. Of particular note is the Tanach Yomi project, in which individuals and groups study a chapter of *Tanach* each day. You can purchase study guides for the program and register online for it.

Emunah Women

ADDRESS: http://emunah.org

DESCRIPTION: The home page of the world's largest religious women's Zionist organization describes the projects of the group in Israel, details news and convention information, offers travel packages, and provides selected articles from its magazine, *Emunah*.

Friends of Israel Disabled Veterans

ADDRESS: http://www.fidv-bh.com

DESCRIPTION: Through this site you can learn about the history and events of the group and the Beit Halochem centers it funds, review a wish list of donations, purchase items from the gift shop, read about a "hero of battle" and view video and photo clips, and participate in online discussion groups.

Hadassah

ADDRESS: http://www.hadassah.org

DESCRIPTION: Through the home page of this American women's Zionist group you can learn about its organization, educational projects, women's health work, advocacy projects, travel missions, international branches, and online events. You can also chat online and find out about the group's convention and employment opportunities and its voter challenge project. The group's publication, *Hadassah Magazine,* is also online and has browsable archives dating back to 1996. Finally, a link to the group's youth movement, Young Judaea, is also available.

International Coalition for Missing Israeli Soldiers

ADDRESS: http://www.mia.org.il/

DESCRIPTION: The soldiers' stories, a P.O.W. chronology, an archive of press articles, and laws and conventions relating to P.O.W.s constitute most of the offerings on this site, which also tells you how you can join the struggle to secure the release of Israeli soldiers missing in action or who are prisoners of war.

Israel Bonds

ADDRESS: http://www.israelbonds.com

DESCRIPTION: The searchable site of this U.S.-based group provides an FAQ and a list of rates and investment opportunities. You can locate local offices and read about delegations and events as well.

Israel Bonds of Canada

ADDRESS: http://www.israelbonds.net

DESCRIPTION: The searchable site of this Canadian-based group describes investment vehicles and benefits, as well as projects sponsored by the group. A list of local offices is also provided.

Jerusalem Center for Public Affairs

ADDRESS: http://www.jcpa.org/

DESCRIPTION: "JCPA is an independent, nonprofit institute for policy research and education serving Israel and the Jewish people since 1976." Details about the principal program areas of study are provided, along with extensive commentary on the center's findings in each of these areas. The site offers an online catalog of the center's publications, selected full-text versions of its newsletters, and the table of contents and abstracts of its journal *Jewish Political Studies Review,* dating back to 1989. This is a rich site of material for those interested in policy research.

Jerusalem Foundation

ADDRESS: http://www.jerusalemfoundation.org.il/

DESCRIPTION: Founded by Teddy Kollek, this group raises money to fund basic community facilities and services in Jerusalem. The home page describes the projects in six areas: Community Services, Sport and Recreation, Religious Services, Social Welfare and Health Services, Education, Arts and Culture, Beautification and Preservation, and Living Together: Pluralism and Coexistence. There is a page devoted to Jerusalem facts and figures as well.

Jerusalem Institute for Israel Studies

ADDRESS: http://www.jiis.org.il/

DESCRIPTION: The searchable site of this think tank on the future of Jerusalem describes the group's work in areas such as religious toleration, the peace process, arbitration between Jews and Arabs, and industrial development. Of particular note are the extensive lists of publications from the group in the areas of its research.

Jewish National Fund

ADDRESS: http://www.jnf.org

DESCRIPTION: This home page describes the group's history and projects, with a focus on its environmental and reforestration agenda. You can also learn about its action areas, community programs, college activities, and travel and tours. In addition, you can plant a tree online.

Jewish National Fund of Canada

ADDRESS: http://www.jnf-canada.org/

DESCRIPTION: This site describes the history of the organization, its fundraising programs, and its tree-planting activities. Of particular note is the educational section entitled "Israel, Landscape of Heritage," created by Mooli Brog and designed by Nurit Reshef. Aimed at children, this area offers instructional material about places and nature in Israel, a selection of songs, stories in English and Hebrew, games, and videos of the country.

Keren Kayemeth Leisrael

ADDRESS: http://www.kkl.org.il

DESCRIPTION: This English and Hebrew home page of the Jewish National Fund in Israel describes the group's history and projects, with a focus on its environmental and reforestration agenda. You can also learn about its youth clubs and educational programs and locate regional offices worldwide. In addition, you can plant a tree online. Of particular note in the Jewish Sources section are the *divrei* Torah by Nehama Leibowitz for 5759 and Simcha Raz for 5760. Also of note is the alphabetical listing of the names of missing persons from Eastern Europe in World War II, whose properties in Israel the KKL managed in the past or manages today.

Na'amat USA

ADDRESS: http://www.naamat.org

DESCRIPTION: "NA'AMAT, Hebrew acronym for 'Movement of Working Women and Volunteers,' is an organization and a movement striving to enhance the quality of life for women, children, and families in Israel, the U.S., and around the world." Its home page describes its history and work in the United States, Israel, and internationally. You can read selected articles from the current and back issues of *Na'amat Woman Magazine,* check events by region of the country, and learn about projects at the top of the organization's agenda.

New Israel Fund

ADDRESS: http://www.nif.org

DESCRIPTION: Dedicated to the strengthening of democracy and social justice, this group's home page in English and Hebrew highlights news about the group and details its events, study tours, issue areas, and volunteer and employment opportunities. The site also lists links to relevant Jewish, Israeli government, news, and Palestinian sites.

Sherut La'am

ADDRESS: http://www.virtualjerusalem.com/clients/wzo/zionet/sherut.htm

DESCRIPTION: Created by Jeffrey C. Lerman, this FAQ describes the Sherut La'am program, an Israeli version of the Peace Corps.

WIZO: Women's International Zionist Organization

ADDRESS: http://www.wizo.org

DESCRIPTION: The English and Hebrew home page of this group, dedicated to the welfare of women and children in Israel, describes the organization's projects, services, and structure and offers a clickable map to locate local offices. You can read articles from *The WIZO Review* and press releases and learn about the group's work at the UN.

Zionist Organization of America

ADDRESS: http://www.zoa.org/

DESCRIPTION: From this home page you can read some of the group's publications and press releases, check its calendar of events, and sign up for an online newsletter. A browsable archive of the newsletter called *ZINC* is available, back to 1998.

THE PALESTINIANS

Palestinian Academic Network

ADDRESS: http://www.planet.edu

DESCRIPTION: This searchable home page in English and Arabic offers access to seven Palestinian universities, along with several research centers and nongovernment sites. Of particular note is the extensive set of links to sites recommended or hosted by the network in areas including Palestinian information, Arab information, Arab university sites, Palestinian education, newspapers, Internet service providers, and general Palestinian sites.

Palestinian National Authority

ADDRESS: http://www.pna.net

DESCRIPTION: The official, searchable home page of the PNA provides links to news stories, editorials, articles, reports, and leaders' speeches. There are also sections on the settlements, the peace process, building Palestine, a daily press review, Jerusalem as the capital of Palestine, Palestine and the UN, the PLO, facts about Palestine, and links to government ministries. Related sites in the areas of academia and research, government and non-overnment institutions, colleges and universities, media and news, Internet service providers, banks, and statistical resources are also available.

THE PEACE PROCESS

Abraham Fund

ADDRESS: http://www.coexistence.org

DESCRIPTION: Committed to coexistence between Jews and Arabs in Israel, this group's home page describes its goals and offers access to local chapters, an interactive quiz, an online newsletter, a list of events, and related links. There is a database of funded projects searchable by organization name, project name, subject area, and funding year, along with an FAQ about how to apply for funding.

Americans for Peace Now

ADDRESS: http://www.peacenow.org/

DESCRIPTION: This searchable site describes the work of this American organization in support of Shalom Achshav, the Peace Now movement in Israel. News updates, calls to action, a calendar of events, and notices of Capitol Hill Conferences are all available here, along with a set of links to peace and Middle East links.

Ariga

ADDRESS: http://www.ariga.co.il/peace.htm

DESCRIPTION: This section of the larger Ariga Web site provides an extensive list of sites from both Israelis and Arabs devoted to the peace process. This is an excellent place to look for resources that support the peace process.

Dor Shalom

ADDRESS: http://www.dorshalom.org.il

DESCRIPTION: The Hebrew home page of this group, the Peace Generation, highlights the group's projects, local chapters, and student activities. There are online discussion groups and an explanation about the group and its goals in English as well.

Golan Heights Information Server

ADDRESS: http://www.golan.org.il/

DESCRIPTION: Hebrew, English, and Russian updates on the struggle to retain the Golan Heights. Of particular note are the links to Golan

Heights-related sites and the extensive hypertext directory of settlements on the Golan.

Jewish-Palestinian Encounter

ADDRESS: http://www.salam-shalom.net/

DESCRIPTION: "Project Encounter is a global movement of people intent on promoting human rights, communication, and reconciliation between peoples in conflict in the Middle East, the Balkans, and around the world." Its home page offers an online forum, along with a description of its projects, conferences, literary corner, and an extensive set of links to relevant and related sites.

Judea Magazine

ADDRESS: http://www.crosswinds.net/~judea/

DESCRIPTION: This publication presents the viewpoint of Jewish settlers on the West Bank. You can receive it free by e-mail or read the current issue and browse old issues back to 1993 online. There is also a subject index covering 1993 to 1998 that is searchable. The site has photos of the region and a map of Jewish settlements in Judea.

Professors for a Strong Israel

ADDRESS: http://www.aquanet.co.il/web/psi/

DESCRIPTION: The home page of this group, which "expresses opposition to the policies of the Rabin Government that endanger the security of the State of Israel," presents the group's views, its statements to the press, an opportunity to join its and related mailing lists, and a document archive of primary source materials supporting its positions. There is a set of related links as well.

Women In Green

ADDRESS: http://www.womeningreen.org/

DESCRIPTION: The home page of this group, which urges caution in the peace process negotiations, describes the group's positions and offers a photo and poster gallery, a mailing list, and links to sites expressing similar views.

Yitzhak Rabin Center for Israel Studies

ADDRESS: http://www.rabincenter.org.il

DESCRIPTION: This English and Hebrew site describes the work of this center devoted to the continuation of the work begun by Yitzhak Rabin when he served as prime minister. There is information on the archive, library, research institute, fellows program, grants, conferences, and public lectures. Details about the educational programs and materials produced by the center are also available, along with extensive sections on the life and words of Yitzhak Rabin and his assassination.

THE PERFORMING ARTS

Jewish Entertainment Resource Guide

ADDRESS: http://www.jewishentertainment.net

DESCRIPTION: "Jewish Entertainment Resources is a worldwide network of entertainers who make all or part of their living through the performance or presentation of Jewish material." You can search the database by performer's name or category. The site provides instructions on how to place a listing in the database as well.

MUSIC

Belz School of Jewish Music

ADDRESS: http://www.yu.edu/belz/

DESCRIPTION: The home page of the cantorial school of Yeshiva University provides information about the school, its current course descriptions and convention, and provides access to the *Journal of Jewish Music & Liturgy.*

Hava Nashira: A Jewish Songleader's Resource

ADDRESS: http://www.uahcweb.org/hanashir/

DESCRIPTION: This home page, maintained by Adrian Durlester, offers a guidebook for song leaders, bibliographies of song books and recordings, a hypertext list of Jewish music publishers and suppliers, and an extensive list of Jewish music links.

Israel Gimel: Israeli Jewish Midi Music Library

ADDRESS: http://members.aol.com/israelmidi/index.html

DESCRIPTION: This site provides an extensive collection of Jewish and Israeli music in midi format. Categories include religious, folk dance, klezmer, and holiday music, along with movie themes. Also included is a set of links to other Jewish music sites.

Israeli Guitar Archive

ADDRESS: http://www.geocities.com/Broadway/Stage/1534/

DESCRIPTION: This English and Hebrew site provides the guitar players' chords and tablatures for Israeli songs by 40 different bands. All songs have Hebrew and English text.

"Jerusalem of Gold"

ADDRESS: http://www.jerusalemofgold.co.il

DESCRIPTION: This site is devoted to a study of the song sung by Naomi Shemer. Included are the history of the song, its lyrics, Jewish sources, translations, musical score, and an explanation of its metaphors. The Resources section details instructional material related to the song.

Jewish Music Heritage Trust

ADDRESS: http://www.jmht.org

DESCRIPTION: Now called the Jewish Music Institute, the goal of this London-based organization is the preservation of the Jewish musical heritage. Its home page describes news about the group and lists its musical publications. There is also a link to Jewish Music Distribution UK, a leading specialist supplier of Jewish CDs, tapes, books, and sheet music.

Jewish Music Web Center

ADDRESS: http://www.jmwc.org

DESCRIPTION: Created by Brandeis University librarian Judith Shira Pinnolis, "the purpose of the Jewish Music WebCenter is to provide a forum for gathering and presenting information on academic, organizational, and personal activities in Jewish music today." Resources are provided in the areas of researching Jewish music, Web resources, getting to the music, places to study, reviews, festivals, organizations, societies and conferences, and general music and library resources. There are listings of announcements and a calendar of events, as well as a bibliography of biographies and a dictionary of Jewish music practitioners. A "featured sites" section is also available. This is an excellent, comprehensive site for anyone looking for a starting point in the area of Jewish music.

Jewish-Israeli Song Lyric Archive

ADDRESS: http://www.netspace.org/~dmacks/shira/archive-index.html

DESCRIPTION: Maintained by Daniel Macks, this page offers a browsable table of Jewish and Israeli song lyrics, arranged alphabetically by title. The lyrics are provided in rtf format, and the page includes instructions for using the archive. Information about the composer and lyricist is also provided.

Klezmer Shack

ADDRESS: http://www.klezmershack.com

DESCRIPTION: Everything you ever wanted to know about klezmer music you can find at this comprehensive, searchable site by Ari Davidow. You can locate people and bands by name and location, radio shows, sheet music, recordings, instruments, organizations, and record label contacts. There are reviews, top 10 lists, news, a calendar of events, and online discussions in Virtual Ashkenaz, as well as an extensive set of links to klezmer articles on the Internet. This is an excellent starting point for anything related to klezmer music.

Klezmer Webring

ADDRESS: http://www.geocities.com/Broadway/Stage/2452/Klezmerring.htm

DESCRIPTION: This is a starting point for klezmer sites, where you can also learn how to add your site to the Web ring.

Ladino Melodies of Sephardic Jews

ADDRESS: http://www.geocities.com/Paris/6256/ladino.htm

DESCRIPTION: Using Real Player, you can listen to more than 20 Sephardic songs, with a particular emphasis on the music of Moroccan Jewry.

MP3 Hebrew Center

ADDRESS: http://www.israeliz.co.il/mp3/

DESCRIPTION: Download samples of the latest in Israeli music from this site.

Zemerl

ADDRESS: http://www.princeton.edu/zemerl/

DESCRIPTION: This site is designed as a comprehensive interactive database about Hebrew, Yiddish, and Ladino Jewish music. The searchable database is arranged by category and lists the song, its composer, its lyricist, and comments about the title. You can add or modify database listings and, in many cases, listen to the songs themselves. There are feature articles, a list of songs the database is looking for, and a bulletin board, as well as a set of Jewish music links. This is an excellent starting point for information on particular Jewish songs.

MUSIC FOR SALE

A Bisl Yidishkayt

ADDRESS: http://www.yiddishmusic.com

DESCRIPTION: This Web site offers Yiddish music, books, and language materials for sale online. Choose from titles in the areas of klezmer, hasidic, cantorial, children's, and holidays. There are lengthy essays about klezmer music and its revival in the United States and Europe. You can also find sheet music, humorous titles, and videos here as well.

HaTaklit

ADDRESS: http://www.shalom3000.com

DESCRIPTION: Describes itself as carrying "the largest collection of Jewish and Israel recordings in the United States," the home page of this store also lists books, videos, and magazines. You can search its catalog or browse in several categories, including Book Best Sellers, Hebrew World, Star of David Movie Festival, Dudu Fisher, and Jerusalem 3000.

Hatikvah Music

ADDRESS: http://www.hatikvahmusic.com/

DESCRIPTION: The searchable home page of this Los Angeles Jewish music store offers online purchases of Yiddish, klezmer, cantorial, Sephardic, Ladino, and children's music and videos. There are sections on bargains, comedy, and the holocaust as well.

Jewish Music

ADDRESS: http://www.jewishmusic.com/ and http://www.tara.com

DESCRIPTION: This extensive online store for Jewish music features books, recordings, software, and videos that are searchable by category, artist, and title. It also serves as the home page for Tara Publishing, a leading publisher of Jewish music. You can check best-sellers, new releases, new additions, sale items, and recommended titles. Of particular note is the virtual listening station, where you can listen to music clips from the store's top 48 albums using Real Player. Samples from Israeli albums are also offered. This is a comprehensive site for music purchases.

Kol Ami

ADDRESS: http://www.sisuent.com

DESCRIPTION: "SISU Home Entertainment is the world's leading supplier of Israeli and Jewish videos, CDs, cassettes, games, and books." Use the e-mail feature to request a catalog.

Mostly Music

ADDRESS: http://www.jewish-music.com/mostly-default.asp

DESCRIPTION: The home page of this Brooklyn Jewish music store allows you to order music and videos online in a variety of categories, including solo artists, groups, choirs, hasidic music, instrumentals, Sephardic and Ladino music, wedding songs, klezmer, children's titles, cantorial music, and Israeli and holiday selections. The site is searchable by artist, album, song, and composer.

NMC

ADDRESS: http://www.nmc-music.co.il

DESCRIPTION: The searchable Hebrew and English home page of this Israeli record company offers a wide range of Israeli and general music for sale online. You can browse by category, check for best-sellers and sales, read the online magazine, and participate in online discussions.

AMERICAN MUSICAL GROUPS

Zamir Choral Foundation of New York

ADDRESS: http://www.zamirfdn.org

DESCRIPTION: The home page of this New York–based choral group features information about the constituent members of the foundation, including Hazamir, the National Jewish High School Choir, the Zamir Chorale, the North American Jewish Choral Festival, and the National Jewish Chorale.

Jewish Collegiate A Cappella Information

ADDRESS: http://www.neima.org/groups.htm

DESCRIPTION: "Ne'ima, which means 'melody' in old Hebrew, is a brand new organization designed to be an umbrella for Jewish music organizations on college campuses." Its home page features an extensive hypertext list of collegiate a cappella groups.

Shlock Rock Website

ADDRESS: http://www.shlockrock.com/

DESCRIPTION: The home page of this American Jewish rock and roll band known for setting Jewish lyrics to rock songs features information about the group and its music, an FAQ, and an opportunity to sign up for its online newsletter. You can also look at its photo album and check its calendar of performances. Of particular note is the group's database of songs, which allows you to search for music by category. Also of note is the educational material compiled by the group to be used in conjunction with its music.

Zamir Chorale of Boston

ADDRESS: http://www.zamir.org

DESCRIPTION: Information about the performance schedule of this choral ensemble is presented on its home page, along with recordings you can purchase online. A complete playlist and much of the group's sheet music are also available, along with several of its newest songs in MP3 format. There is information on the Renaissance composer Salamone Rossi and links to Jewish musical resources. Of particular note are the extensive, hypertext list of Jewish choral sheet music publishers, the lengthy bibliography of materials on Jewish music, and the database Zam'ru. The database, an index of Jewish choral music, is searchable by nine different criteria and is arranged in alphabetical order by composer.

Country Yossi

ADDRESS: http://www.countryyossi.com

DESCRIPTION: This New York–based family magazine offers articles about Torah, Israel, books, humor, music, controversial topics, and health and has columns on advice, health, and letters to the editor, all from a religious Jewish perspective. You can read archives dating back to 1996 and listen to selections from Country Yossi's albums using Real Player.

ISRAELI MUSICAL GROUPS

Israel Audio and Music Sites

ADDRESS: http://www.act.co.il/topics/israel.html

DESCRIPTION: ACT, an online Hebrew and English music magazine, presents an extensive set of links to Israeli recording studios, companies and organizations, media, radio, television, listservs, and individual Israeli musical artists.

Israel Opera Company

ADDRESS: http://www.israel-opera.co.il

DESCRIPTION: From this site you can find out about the history of the opera company and its current productions, education program, national stars, and international co-productions. Ticket and subscription information is provided, along with a seating chart of the opera house.

Israeli Philharmonic Orchestra

ADDRESS: http://www.ipo.co.il/

DESCRIPTION: Information in English and Hebrew on the history, music director, and orchestra members is available at this site, along with a listing of concerts and subscription prices. News about the orchestra and a listing of special concerts are also available. You can order tickets through Israel's online central booking service called Cartisim at http://www.cartisim.co.il.

Muzica

ADDRESS: http://www.muzica.co.il

DESCRIPTION: This Hebrew-language online magazine follows the Israeli music scene. You can read current columns and articles from the archives dating back to 1999, participate in online discussions, and listen to music clips in MP3 format.

DANCE

Dance Hall

ADDRESS: http://www.dancehall.co.il

DESCRIPTION: This online English and Hebrew magazine about Israeli folkdancing includes a database of Israeli folk dance sites searchable by country and city, listings of nostalgia dance sessions, and a database of dance sessions in Israel, searchable by instructor, city, and time of day. You can also look for a partner for pair dances.

Israelidance.com

ADDRESS: http://www.israelidance.com

DESCRIPTION: In addition to hosting the home pages of a number of folk dance groups, this site's most noteworthy resource is its database of more than 1,200 dances searchable by name, type of dance, and choreographer. You can also search for dance sessions worldwide and find information about dance camps.

Kesher LeMachol

ADDRESS: http://orion.webspan.net/~hgpklm/

DESCRIPTION: "Kesher LeMachol is a newsletter of Israeli dance and related events worldwide published six times per year by Honey Goldfein-Perry." The newsletter's home page provides class listings in the New York area and a history of dance camps throughout the United States. Of particular note is the dance index of 3,000 dances that can be ordered in print or electronic format. Information on the dance, including its history, recording, and steps, is provided.

THEATER AND FILM

Alden Films

ADDRESS: http://www.aldenfilms.com

DESCRIPTION: Browse the online catalog of this Jewish video provider for titles in the areas of Israel, the Holocaust, Jewish Literature, American Jewry, Judaism, Jews in Other Lands, Jewish Death and Mourning, Jerusalem, and Archaeology. "Included in the index are videos on Israel that are currently available for free (up to four videos) to educators, clergymen, and librarians in the tri-state region (NY, NJ, CT)."

Ergo Media Jewish Video Catalog

ADDRESS: http://www.jewishvideo.com

DESCRIPTION: This online catalog allows you to search for and purchase videos in the categories of Israel at 50, North America's Jews, Yiddish, the Holocaust, Israel, Classic Israeli Films, Jews around the World, Jewish Life and Tradition, and Children.

Jewish Film Archive

ADDRESS: http://www.jewishfilm.com/

DESCRIPTION: Created by Larry Mark, this site is "a not-for-profit archive of information on Jewish films and Jewish Film Festivals." You can view listings by title, subject, and year of distribution and browse the links to film festivals and acting awards.

National Center for Jewish Film

ADDRESS: http://www.jewishfilm.org

DESCRIPTION: The home page for this center, housed at Brandeis University, details information about new releases and special events. Of particular note are the browsable database of films in distribution, arranged by category and available for sale, and the listing of film screenings worldwide.

Research Library and Archives of Jewish Theater

ADDRESS: http://members.tripod.com/~jtheater/

DESCRIPTION: "This site is designed for those interested in the research of Jewish theater. Its focus is the study of Jewish national art theater as a cultural and social phenomenon of the late 19th–20th centuries, as well as histories of particular theatrical enterprises: GOSET (Russia), Habima (Russia, Palestine, Israel), Artef (USA), etc. The site comprises a wide scope of materials, including scholarship and documentary sources along with graphic images and links to electronic resources." There are indices of articles, pictures, bibliographies, primary sources, and Internet resources. The entire site is searchable.

Second Avenue Online

ADDRESS: http://www.yap.cat.nyu.edu

DESCRIPTION: This project, based at New York University, hopes to record the history of the American Yiddish theater. The site includes a history of Yiddish theater, an encyclopedia of theatrical biographies and shows accompanied by audio and video clips, and illustrated articles on Yiddish theater. In the spotlight section you can watch animated productions. The archives provide a list of Yiddish theater resources, and the digital library houses bibliographies and tapes relating to Yiddish theater studies. An events calendar and chat room are offered as well. The entire site is searchable.

PERSONALS

Jewish Geography

ADDRESS: http://www.jewishgeography.org

DESCRIPTION: Play Jewish Geography online at this site, where you can search for people by keyword or by hometown, college, or group affiliation. You can register yourself for free and sign up for an online newsletter as well.

GAY AND LESBIAN COMMUNITIES

Twice Blessed: The Jewish GLBT Archives Online

ADDRESS: http://www.usc.edu/isd/archives/oneigla/tb/

DESCRIPTION: Johnny Abush of Toronto created these archives, that now reside at the University of Southern California. There are resources in the areas of news, health, marriage, liturgy, the Holocaust, *tzedakah*, shopping, books, films, plays, and recordings. In addition, a number of indices and lists are provided, including U.S. and international directories and lists of discussion groups, chat rooms, personals and matchmaking, newsletters, and magazines and Webzines.

SINGLES

Single Jewish Woman's Website

ADDRESS: http://www2.acd-pc.com/~rsusselj/index.html

DESCRIPTION: Despite its name, this site, created by Rachel Furman, is aimed at Jewish singles of both sexes and "lists dating services, matchmaking services, singles groups, events, newsletters, and miscellaneous sites, as well as sites with advice, suggestions, and humor appropriate to the single Jew in search of his or her *basherte*." The lists described in each category identify whether the service is free or fee-based, the observance level of the participants, and the geographical locations covered. This is an excellent starting point for information for all Jewish singles.

Ark Electronic Shadcenter

ADDRESS: http://www.arkline.com

DESCRIPTION: You can search the database for free by gender and level of observance, correspond anonymously with members by e-mail, and participate in chat rooms and a discussion with a psychologist.

Basherte

ADDRESS: http://www.basherte.com

DESCRIPTION: Aimed at Jews who are looking as much at their spiritual development as at their dating, this site describes the group's workshop, its Israel tours, and its schedule of events. For a fee you can search the online database.

J-Mates

ADDRESS: http://www.jmates.com

DESCRIPTION: This site will allow you to post a profile and search the database for free. Other services have a fee attached and are described on the site. The site is available in Spanish and Portuguese as well.

Jewish Introductions

ADDRESS: http://www.jewishintroductions.com

DESCRIPTION: This site describes the benefits of subscribing to the introduction service and provides an FAQ, a list of dating tips, and an explanation of how the service works.

Jewish Match

ADDRESS: http://www.jewishmatch.com

DESCRIPTION: Read the advice columns and articles on travel, health, dining, dating etiquette, and romance and join the chat group in the online magazine for singles. You can also search the database by gender, age, and location and check the calendar of events.

Jewish Matchmaker System

ADDRESS: http://www.yenta.email.net

DESCRIPTION: You can fill out an online questionnaire for a free trial membership. Your identity will be concealed unless you choose to reveal it.

Jewish Quality Singles

ADDRESS: http://www.jqs.com

DESCRIPTION: "All areas on this site are free to view. If you would like to contact any members and/or post your own ad, you must become a member yourself," for which there is a fee. You can also sign up for a newsletter with events relevant to your zip code.

Jewish Singles Connection

ADDRESS: http://www.thejewishpeople.org

DESCRIPTION: Part of a project funded by the Federation of Cleveland, the site features a database of singles' activities and travel programs throughout the United States and Canada, searchable by geographic location. You can add your profile to the personals section for free and also read about success stories.

Jewish Singles in Brazil

ADDRESS: http://www.jewsinglesite.com.br

DESCRIPTION: This site, in Portuguese, English, and Spanish, offers an online tour and FAQ highlighting its services. Of particular note is the extensive set of links to Jewish and general sites, with a particular emphasis on Latin America.

JDate: Jewish Singles Network

ADDRESS: http://www.jdate.com

DESCRIPTION: Free registration is offered to this site that describes itself as "the largest Jewish singles network on the Internet." The home page describes the costs and conditions of the service and the group's cruise and highlights success stories.

Jewish Singles News

ADDRESS: http://www.jewishsinglesnews.com

DESCRIPTION: Describing itself as "the largest newspaper for Jewish singles ages 21–88 in the country," the listings in this Web site cover the New York, New Jersey, and Connecticut singles communities. It offers readers and subscribers a list of monthly calendar of events, a singles' travel calendar, personal ads, tips on dating, and feature columns.

Jewishsingles.net

ADDRESS: http://jewishsingles.net

DESCRIPTION: Free registration provides you with a variety of services, including a worldwide database you can search by gender, location, and age. Additional services are available for a fee.

NewFlame.com

ADDRESS: http://www.newflame.com

DESCRIPTION: The site for this Jewish dating service for singles in the United Kingdom and Europe allows you to search its database by a number of parameters for free. If you choose to contact someone from the database, there is a fee involved. You can also add yourself to the database.

Nice Jewish Singles

ADDRESS: http://www.nice-jewish.com

DESCRIPTION: This site allows you to "search through thousands of profiles to find people who meet your specific criteria based on interests, lifestyle, location, and more. Then send messages to the people whom you have chosen, quickly and anonymously from the comfort of your own home or office." You can create an anonymous e-mail address at the site through which to communicate.

Orthodox Connection

ADDRESS: http://www.the-wire.com/shadchan

DESCRIPTION: "Orthodox Connection is a confidential and discreet computer-aided matchmaking service for clients who are Shomer Shabbos and keep a kosher home." Its four offices in the United States and Canada offer a personal interviewing process. Fees for registering are outlined.

SCIENCE

Israel Science and Technology Homepage

ADDRESS: http://www.science.co.il

DESCRIPTION: This home page, created by Dr. Israel Hanukoglu when he served as science adviser to the Israeli prime minister, functions as a clearinghouse of information about Israeli sites and information relating to agriculture, biosciences, chemistry, computer science, earth and environment, economics, education, engineering, the Internet, mathematics, medical sciences, physics, psychology, social sciences, statistics, and technology. The entire site is searchable. This is an excellent starting point for all types of scientific information.

Association of Orthodox Jewish Scientists

ADDRESS: http://www.aojs.org/

DESCRIPTION: Information on the activities and publications of this international group, based in New York, whose goal is "science in the service of Torah."

Israeli Association of Electronics Industries

ADDRESS: http://www.iaei.org.il

DESCRIPTION: From this home page that profiles the Israel electronics industry, you can learn about the organization and its members, as well as international cooperation ventures and investment incentives. Companies participating in job fairs are listed, as well as upcoming events. Of particular note is the database of members, searchable by company name, product category, employee size, and annual revenue.

Jewish Scientist Network

ADDRESS: http://www.jsn.org/jsnhome.html

DESCRIPTION: This site serves as a clearinghouse for announcements, articles, pointers to articles, book reviews, historical notes, hyperlinks, editorials, comments, and suggestions that the Webmasters have categorized into 44 subject areas.

SEPHARDIM

Sephardi Connection

ADDRESS: http://sephardiconnect.com

DESCRIPTION: The main features of this site are the forums built around the subjects of Sephardic Judaism and *Sephardim*; their history, culture, literatures, languages, and genealogy; and their past, present, and future struggles and concerns. You can sign up for more than 14 groups and view links to museums, music, news, and holiday material of Sephardi interest.

Worldwide Sephardic Community

ADDRESS: http://www.bsz.org

DESCRIPTION: Created by Shaarei Zion Congregation in Brooklyn, this large directory of Sephardic sites is arranged by category and covers the origins and definition of Sephardic Jewry, genealogy, food, music, synagogues, and other Sephardic organizations. There is also a gateway to the Brooklyn Sephardic community, with news, chat rooms, a calendar of events, a searchable database of *minyanim*, classified ads, music, and links to other sites about Syrian Jewry. The last searchable directory covers over 1,000 home pages of Jewish interest, with a special emphasis on Sephardic Jews. This is an excellent portal for material about the Sephardic community, particularly Syrian Jewry.

European Sephardic Institute

ADDRESS: http://www.sefarad.org/

DESCRIPTION: In English, Spanish, and French, this searchable site has areas about the group's goals and membership, along with links to its hosted publications, the Sephardic world on the Internet, Israel, and the Jewish communities of Belgium. Social announcements, a discussion forum, and a guestbook are also available. You can sign up to be part of the group's listserv as well.

Ivri-Nasawi

ADDRESS: http://www.ivri-nasawi.org/

DESCRIPTION: This home page of the New Association of Sephardi/Mizrahi Artists & Writers International offers news and information about the group, a calendar of events, a bulletin board for discussion, and details about the National Sephardi Literary Contest. Full text of the organization's newsletter is available, along with archives dating back to the end of 1999.

Portuguese Jewry

ADDRESS: http://www.saudades.org

DESCRIPTION: Created by Rufina Bernardetti Silva Mausenbaum, this site provides access to resources and books about the community. It also offers individuals the opportunity to share their memories about the Portuguese Jewish experience and participate in the discussion forum. Links to Sephardic Jewish sites are also available.

Rhodesli Sepharidic Ring

ADDRESS: http://www.geocities.com/Heartland/Valley/2177/rhoserng.htm

DESCRIPTION: Owned by Petros Michailidis, this ring unites sites dealing with the Sephardic Community of Rhodes Greece.

Routes of Sefarad

ADDRESS: http://www.redjuderias.org

DESCRIPTION: A Spanish-language site that highlights the cities in which Jews lived and the legacies they left behind.

Sephardi/Mizrahi Studies Caucus

ADDRESS: http://www.princeton.edu/~rsimon/ssc.htm

DESCRIPTION: Begun in 1998, "the central aim of the Sephardi/Mizrahi Studies Caucus is to promote the integration of Sephardi and Mizrahi Studies into general Jewish Studies, both in teaching and in scholarship." This home page, maintained by librarian Rachel Simon, provides links to organizations and resources, scholars and their research, courses, syllabi, conferences, and grants in the field.

Sephardim.Org

ADDRESS: http://www.sephardim.org

DESCRIPTION: Created by David Silvera, this site focuses on Jamaican Jewry and includes a section on the community's history and genealogical resources. There is also an area describing the history of Neveh Shalom, the synagogue in Spanish Town. Of particular note is the section on Spanish and Portuguese liturgy, that provides sample sound files for Shabbat and the holidays, as well as the Torah and Haftorah cantillations.

Tunisian Jews

ADDRESS: http://www.harissa.com/

DESCRIPTION: Through this searchable site in English and French you can learn about the history, religion, customs, arts, food, and music of the Tunisian community. There are also ads, a chat room, photos, and a hypertext list of Tunisian cities.

SOCIAL ACTION

Just Tzedakah

ADDRESS: http://www.just-tzedakah.org

DESCRIPTION: This extensive site is aptly subtitled "The Web Resource for Donors to Jewish Charities." It has sections on halachic guidelines for donations, complete with *ma'aser* calculator, what Jewish law teaches about *tzedakah*, community guidelines for donations, fundraising techniques, and online giving. Of particular note is the searchable database of Jewish charitable organizations, with reports detailing how their money is spent. This is an outstanding resource for information on Jewish charities.

Yashar

ADDRESS: http://www.israel-nonprofit.org OR http://www.intournet.co.il/yashar/index.htm

DESCRIPTION: The goal of YASHAR, which means "direct" is "the maintenance of a listing of Israeli nonprofit organizations for the purpose of providing donors with information about nonprofit organizations in the State of Israel." Organizations are listed by area of interest, and each entry details the group's history, goals, activities, membership, policies, scope, affiliations, funding needs, and contact information. The site also provides tax information and links to other charitable sites. This is an excellent directory of Israeli nonprofit organizations.

American Jewish Society for Service

ADDRESS: http://www.ajss.org

DESCRIPTION: Similar to Jimmy Carter's Habitat for Humanity, the goal of this group is to give young people an opportunity to serve their fellow men in need by participating in voluntary summer work camps throughout the United States, constructing or repairing communal buildings and homes. Its home page describes the program and has a question and answer section and an application.

Domestic Abuse and the Agunah Problem

ADDRESS: http://users.aol.com/agunah/index.htm

DESCRIPTION: Maintained by social worker Mark Cwik, this page provides articles on domestic abuse, Jewish abuse, and the *agunah* problem; halachah, documents, and responsa on Jewish family law; a bibliography of articles and books on these topics; a directory of resources for victims of Jewish domestic abuse, including shelters and contact persons; resources for *agunot*, including agencies and contact persons; personal stories; and links to other relevant sites.

Jewish Fund for Justice

ADDRESS: http://www.jfjustice.org

DESCRIPTION: The goal of this group is to "assist community-based groups to support programs that promote self-sufficiency and sustainable solutions to problems." Its home page describes its goals, its grants and recipients, and guidelines for requesting funding. You may order the group's educational materials online.

American-Israeli Cooperative Enterprise

ADDRESS: http://www.us-israel.org/

DESCRIPTION: The enterprise's goal is "to strengthen the U.S.–Israel relationship by developing social and educational programs in the U.S. based on innovative, successful Israeli models that address similar domestic problems, and bringing novel U.S. programs to Israel." Its extensive and searchable site has a section on its publications that can be read in full text online. Of particular note are the group's reports on relationships between most individual U.S. states and Israel. Also of note is the in-depth resource center, with articles on numerous topics of Jewish interest. Finally, the site houses a noteworthy virtual tour of Israel. This is a rich and well-created site that provides excellent resources in a variety of areas.

Adoption

ADDRESS: http://www.starsofdavid.org/

DESCRIPTION: "Stars of David International is a nonprofit information and support network for Jewish and partly Jewish adoptive families of all sizes, ages, and origins." Its home page provides a directory of local chapters, along with a calendar of events and membership information. You can find out about volunteer opportunities as well. Of particular note are the links to Jewish and general adoption resources online and the bibliography of articles and books on Jewish adoption.

American Jewish Committee

ADDRESS: http://ajc.org

DESCRIPTION: The mission of this group is to "safeguard the welfare and security of Jews in the United States, in Israel, and throughout the world; strengthen the basic principles of pluralism around the world, as the best defense against anti-Semitism and other forms of bigotry; and enhance the quality of American Jewish life by helping to ensure Jewish continuity and deepen ties between American and Israeli Jews." Its searchable home page provides access to its action alerts, press releases, regional chapters, and events. It has sections on programs relating to Jewish life, Israel, international issues, and domestic problems. The full text of its publications is available online, as are the ads the group has run in publications nationwide.

American Jewish World Service

ADDRESS: http://www.ajws.org

DESCRIPTION: The home page of this relief organization describes the programs it sponsors worldwide, arranged by continent. You can learn how to participate in its volunteer corps and outreach activities.

B'tselem

ADDRESS: http://www.btselem.org

DESCRIPTION: The Hebrew and English home page of the Israel Information Center for Human Rights in the Occupied Territories describes the work of the group, and provides access to primary source documents in the area of human rights and to a catalog of publications. You can sign up to receive an online newsletter and check the list of links to human rights sources online.

Congress of Secular Jewish Organizations

ADDRESS: http://www.csjo.org

DESCRIPTION: "The Congress of Secular Jewish Organizations is composed of independent organizations whose unity of purpose is a secular expression of our Jewish heritage, with particular emphasis on the cultural and ethical precepts of Jewish learning." Its home page features information about its events, scholarships, and employment opportunities. You can access its constituent organizations, browse its catalog of publications, and check its annotated list of resources as well.

Ezras Torah Relief Fund

ADDRESS: http://www.ezrastorah.org

DESCRIPTION: "Ezras Torah is a nonprofit Jewish relief organization that specializes in supplying funds to needy Torah families in Israel and the world over." You can learn about the group's history and programs and order a copy of its halachic luach.

HIAS: The Hebrew Immigrant Aid Society

ADDRESS: http://www.hias.org

DESCRIPTION: The home page of this immigrant and resettlement group details the history of the organization and news updates about it, as well as provides access to local offices. Information is also given on its scholarships and convention, and there are links to other immigrant and refugee sites. Of particular note are the sections on facts and figures that detail immigration statistics dating back to 1954, the legislative update section that describes current congressional action affecting immigrants, and the extensive section on immigration information.

JCC Association

ADDRESS: http://www.jcca.org

DESCRIPTION: From the home page of this umbrella organization of Jewish Community Centers, you can find member centers and camps and check job listings and relevant Jewish links. There is information on the Maccabi Games, an early childhood resource center, Israel programs, and the group's biennial convention. Special sections for members offer additional services, including a private intranet service. Finally, there is a link to the Jewish Welfare Board's chaplains.

Jewish Abuse Domestic Violence Hotline

ADDRESS: http://www.jewishabuse.org/

DESCRIPTION: "The mission of Community Help and Abuse Information, CHAI, is to create a supportive environment that addresses domestic abuse in the Jewish community through advocating for victims, educating the community, and raising awareness about available options." Its home page describes its programs, a calendar of events, information for victims, and tips on recognizing child abuse and domestic violence.

Jewish Braille Institute

ADDRESS: http://www.jewishbraille.org

DESCRIPTION: Learn about the projects of this institute dedicated to the integration of the blind and visually impaired into Jewish life from this home page. Details are provided about children's and youth programs, college and professional education, assistance to the elderly, programs in Israel, outreach to Eastern European and Soviet Jews, and community-based activities. You can learn about volunteer opportunities, library services, and magazines available to the blind and read the current issue of the newsletter *Points.*

Jewish Prisoner Services International

ADDRESS: http://www.jewishprisonerservices.org/

DESCRIPTION: From this Web site you can check the services offered by this group that is dedicated to the welfare of Jewish prisoners throughout the world. You can locate regional offices, read press releases, and learn about its pen pal program. A set of relevant links is also provided.

Jewish War Veterans

ADDRESS: http://www.penfed.org/jwv/home.htm

DESCRIPTION: The home page of this American veterans group concentrates on information about its convention and also lists the group's resolutions.

Jewish Women International

ADDRESS: http://www.jewishwomen.org

DESCRIPTION: "Focusing on family violence and the emotional health of children, Jewish Women International strengthens the lives of women, children, and families through education, advocacy, and action." Its home page describes the group's history and programs in the areas of domestic violence and child abuse and provides access to its press releases and chapters worldwide. There is a section on career opportunities and a members-only area as well.

Jews in Recovery from Alcoholism and Drug Abuse

ADDRESS: http://www.jacsweb.org/

DESCRIPTION: From this home page you can find access to the group's local meetings, arranged by state, and read about the spiritual sources of its program and personal stories of its participants. A library of materials and numerous bibliographies are also available.

Joint Distribution Committee

ADDRESS: http://www.jdc.org

DESCRIPTION: The home page of this group, known for its rescue and relief programs worldwide, describes its work, details its global, nonsectarian activities arranged by region, and provides a searchable library of its news stories.

Mazon

ADDRESS: http://shamash.org/soci-action/mazon/

DESCRIPTION: Meaning "sustenance" in Hebrew, Mazon is dedicating to eradicating hunger in America. Its home page describes its work and programs, the state of hunger in America, the Jewish tradition of *tzedakah*, and a financial statement of the group.

National Council of Jewish Women

ADDRESS: http://www.ncjw.org

DESCRIPTION: The home page of this group of "advocates for social justice" describes the issues and advocacy positions of the group, along with its programs and projects, and highlights the organization's efforts in the areas of voting, gun control, and child-care. You can read articles from the current issue of the *NCJW Journal* and check articles back to 1998. Other publications from the organization are also available online, along with links to Web sites dealing with social action issues.

Nisan Young Women Leaders

ADDRESS: http://www.nisan.org

DESCRIPTION: Nisan Young Women Leaders seeks to develop the leadership potential of Jewish and Arab Israeli young women. Its home page describes the programs of the group, gives news about its activities, and offers an area for members. Of particular note is the resource center, that provides a database of career mentors, along with links to sites of interest to young women.

Ohel: Jewish Children and Family Services

ADDRESS: http://www.ohelfamily.org/

DESCRIPTION: Ohel is an agency servicing children who are neglected, are abused, and suffer from mental illness and developmental disabilities. Its focus is on the religious community. From its Web site you can find out about its programs, speaker's bureau, events, and volunteer opportunities. The library provides some articles on child abuse and neglect, and samples of children's work are also available.

Shalem Center

ADDRESS: http://www.shalem.org.il

DESCRIPTION: The English and Hebrew home page of this research institution which studies Jewish social thought and Israeli public policy, describes the group's work and provides access to details about its graduate and senior fellowships. You can read selected articles from the center's journal, *Azure,* and search its archives, as well as order its books online.

Shalom Center

ADDRESS: http://www.shalomctr.org/

DESCRIPTION: Directed by Rabbi Arthur Waskow, the Shalom Center "brings Jewish spirituality, tradition, and experience to bear on issues of *tikkun olam*—pursuing peace, seeking justice, healing the earth, and building community." Its section entitled "Worlds of Action" contains articles on peace, justice, healing the earth, and community. The area on Study lists the group's teachers, books, and tapes and provides a set of relevant links to Web sites. The section called "Worlds of Spirit" has *divrei* Torah for each week of the year, for holidays, and for lifecycle events, along with writings about the main prayers of the *siddur.*

Tzedek

ADDRESS: http://www.tzedek.org.uk

DESCRIPTION: Based in the United Kingdom, Tzedek is a Jewish overseas development and educational charity that provides direct support to the developing world and educates the Jewish community as to the causes and effects of poverty. In addition, Tzedek organizes an Overseas Volunteer Programme in which Jewish volunteers work for up to eight weeks during the summer at development projects in Africa and Asia. Its searchable home page describes this project and other programs and events, articles about the organization, and links to other

Jewish sites. You can participate in a chat room and join online discussions as well.

United Jewish Appeal

ADDRESS: http://www.uja.org/ and http://www.ujc.org and http://www.jewishfedna.org and http://www.jewishcommunities.org

DESCRIPTION: Now the United Jewish Communities, this home of North America's federations describes the group's mission, details about its campaign and recipients of its funds. There is a searchable directory of local chapters, press releases, news, and a national calendar of events as well. You can also browse the national and family mission tours listed.

United Jewish Communities: The Federations of North America

ADDRESS: http://www.uja.org/ and http://www.ujc.org and http://www.jewishfedna.org and http://www.jewishcommunities.org

DESCRIPTION: Formerly known as the United Jewish Appeal, this home of North America's federations describes the group's mission and details about its campaign and recipients of its funds. There is a searchable directory of local chapters, press releases, news, and a national calendar of events as well. You can also browse the national and family mission tours listed.

Wolk Center for the Jewish Deaf

ADDRESS: http://www.infoshop.com/wolkcenter

DESCRIPTION: The home page of this Rochester, New York–based group describes the center's work and its conference and allows you to sign up for its online discussion group.

Yad Sarah

ADDRESS: http://www.yadsarah.org.il/

DESCRIPTION: The Hebrew and English home page of this largest volunteer organization in Israel which provides "a spectrum of free or nominal cost services to help sick, disabled, and elderly people remain at home," describes its history and services. You can also learn about Israeli innovations in health care, mission tours, and volunteer opportunities and sign up for an online newsletter. Of particular note is the directory of easy-access sites for tourists in Israel.

Ziv Tzedakah Fund

ADDRESS: http://ziv.org

DESCRIPTION: Danny Siegel's wonderful Tikun Olam projects are described in the searchable home page of this organization, which distributes money to small groups and individuals worldwide who are looking to make a difference. You can read the annual report and find out about books by Danny Siegel. The group has published a *tzedakah* curriculum, that is also available for sale. Of particular note is the section of "116 Practical Mitzvah Suggestions."

ORT

ADDRESS: http://www.ort.org

DESCRIPTION: "ORT, founded in 1880 in St. Petersburg, is today a global, nonprofit organization, meeting the education and training needs of contemporary societies around the world." The site is divided into six major areas. The first provides organizational information, including access to local chapters and departments, press releases, publications list, and events. The Jewish Educational Resources section provides links, with an emphasis on British Web sites. The Global Campus area is notable for its online educational programs, including Navigating the Bible, EnglishSpace, and a host of Jewish instructional materials. The Jewish Community section houses a number of organizations' home pages, and the Cyberspace area lists relevant Jewish links.

STUDENTS

UNIVERSITY GROUPS

Hillel

ADDRESS: http://www.hillel.org

DESCRIPTION: The home page of this international Jewish university students' organization details the group's work, educational programs, public policy stances, departments, travel and summer opportunities, conferences, and employment openings. Using Real Player, you can listen to and view clips from the group's audio-visual library. Listings for programming resources, scholarships, awards, and discussion groups are available as well. Of particular note is the guide to Jewish life on campus, that is searchable by name of school, country, and region. This is an excellent starting point for students looking for information about Jewish life on campus.

Association des Etudiants Juifs

ADDRESS: http://www.aej-france.org

DESCRIPTION: The French-language page of this national Jewish students' association describes its history, goals, and vacation programs, along with a list of relevant links.

Kesher

ADDRESS: http://www.keshernet.com

DESCRIPTION: The home page of this organization for Reform students has sections for high school students, college students, congregations, campus leaders, and campus professionals. Resources provided include a directory of members, a guidebook for song leaders, and information about grants. You can join a listserv and find details about the group's annual convention. Of particular note is the section aimed at high school students that offers guidelines for choosing a college with a Jewish presence.

Koach

ADDRESS: http://www.uscj.org/koach

DESCRIPTION: The searchable home page of this organization for Conservative students describes the goals and activities of the group. You can read the organization's newsletter, sign up for a listserv, and check the Jewish holiday information provided. The Resources section helps students choose a college and guides them toward study in Israel, building a personal Jewish library, and considering careers in the Jewish community.

National Jewish Law Students Association

ADDRESS: http://www.seamless.com/njlsa/

DESCRIPTION: From this home page you can learn about the activities, publications, and annual conference of this group that seeks to build bridges within and outside the Jewish community. A listing of community events, a guest book, and an online newsletter are available. You can locate local chapters of the group through the links section, along with a list of relevant Jewish and legal sites.

Union of Jewish Students of Great Britain and Ireland

ADDRESS: http://www.ujs.org.uk

DESCRIPTION: The home page of this university group describes its mission and events and its educational program in Israel and provides links to the Web sites of local chapters, along with other relevant Jewish and student home pages.

YOUTH GROUPS

ANJY: A Network for Jewish Youth

ADDRESS: http://www.anjy.org/

DESCRIPTION: ANJY is a national training, resource, and development agency with 130 affiliated clubs and organizations in Britain. It recently merged with the UJIAs Makor Educational Resource Centre, forming the largest network of youth services in the United Kingdom. Its home page provides news about the group, along with a chat room, listservs, and links to relevant Jewish and social action sites. The site is most notable for its resources, including the Ultimate Jewish Youth Groups Guide and a full-text game book.

Betar-Tagar

ADDRESS: http://www.betar.org/

DESCRIPTION: Betar is a youth group associated with the Revisionist movement, and Tagar is the group's college division. Its Web site provides information on local and national programs, Israel tours, *aliyah*, activism campaigns, and online chats. You can browse an international directory of local chapters arranged by region and city, play online e-games, and download many of the group's publications as well. A list of relevant links is also provided.

Bnei Akiva of the United States and Canada

ADDRESS: http://www.bneiakiva.org

DESCRIPTION: "Bnei Akiva is dedicated to bringing Torah Va'Avodah Religious Zionism to North America." Its searchable Web site features information about its national and summer programs and provides listings of fund raising and educational programming ideas. You can also read the group's monthly publication, *Akivon*, and download its weekly *divrei* Torah, *Likrat Shabbat.*

Habonim Dror

ADDRESS: http://www.habonimdror.org/

DESCRIPTION: "Habonim Dror is a Labor Zionist youth movement with summer camps and local chapters throughout the United States and Canada." Its home page describes its Israel programs and provides a searchable directory of its summer camps and local chapters. You can read the group's publication *BaTnua* online as well. A list of Jewish sites is also available.

Hashomer Hatzair

ADDRESS: http://www.hashomer.org

DESCRIPTION: Part of the International Progressive Zionist Movement, Hashomer Hatzair's Web page describes the group's events and programs, summer camp, and mailing lists. Also provided is a directory of worldwide chapters and local chapters in North America. A set of relevant Jewish links is available as well.

Ideanet

ADDRESS: http://www.jewishyouth.com

DESCRIPTION: Created by Avi Frier, IdeaNet provides resources for Jewish youth professionals. You can sign up for an online subscription and browse the archives dating back to 1996. Information about a paid subscription to the compendium, which organizes resources by subject, is also available, as is a listing of job opportunities. Of particular note is the extensive set of links to Jewish sites in 18 categories, including camps, educators' resources, children and teen sites, Jewish crafts and activities, and youth groups.

Israel Scouting Network

ADDRESS: http://israel.scout.net/

DESCRIPTION: From this home page you can learn about the organization and trappings of the Israeli Scout movement. The site features links to the home pages of local scout troops throughout the country.

Israel Youth Groups

ADDRESS: http://www.geocities.com/Pentagon/Barracks/8945/imageindex.html

DESCRIPTION: Choose *Peulot* from the listings on this Hebrew language site, and you will have access to the home pages of the major Israeli youth groups. The site also houses a good collection of educational links in the Sifriyah section that are arranged by topics, including many Jewish subjects.

National Jewish Committee on Scouting

ADDRESS: http://www.shamash.org/scouts/

DESCRIPTION: "The mission of National Jewish Committee on Scouting is to promote Boy Scouting among Jewish youth, to help Jewish institutions and local council Jewish committees to provide Scouting opportunities for Jewish youth, and to promote Jewish values in Scouting through program help and the religious emblems program." The group's home page describes the emblems, provides a calendar of events, and gives full-text access to its publications. You can sign up for a listserv and check other scouting resources as well. There are also directories of regional subcommittees and Jewish-sponsored scout troops worldwide.

National Jewish Girl Scout Committee

ADDRESS: http://www.njgsc.org/

DESCRIPTION: The National Jewish Girl Scout Committee is a nonprofit organization that works in cooperation with Girl Scouts of the USA to promote the Jewish Girl Scout award and to encourage cultural exchanges with the Israel Boy and Girl Scouts Federation. Its home page describes the award and lists the group's publications.

NCSY: National Council of Synagogue Youth

ADDRESS: http://www.ou.org/ncsy/

DESCRIPTION: The home page of this Orthodox youth group is divided into two sections—Programs and Summer Activities. The Programs section features national events and projects, *divrei* Torah, chat groups, e-mail lists, and access to local chapters and the group's affiliate Yachad, aimed at disabled youngsters. The Summer section describes the group's camps and Israel programs.

USY: United Synagogue Youth

ADDRESS: http://uscj.org/usy/

DESCRIPTION: USY is the high school affiliate of the Conservative movement in the United States. Its searchable home page describes its programs in the United States and Israel, its social action projects, and its educational programs. You can join a listserv and participate in chat room discussions as well. From the Bookshelf section you can read *Achshav* in Adobe Acrobat format, dating back to 1997, check newsletters, press releases, and publicity materials. The People section helps you locate regional chapters. Of particular note is the browsable program bank index.

Young Judaea

ADDRESS: http://www.youngjudaea.org

DESCRIPTION: As of this writing, the home page of this Zionist youth group sponsored by Hadassah was under construction. The site does have its 1998 continuity study uploaded.

TRADITIONAL JEWISH STUDIES

Project Genesis

ADDRESS: http://www.torah.org

DESCRIPTION: Through e-mail newsletters, Project Genesis offers free, online courses aimed at beginning, intermediate, and advanced students, as well as teenagers. Courses in a variety of foreign languages are also available. Of particular note is the Jewish Learning Index, which contains hypertext lists of Jewish learning institutions in Israel, in the Diaspora, and online, along with an extensive set of other similar resources. This is an excellent starting point for anyone looking for an online course.

TorahNet

ADDRESS: http://uahc.org/torahnet/

DESCRIPTION: Eric Simon's very comprehensive, annotated guide to traditional Jewish studies online is an excellent starting point for anyone looking for online Torah study. Its contents include sections on Torah Study on the Web, Major Archives, Other Torah Related Pages, Torah for Children, Internet Subscription Lists, Talmud Study/Daf Yomi, Torah-Related and Jewish Distance Learning, and Torah and Talmud Texts on the Internet.

Aish HaTorah

ADDRESS: http://www.aish.com

DESCRIPTION: Aish HaTorah offers educational programs in traditional Judaism worldwide. Its searchable home page, available in English, Hebrew, Russian, and Spanish, includes sections on Jewish issues, dating, family, spirituality, Jewish literacy, the Holocaust, the weekly Torah portion, and holidays. It also describes its online and offline seminars and programs in Israel. You can ask a rabbi questions and sign up for a number of listservs as well.

CrownTowers Web Torah Guide

ADDRESS: http://www.geocities.com/athens/forum/7332/summary.html

DESCRIPTION: A summary guide to Torah study online.

Gates of Jewish Heritage

ADDRESS: http://www.jewishgates.org/

DESCRIPTION: Created by Rabbi David Lipman, this searchable site offers information in several categories. "In History, you can connect to different periods and different personalities. Under Torah, you can go to the week's portion, past portions, or additional Torah materials such as rabbinic midrash and modern commentaries. In Talmud, you can try a passage, you can pick a whole topic with a variety of relevant Talmud chunks, or you can check out the entire archives." There are suggestions for a home Judaica library as well. Of particular note is the extensive hypertext index, arranged by topic.

Halacha World Center

ADDRESS: http://www.halacha.net

DESCRIPTION: Based in Jerusalem, "The Beit Shlomo Institute mediates halachic questions received from all over the world, and directs them to leading decisors of halachah." Its HalachaNet archives provide responsa to questions and answers about Shabbat, Pesach, mourning, *kashrut*, medical ethics, business issues, education, community relations, and even gardening. A list of participating *poskim* is provided, as is free bibliographical information.

Hypertext Page of Talmud

ADDRESS: http://www.ucalgary.ca/~elsegal/TalmudPage.html

DESCRIPTION: This site by Eliezer Segal makes excellent use of the Web's capabilities by providing a clickable page of Talmud for the reader to explore. Click on a portion of the image of the Talmud page and you will be transported to a site offering detailed information on when, where, and why the text was composed.

Jewish Interactive Studies

ADDRESS: http://www.jewishstudies.org

DESCRIPTION: Register for an interactive course in the foundations of Judaism, Bible, or ethics at this site directed by Rabbi Moshe Zauderer.

Jewish Law

ADDRESS: http://www.jlaw.com

DESCRIPTION: Compiled by the Orthodox Union and a group of law firms.

Modia

ADDRESS: http://www.modia.org/

DESCRIPTION: This French-language site offers an extensive collection of articles on all aspects of Jewish life and religion, Israel, and Hebrew. You can also sign up for an online newsletter.

Think Jewish International

ADDRESS: http://www.thinkjewish.com/

DESCRIPTION: Sponsored by Lubavitch, "this Web site is dedicated to encouraging Jews worldwide to start thinking Jewish by presenting high quality audio lectures and classes offered by some of the greatest Jewish thinkers of our time." You can listen to many of the lectures using Real Player and sign up for a weekly newsletter online.

Torah Trup Tutor

ADDRESS: http://www.mat.net/~ewackerm/

DESCRIPTION: Created by Ellie Wackerman, this site provides recordings of cantillations in both .wav and Real Player formats. Cantillations covered include the Torah, Haftorah, Purim, Shalosh Regalim, Eicha, and High Holidays. You can also request tapes made to order, and a list of related links is provided.

Virtual Beit Midrash

ADDRESS: http://www.vbm-torah.org

DESCRIPTION: Sponsored by Yeshivat Har Etzion, this site uses e-mail to send out weekly yeshiva-style lessons to subscribers, who can then communicate with course instructors. Courses are offered in *Tanach*, Talmud, halachah, Jewish philosophy, and holidays, and a number of introductory classes are provided as well. Samples of each course are available through the archives. You can check the tables of contents of a number of the yeshiva's publications and find out about the programs offered in the yeshiva itself. There is also a set of links to similar learning sites provided.

Virtual Torah

ADDRESS: http://www.virtualtorah.org/

DESCRIPTION: From this site you can learn a mitzvah a day, read a *dvar* Torah, ask a rabbi a question, and find classes about Judaism for Beginners, the weekly Torah reading, the Book of Proverbs, Ethics of the Fathers, the holidays, and Jewish living. There is a biographical listing of Jewish leaders and a dictionary of Jewish terms as well. An extensive set of links is also provided. Of particular note is the "Bracha Machine," which allows you to input the name of a food and receive the name of the blessing said over it in return.

DISCUSSIONS OF TRADITIONAL JEWISH STUDIES

Aish HaTorah Mailing Lists

ADDRESS: http://www.aish.edu/learning/maillists/lists.htm

DESCRIPTION: Aish HaTorah houses 15 different listservs, all of which are described at this site.

B'Or HaTorah

ADDRESS: http://www.borhatorah.org/home/home.html

DESCRIPTION: Edited by Professor Herman Branover, *B'Or HaTorah* is an online periodical that is subtitled, "A Journal of Science, Art, and Modern Life in the Light of the Torah." You can read an article from the current issue and check the tables of contents of issues back to 1982. Details on ordering books and media productions and back issues of the journal are provided, along with information on the group's conference. You can also sign up to receive a weekly newsletter.

Daf Yomi Advancement Forum

ADDRESS: http://www.shemayisrael.co.il/dafyomi2/

DESCRIPTION: Maintained by Rabbi Mordecai Kornfeld, *rosh kollel* of Kollel Iyun Hadaf in Har Nof, Jerusalem, this forum provides a calendar for *daf yomi* study. In addition, for each *daf* there are insights, background information, a review of the *daf*, a point-by-point summary, and charts and graphics. Browsable archives arranged by *masechet* are also available. You can join a variety of listservs as well.

List of Jewish Learning Lists

ADDRESS: http://ourworld.compuserve.com/homepages/Susieq/lists.htm

DESCRIPTION: Created by Susan Ehrenfeld, this list is a good starting point for those searching for an online Jewish studies discussion. The list includes a description of the subject material covered, the e-mail address to send to, and the message to include in order to subscribe. Although the list dates back to 1996, it is still a good starting point.

Mail Jewish Torah and Halacha

ADDRESS: http://www.shamash.org/mail-jewish/

DESCRIPTION: Maintained by Avi Feldblum, this Web site houses the discussions of the listserv Mail Jewish, the oldest Torah- and halachah-based computer mailing list. "Mail Jewish was founded in 1986 for the purpose of discussing Jewish topics in general within an environment where the validity of halachah and the halachic process is accepted, as well as for the discussion of topics of halachah." From this site you can search the listserv's archives, browse a subject index to them, check the hypertext edition, and read articles in the list serv's special topics collections. Of particular note are the articles and Information about Rav Soloveicheck *zt"l* and the collection of rabbinical statements and reactions following the Rabin assassination.

Torah Tapes

ADDRESS: http://www.torahtapes.com

DESCRIPTION: Compiled by Eugene Hurewitz, this site lists tapes for sale by 26 well-known Orthodox leaders.

INSTITUTIONS OF TRADITIONAL JEWISH STUDIES

Baltimore Hebrew University

ADDRESS: http://www.bhu.edu

DESCRIPTION: Learn about the history, course offerings, faculty, resources, and services of this school, which offers undergraduate, graduate, continuing education, and elderhostel programs. You will also find links of Jewish interest, to sister institutions, and to the surrounding community near Baltimore Hebrew University.

Gratz College

ADDRESS: http://www.gratzcollege.edu

DESCRIPTION: The home page of this Philadelphia school describes the programs of its college, high school, and continuing education programs. Information on the library and its special collections are also available.

Hebrew Institute of Boston

ADDRESS: http://www.hebrewinstituteofboston.org/

DESCRIPTION: The home page of this school describes its unique course offerings and services in the areas of Translation and Notarization, Israeli Art and Customized *Ketubbot*, Consultation on Hebrew Teaching Techniques and Program Developments, Hebrew Courses for Professionals, Hebrew Kindergarden, and teaching for the Bagrut, the Israeli Matriculation Exams.

Hebrew Theological College

ADDRESS: http://www.htcnet.edu

DESCRIPTION: The home page of this school, located in Skokie, Illinois, describes the yeshiva programs for men and women, aimed at university age and high school age students. There is information about the school's summer camp and its community service program. Of particular note is the college's library catalog, which can be searched online.

Hebrew Union College

ADDRESS: http://www.huc.edu

DESCRIPTION: With branches in Cincinnati, Los Angeles, New York, and Jerusalem, this school is "the academic, spiritual, and professional development center for Reform Judaism." Its searchable home page describes the school and its degree programs, rabbinical training, faculty, courses, and admissions requirements, as well as its adult learning and outreach programs. Alumni can sign up for a listserv. Online directories for staff and students are available as well. Of particular note is the school's library, which can be searched online, as well as the listing of publications by faculty members that are available in full text.

Institute of Traditional Judaism

ADDRESS: http://www.utj.org/metivta/index.html

DESCRIPTION: Part of the Union for Traditional Judaism based in Teaneck, New Jersey, this home page describes the *beit midrash*, continuing education, and rabbinical programs of the school, along with details about its faculty and students.

Jewish Theological Seminary of America

ADDRESS: http://www.jtsa.edu

DESCRIPTION: The searchable home page of this New York–based school of the Conservative movement describes the departments, curriculum, admissions policies, and faculty of the institution. Details about student life, degree requirements, rabbinical and cantorial programs, and outreach activities are also provided. The Learn Online section offers access to publications, listservs, mini-lessons, and other educational resources. There is a student e-mail directory, an online tour of the facility, and an alphabetical index to the Web site's contents. Of particular note is the extensive library section that provides an online searchable catalog of one of the world's premier Judaica collections, as well as striking online exhibits.

Kollel: A Center for Liberal Jewish Learning

ADDRESS: http://www.kolel.org

DESCRIPTION: Kollel offers courses in Toronto, as well as the online courses described on its Web site. You can explore the weekly parsha, read book reviews, learn about the holidays, participate in online discussions with the Reb on the Web, and purchase tapes of kollel classes. Information on faculty, details about course registration, and archives of the discussion groups are available, along with a reading list and a set of relevant links.

Leo Baeck College

ADDRESS: http://www.lb-college.demon.co.uk

DESCRIPTION: Based in London, this school prepares rabbis for serving the Reform community. Its home page describes the school's academic programs and its history, faculty, and library. A set of relevant links is also provided.

London School of Jewish Studies

ADDRESS: http://www.brijnet.org/lsjs/index.html

DESCRIPTION: "The London School of Jewish Studies (formerly Jews' College, London) is a modern Orthodox academic institution, representing a type of Orthodoxy open to that which is best in the general culture." From its home page you can learn about its part-time and full-time undergraduate and graduate programs, its evening courses, intercollegiate courses, and technical and vocational training. Information about the school's faculty and publications is also available.

Maqom

ADDRESS: http://www.maqom.com/

DESCRIPTION: Founded by Rabbi Judith Abrams, Maqom is "a cyberschool for adult Talmud study." Its searchable site allows you to sign up for free Talmud study by e-mail. You can search the listserv's archives, consult an annotated bibliography about talmudic literature, and check the list of relevant Web sites.

Ohr Somayach

ADDRESS: http://www.ohr.org.il/

DESCRIPTION: The searchable home page of this Jerusalem based institution describes its departments, programs of study, and outreach programs for overseas students during the summer and winter breaks and after high school. It also houses a wide range of resources, including an extensive section on exploring Jewish thought, literature, and humor; a large collection of full-text publications; and a catalog of audiotapes that you can listen to with Real Player. Of particular note are the e-mail directories of faculty and alumni, the archives of the 25 listservs hosted by the organization, the section on the Jewish holidays, and the archives of the *daf yomi* studies. This is a large and impressive site with many areas to explore.

Reconstructionist Rabbinical College

ADDRESS: http://rrc.edu

DESCRIPTION: The searchable home page of this Philadelphia-based school describes the departments, curriculum, admissions policies, and faculty of the institution. Details about student life, degree requirements, scholarships, and internships are also provided.

Spertus College

ADDRESS: http://www.spertus.edu/College.html

DESCRIPTION: The searchable home page of this Chicago-based school describes the Jewish Studies degree programs and the courses in the Center for Nonprofit Management. Details about the current lecture series and continuing education courses are also available.

Information about the museum, library, Holocaust center, and Chicago Jewish Archives is provided as well.

Touro College

ADDRESS: http://www.touro.edu

DESCRIPTION: The home page of this New York–based institution describes the undergraduate and graduate programs the school offers in the United States and Israel. Information about the school's departments and faculty is also available. Of particular note is the online course section, which lists current courses with their associated Web sites. Courses from previous semesters are archived.

University of Judaism

ADDRESS: http://www.uj.edu

DESCRIPTION: Based in Los Angeles, this school represents the Conservative movement on the West Coast. Its searchable home page describes the faculty and programs of the school in its college of arts and sciences and its graduate and rabbinical schools, as well as its admissions requirements. There is also information about the school's extension program, elderhostel, conferences, think tanks, writers' institute, performing arts series, gallery, and sculpture garden. The Links section provides access to general and Jewish resources in Los Angeles and Jewish communal, news, and educational sites.

Virtual Beit Hamikdash

ADDRESS: http://www.neveh.org/mikdash/

DESCRIPTION: This VRLM model of the Second Temple in Jerusalem can be viewed from a variety of perspectives and provides a walk-through map of the building. This site also houses photos of the Beit Hamikdash Model, situated in the Kotel Tunnel in Jerusalem.

Yad Harav Nissim

ADDRESS: http://www.jewishworld.co.il/HebWeb/yad/

DESCRIPTION: Originally founded as an institute for the preparation of rabbis and rabbinical judges in Israel, this institute's home page describes its rabbinical training program and publishing house.

Yakar Center

ADDRESS: http://www.yakar.org/

DESCRIPTION: This learning community in Jerusalem describes itself as "a center for education, social concern and spiritual expression that reaches out to all." Its programs of "tradition and creativity" are described at the site, and you can sign up for a discussion group as well.

Yeshiva University

ADDRESS: http://www.yu.edu

DESCRIPTION: The searchable home page of this New York-based Orthodox institution describes its undergraduate, graduate, professional, rabbinical, and cantorial programs, along with information about its museum and high schools. Details about faculty, admissions requirements, student services, and athletics are provided, and there is a searchable e-mail directory. Of particular note are the university's libraries, which are searchable online.

Yeshivat Chovevei Torah

ADDRESS: http://www.yeshivatCT.org

DESCRIPTION: This is the home page of the New York school whose "mission is to inspire and train men and women to enter professionally into Jewish religious leadership—so as to shape the spiritual and intellectual character of the Jewish community in consonance with modern and open Orthodox values and commitments." Its home page describes its undergraduate, rabbinical, and adult education programs and its faculty.

Yeshivat Mercaz HaRav

ADDRESS: http://www.mercazharav.org

DESCRIPTION: This English and Hebrew site describes the work of this "center for Torah and leadership," including its programs and *roshei yeshiva*. You can purchase the publications of Mercaz HaRav Kook here. Of particular note is the extensive collection of Torah *shiurim* that is indexed by rabbi and browsable by subject. Similarly, there is a large collection of *divrei* Torah, arranged by parsha.

TRAVEL

Jewish Destinations

ADDRESS: http://www.jewishdestinations.com

DESCRIPTION: Based on the research of travel writer Oscar Israelowitz, this site provides a database of more than 6,000 kosher restaurants, synagogues, tourist attractions, and other travel services searchable by city and state. There are listings for Israel as well.

Jewish Travel

ADDRESS: http://www.jewishtravel.com

DESCRIPTION: This home page, created by Shelley Frier List, offers access to selected links in the areas of Jewish and general travel, the travel community, and listings and bookings. There are sections on Israel, singles, family, and business travel, as well as an article on *kashrut* when visiting Disney World.

Jewish Travel Network

ADDRESS: http://www.jewish-travel-net.com/

DESCRIPTION: This site features home hospitality and exchange programs for Jewish travelers. You can offer your services as a host or contact for free, but there is a fee for receiving listings, a sample of which is offered on the home page. You can view listings in the areas of travel services, student and singles services, rentals, B&Bs, and hotels for free as well.

JewishTravel.org

ADDRESS: http://www.jewishtravel.org/

DESCRIPTION: Part of the Jewish Family and Life collection of online magazines, this searchable site offers feature articles about Jewish travel.

New York Guide for Israelis and Jews

ADDRESS: http://www.nyway.com

DESCRIPTION: This site, in English and Hebrew, is a searchable, online travel guide highlighting places of interest to Israelis and Jews in New York. The database of resources is browsable, with listings in 14 categories. There are discussion groups you can join as well.

WOMEN

Jewish Feminist Resources

ADDRESS: http://world.std.com/~alevin/jewishfeminist.html

DESCRIPTION: Created by Adina Levin, this site provides links divided into the categories of art; Judaism, past and present; organizations; periodicals; and Web sites. This is an excellent subject guide.

Annotated Bibliography and Guide to Archival Resources on the History of Jewish Women

ADDRESS: http://www.library.wisc.edu/libraries/WomensStudies/jewwom/jwmain.htm

DESCRIPTION: Created by librarian Phyllis Holman Weisbard, this1997 bibliography is a slightly modified version of the one found in *Jewish Women in America: An Historical Encyclopedia,* edited by Paula E. Hyman and Deborah Dash Moore. It provides a searchable format for the books, periodicals, collections, and archival resources listed.

Bridges: The Jewish Feminist Journal

ADDRESS: http://www.pond.net/~ckinberg/bridges/

DESCRIPTION: You can read a sample from this journal and browse the tables of contents of older issues dating back to 1990. You can sign the guest book, post to a community bulletin board, and check the guidelines for writers as well. A set of feminist and Jewish Internet links is also provided.

International Council of Jewish Women

ADDRESS: http://www.icjw.org.uk/

DESCRIPTION: This page describes the worldwide projects of this organization in the areas of aiding women in enterprise or professions; health-related projects; work with children, the elderly, and the disabled; and training programs. News and events about the organization are also provided, along with a list of links to similar sites.

Jewish Feminist Resources

ADDRESS: http://www.jew-feminist-resources.com/

DESCRIPTION: Created by Renee Primack, this searchable site has sections on ritual and liturgy, Torah commentary, sermons, recipes, stories, and events. You can sign up for a listserv, check the message boards, and purchase books, music, and gifts online.

Jewish Women on the Frontier

ADDRESS: http://www.jewishwomenexhibit.com

DESCRIPTION: Created by the Jewish Historical Society of the Upper Midwest, this online exhibit describes the journey to the frontier and Jewish life inside and outside the home. You can read impressions of the exhibit and post your own responses.

Jewish Women's Archive

ADDRESS: http://www.jwa.org/main.htm

DESCRIPTION: "The mission of the Jewish Women's Archive is to uncover, chronicle and transmit the rich legacy of Jewish women and their contributions to our families and communities, to our people and our world." Its Resource section features educational materials, a bat mitzvah guide, a speakers list, recommended reading, and links to relevant Web sites. The searchable virtual archive and Exhibits areas present displays on Rebecca Gratz, Emma Lazarus, Molly Picon, Justine W. Polier, Hannah G. Solomon, and Lillian Wald.

Jewish Women's Web Ring

ADDRESS: http://www.geocities.com/Heartland/Hills/1330/women.html

DESCRIPTION: This site is a starting point for Web sites dealing with writing by and about women, the laws of *niddah, mikveh* information, and material from Chabad.

Lilith

ADDRESS: http://www.lilithmag.com

DESCRIPTION: Articles from this independent Jewish women's magazine are available here along with information on reprints packets, internship opportunities, and details on how to write for the magazine.

National Council of Jewish Women

ADDRESS: http://www.ncjw.org

DESCRIPTION: The home page of this group of "advocates for social justice" describes the issues and advocacy positions of the group, along with its programs and projects, and highlights the organization's efforts in the areas of voting, gun control, and childcare. You can read articles from the current issue of the *NCJW Journal* and check articles back to 1998. Other publications from the organization are also available online, along with links to Web sites dealing with social action issues.

WIZO: Women's International Zionist Organization

ADDRESS: http://www.wizo.org/

DESCRIPTION: The English and Hebrew home page of this organization describes its programs in support of women and children, new immigrants, and senior citizens. You can read the group's magazine WIZO Review and find out about its work with the United Nations. A clickable map leads you to local chapters throughout the world.

Women and the Holocaust

ADDRESS: http://www.interlog.com/~mighty/

DESCRIPTION: This site, created by Joan Ringelheim, explores the fate of women during the Holocaust through personal reflections, poetry, book reviews, and interpretive academic essays. There are tributes to women rescuers and partisan fighters as well. Of particular note are the extensive bibliography and lists of relevant Internet resources on the topic.

Women in Judaism

ADDRESS: http://www.utoronto.ca/wjudaism/

DESCRIPTION: "Women in Judaism: A Multidisciplinary Journal is an academic, refereed journal published exclusively on the Internet, devoted to scholarly debate on gender-related issues in Judaism." The full text of the current issue can be found here, along with archives dating back to 1997. Information on other publications, including the projected online *Women in Judaism Encyclopedia,* is available as well.

YIDDISH

National Yiddish Book Center

ADDRESS: http://www.yiddishbookcenter.org

DESCRIPTION: Founded by Aaron Lansky and located in Amherst, Massachusetts, this center is "dedicated to rescuing unwanted and discarded Yiddish books and sharing the treasures they contain" with research libraries worldwide. The home page describes the center and its programs, exhibits, and courses. There is an online virtual tour of the center, as well as details on how to donate books to the center and order sheet music from it. You can view the tables of contents and selected articles from the center's publication *Pakn Treger* and access its archives, dating back to 1997.

Virtual Shtetl

ADDRESS: http://metalab.unc.edu/yiddish/

DESCRIPTION: Although this site by Iosif Vaisman has not been updated since 1998, it still provides a virtual environment for exploring Yiddish language and culture. The Library section provides lists of books, articles, newspapers, dictionaries, statistics, catalogs, and bibliographies about Yiddish, as well as access to a bookstore for online purchases. The Synagogue area displays images and links to synagogue listings and hasidic *shtebilach*. Yiddish educational resources are available from the School section. The Memorial area houses genealogical information and material on pogroms and the Holocaust. The Post Office lists Yiddish discussion groups, radio stations, and newspapers. In the Train Station you can find worldwide maps of the *shtetl*, while the Art section lists galleries, events, and theatrical, musical, and movie productions. Finally, the Kitchen provides family recipes. This is still an excellent and well-organized starting point.

YIVO

ADDRESS: http://www.yivoinstitute.org/

DESCRIPTION: "Founded in 1925 in Vilna, Poland, as the Yiddish Scientific Institute and headquartered in New York since 1940, YIVO is devoted to the history, society, and culture of Ashkenazic Jewry and the influence of that culture as it has developed in the Americas. As the only pre-Holocaust scholarly institution to transfer its mission to the United States, YIVO is the preeminent center for the study of East European

Jewry and Yiddish language, literature, and folklore." Its home page describes the YIVO Library and Archives, the world's largest collection of Yiddish books, and its scholarly publications, conferences, cultural programs, lectures, exhibitions, and courses. Portions of the library's holdings in various subject areas are available in table format. This is a treasure trove of materials related to Yiddish and is an excellent starting point for any studies in this area.

A Bisl Yidishkayt

ADDRESS: http://www.yiddishmusic.com

DESCRIPTION: This Web site offers Yiddish music, books, and language materials for sale online. Choose from titles in the areas of klezmer, hasidic, cantorial, children's, and holidays. There are lengthy essays about klezmer music and its revivals in the United States and Europe. You can find sheet music, humorous titles, and videos here as well.

Avivale's Yiddish Page

ADDRESS: http://www.starkman.com/aviva/yiddish.html

DESCRIPTION: Created by Aviva Starkman, this site provides an annotated list of Yiddish links in the areas of humor and stories, organizations, events, people, and resources, along with a list of universities that offer Yiddish courses.

Der Bay

ADDRESS: http://www.derbay.org

DESCRIPTION: The goal of this group "is to foster the preservation and continued propagation of the Yiddish language (*mame-loshn*) and the associated Yiddish culture, music, theater, literature and poetry." To that end, this Anglo-Yiddish searchable newsletter provides an international calendar of Yiddish events; a comprehensive list of Yiddish teachers, clubs, performers, and klezmer groups; a list of translators; a pen pal service; and access to The Yiddish Network (TYN), whose 181 Yiddish enthusiasts send in information and act as contacts for travelers worldwide. An FAQ and a list of colleges and organizations with Yiddish instruction are also available. Of particular note is the extensive Yiddish word list with vocabulary arranged by subject, the lengthy list of Yiddish and Jewish Web links, and the index to three major Yiddish songbooks.

Glossary of Yiddish Expressions

ADDRESS: http://www.ariga.com/yiddish.htm

DESCRIPTION: This alphabetical listing of Yiddish expressions was created by Michael Fein from http://www.pass.to, who allowed its reposting at Ariga.

Klezmer Shack

ADDRESS: http://www.klezmershack.com

DESCRIPTION: Everything you ever wanted to know about klezmer music you can find at this comprehensive, searchable site by Ari Davidow. You can locate people and bands by name and location, radio shows, sheet music, recordings, instruments, organizations, and record label contacts. There are reviews, top 10 lists, news, a calendar of events, and online discussions in Virtual Ashkenaz, as well as an extensive set of links to klezmer articles on the Internet. This is an excellent starting point for anything related to klezmer music.

Klezmer Webring

ADDRESS: http://www.geocities.com/Broadway/Stage/2452/Klezmerring.htm

DESCRIPTION: This is a starting point for klezmer sites, where you can also learn how to add your site to the Web ring.

Second Avenue Online

ADDRESS: http://www.yap.cat.nyu.edu

DESCRIPTION: This project, based at New York University, hopes to record the history of the American Yiddish theater. The site includes a history of Yiddish theater, an encyclopedia of theatrical biographies and shows accompanied by audio and video clips, and illustrated articles on Yiddish theater. In the Spotlight section you can watch animated productions. The archives provide a list of Yiddish theater resources, and the digital library houses bibliographies and tapes relating to Yiddish theater studies. There is an events calendar and a chat room as well. The entire site is searchable.

Sholom Aleichem

ADDRESS: http://www.sholom-aleichem.org

DESCRIPTION: At this site devoted to the world and work of the Yiddish writer, you can find memoirs, commentary, and reviews, translations and bibliographies, and multimedia productions. Information about the Sholom Aleichem Memorial Foundation and the Beth Sholom Aleichem in Tel Aviv is also available, along with access to a number of bulletin board discussions. The Sholom Aleichem Network contains two other sites of interest: Tevye.net, with links to Yiddish home pages, and Mottel.com, where you can buy books by the Yiddish writer. Of particular note is the collection of journal articles from RAMBI on Sholom Aleichem.

Tevye.Net

ADDRESS: http://tevye.net/links/

DESCRIPTION: Part of the Sholom Aleichem Network, this searchable site offers a Yahoo-style listing of Yiddish links, arranged into 19 categories.

Workmen's Circle

ADDRESS: http://www.circle.org

DESCRIPTION: "The Workmen's Circle/Arbeter Ring, founded in 1900, fosters Jewish identity and participation in Jewish life among its members through Jewish, especially Yiddish, culture and education, friendship, mutual aid, and the pursuit of social and economic justice." Its home page provides access to its local chapters; describes its programs for children, adults, and families, including summer camps; details its member benefits and points of view; and lists its calendar of educational activities.

Yiddish Atlas Project

ADDRESS: http://www.columbia.edu/cu/cria/Current-projects/Yiddish/herzog.html

DESCRIPTION: This home page describes the creation of The Language and Culture Atlas of Ashkenazic Jewry and offers access to its archive of 6,000 hours of spoken Yiddish, the largest and geographically most diverse record of living Yiddish. You can hear how speakers from different areas of the world pronounce 13 sample words and phrases.

Yiddish Voice

ADDRESS: http://www.yiddishvoice.com and http://www.yv.org

DESCRIPTION: The home page of this Brookline, Massachusetts, Yiddish-language radio show, serving Boston's Yiddish-speaking community, also serves as an Internet resource for listeners outside its broadcast area. Program schedules are listed, along with news and access to other radio shows and Yiddish links on the Internet. You can listen to sample interviews and music with Real Player, read about recent programs, and purchase items from the station's gift shop. There's even a live interview with Sholom Aleichem available. This is a good collection of Yiddish-related materials.

Yiddish Web

ADDRESS: http://www.yiddishweb.com

DESCRIPTION: This French-language site provides a short history of Yiddish, information on Yiddish writers, a selection of phrases, a discussion group, and information on the Medem Library in Paris, the largest Yiddish library in Europe. You can also read the current issue of the group's newsletter and browse archives dating back to 1996.

Yiddish Web Sites

ADDRESS: http://www.columbia.edu/cu/cria/Current-projects/Yiddish/list.html

DESCRIPTION: Created by Dr. Judith Klavans of Columbia University, this site lists Yiddish Web sites in the areas of language, literature, history, music, and radio.

GLOSSARY

Aliyah: Immigration to Israel. Comes from the Hebrew word meaning "to ascend."

Amud: A page of Talmud; one side of a *daf.*

Ashkenazic: Literally, "Germanic." Refers to Jews who trace their ancestry to Central and Eastern Europe.

Baal Teshuvah: A newly observant Jew.

Beit Midrash: A study house designed primarily for the study of traditional texts.

Chabad: Describes the Lubavitch hasidic group.

Chafetz Chayim: Title of a book by Rabbi Israel Meir Ha-Kohen (1835–1933), who become known by this appellation. Leader of the mussar, or ethics, movement.

Chametz: Leavened food that is not permissible to eat on Passover.

Cholim: Those who are ill in the community, on whose behalf prayers and psalms are recited.

Daf: A leaf of a Talmud volume. A *daf* is made up of two pages, or *amudim.*

Daf Yomi: A method of dividing up a Jewish text into sections and studying a portion of it each day, so that it may be covered completely in a year.

Divrei Torah: A comment on the portion of the Torah read in the synagogue each week.

Eretz Yisrael: Hebrew for the Land of Israel.

Eruv: A boundary constructed to create a common area in which one may carry on Shabbat. Plural is *eruvim.*

Etrog: A lemon-like fruit used during the holiday of Sukkot. Plural is *etrogim.*

Genizah: A repository for worn-out sacred texts.

Haggadah: The book used during the Passover evening meal, recounting the story of the Exodus from Egypt. Plural is *Haggadot*.

Halachah: Jewish law as expounded in the Talmud and codified in a variety of Jewish law codes.

Hashkafah: Philosophical underpinnings of Jewish laws and traditions.

Hesder: A type of yeshiva study in Israel that allows men to combine study of Torah with military service.

Kashrut: Jewish dietary laws.

Ketubah: The Jewish marriage contract.

Ketuvim: The third section of the Jewish Bible, also called Writings.

Kiddush: Blessing made over wine.

Klitah: The process of being absorbed into Israeli society.

Knesset: The Israeli parliament.

Kol Yisrael: The Israeli radio broadcasting authority.

Kotel: The Western Wall in Jerusalem.

Likud: A right-wing Israeli political party.

Luach: Hebrew for "calendar." A day-by-day description of the religious ritual of the synagogue.

Maaser: The practice of tithing, or giving 10 percent of one's income to charity.

Maharal: Rabbi Yehudah Loewe, a 16th-century rabbi, known as the Maharal from Prague.

Malbim: Rabbi Meir Leibush Malbim, who lived from 1809 to 1879.

Mapam: An Israeli political party.

Masechtah: A tractate of the Talmud. There are 63 *masechtot* in total.

Megillah: The Book of Esther, read in synagogue on Purim.

Menorah: The eight-branched candleholder used during Chanukah.

Mezuzah: A small case affixed to doorposts of Jewish homes. Contains small manuscripts on which are written the commandments to remember and observe Jewish law.

Mikvah: A small bath or pool used for ritual immersion. Plural is *mikvaot*.

Mishnah Brurah: Composed by the Chafetz Chayim, this is a six-volume commentary on the first part of the *Shulchan Aruch,* known as *Orach Chayim.*

Mohel: Specialist who performs circumcisions. Plural is *mohelim.*

Moshiach: Hebrew for "messiah."

Olim: Plural of *oleh.* New immigrants to Israel.

Omer: A measure of barley that was brought each day to the Temple between Passover and Shavuot. Each night in this 50-day period Jews count another day toward Shavuot. Calendars have been devised to aid in this counting process.

Parsha or parshat hashavua: The portion of the Torah read each week in the synagogue.

Pidyon Shevuyim: The commandment regarding the redemption of those taken captive through war or kidnapping.

Pirke Avot: Translated as "Ethics of the Fathers" or "Chapters of the Fathers." Portion of the Talmud that focuses on ethical teachings.

Rambam: Rabbi Moses Maimonides, Jewish scholar, who lived from 1135 to 1204.

Ramban: Rabbi Moses ben Nachman, Jewish scholar who lived from 1194 to 1270.

Rebbe: The leader of a hasidic group.

Rosh Yeshiva: The head of a yeshiva.

Seder: The Passover evening meal.

Sephardic: Refers to Jews who trace their ancestry to Spain. Expelled from there by the Inquisition, Sephardic Jews spread throughout the world, concentrating in countries around the Mediterranean Sea.

Shiur: Literally, "lesson." Traditional yeshiva-style lecture given by a rebbe or teacher. Plural is *shiurim*.

Shoah: The Hebrew term for the Holocaust.

Shulchan Aruch: Jewish code of law written by Rabbi Joseph Karo (1488–1571).

Simcha: A joyous event.

Sukkah: A small hut with a thatched roof, in which Jews eat during the holiday of Sukkot.

Taamei Hamitzvot: Reasons for the commandments.

Takkanah: A rabbinical ordinance.

Tanach: The three major sections of the Jewish Bible.

Tehillim: Psalms recited during times of distress.

Tikkun Olam: Projects aimed at making the world a better place.

Torah: Specifically, the first five books of the Bible. More generally, taken to encompass the entire compendium of Jewish teachings.

Trope: The notes to which the Torah is chanted in the synagogue.

Tzahal: The Hebrew acronym for "Tzava Haganah LeYisrael," the Israeli Defense Force.

Tzitzit: Fringes that are affixed to the corners of a tallit, or prayer shawl.

Ulpanim: Plural of *ulpan*. An intensive method of learning Hebrew.

Yahrzeit: Yiddish for "year's time." Marks the anniversary of a consanguinial relative's death.

Yeshivot: Plural of yeshiva. An institution of intensive Jewish study focusing on religious texts.

Yom HaAtzmaut: Israel Independence Day.

Yom Yerushalayim: The holiday that celebrates the reunification of Jerusalem in 1967.

Zemirot: Special songs sung at Shabbat meals.

Zohar: The fundamental work of Jewish mysticism.

INDEX

THIS BOOK IS AVAILABLE ONLINE!!

The print version of this book is your passport to the full, searchable text online

Just go to

http://www.jewishinternetguide.com

For username, put in your full e-mail address

For password, use the last word on page 50 of this book

KEEPING THIS BOOK CURRENT

Changes and updates to the material in this book will be noted on the author's home page

at:

http://www.jewishinternetguide.com

WHO HAVE WE MISSED?

In the ever-changing world of the Internet, references in print format are usually out of date even before they are published. If you know of any new listings or corrections, please let us know so that our next edition will be as comprehensive as possible.

Readers may reach the author by e-mail at

dromm@yahoo.com